ORNITHOPARCHUS/DOWLAND

A Compendium of Musical Practice

American Musicological Society-Music Library Association Reprint Series

Dover Publications, Inc., New York, in cooperation with the American Musicological Society and the Music Library Association, has undertaken to bring back into print a select list of scholarly musical works long unavailable to the researcher, student and performer. A distinguished Committee representing both these professional organizations has been appointed to plan and supervise the series, which includes facsimile editions of indispensable historical, theoretical and bibliographical studies as well as important collections of music and translations of basic texts. To make the reprints more useful and to bring them up to date, new introductions, supplementary indexes and bibliographies, etc., have been prepared by qualified specialists.

Sir John Hawkins, *A General History of the Science and Practice of Music*
W. H., A. F., and A. E. Hill, *Antonio Stradivari, His Life and Work*
Curt Sachs, *Real-Lexikon der Musikinstrumente,* new revised, enlarged edition
Charles Read Baskervill, *The Elizabethan Jig and Related Song Drama*
George Ashdown Audsley, *The Art of Organ-Building,* corrected edition
Emanuel Winternitz, *Musical Autographs from Monteverdi to Hindemith,* corrected edition
William Chappell, *Popular Music of the Olden Time,* 1859 edition
F. T. Arnold, *The Art of Accompaniment from a Thorough-Bass as Practised in the 17th and 18th Centuries*
The Breitkopf Thematic Catalogue, 1762-1787, with new introduction and indexes by B. S. Brook
Andreas Ornithoparchus, *Musice active micrologus,* together with John Dowland's translation, *A. O. his Micrologus, or Introduction, Containing the Art of Singing*
Denis Stevens, *Thomas Tomkins, 1572-1656*
Thoinot Arbeau, *Orchesography* (translated by Mary Stewart Evans)
Edmond vander Straeten, *La Musique aux Pays-Bas avant le XIXe siècle*
Frits Noske, *La Mélodie française de Berlioz à Duparc* (translated by Rita Benton)

A.M.S.-M.L.A. JOINT REPRINT COMMITTEE

Sydney Beck, New England Conservatory of Music
Barry S. Brook, City University of New York
Hans Lenneberg, University of Chicago
James W. Pruett, University of North Carolina
Gustave Reese, New York University

ORNITHOPARCHUS/DOWLAND

A Compendium of Musical Practice

———◆———

Musice active micrologus

BY ANDREAS ORNITHOPARCHUS

*Andreas Ornithoparcus His
Micrologus, or Introduction:
Containing the Art of Singing*

BY JOHN DOWLAND

———◆———

With a new Introduction, List of Variant Readings
and Table of Citations of Theorists

by

GUSTAVE REESE

*Professor of Music, Graduate School of Arts and Science,
New York University*

and

STEVEN LEDBETTER

*Assistant Professor of Music,
Dartmouth College*

DOVER PUBLICATIONS, INC., NEW YORK

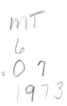
Published in Canada by General Publishing Company, Ltd.,
30 Lesmill Road, Don Mills, Toronto, Ontario.
Published in the United Kingdom by Constable and Company, Ltd., 10 Orange Street, London WC2.

This Dover edition, first published in 1973, is an unabridged
and unaltered reproduction of the following two volumes:
(1) *Musice active micrologus*, by Andreas Ornithoparchus,
published by Valentin Schumann, Leipzig, November 1517
(second edition; the first edition was January 1517).
(2) *Andreas Ornithoparcus His Micrologus, or Introduction:
Containing the Art of Singing*, by John Dowland, published by
Thomas Adams, London, in 1609 (a translation of *Musice active
micrologus*).
Further bibliographical information about these two volumes
will be found in the Introduction.
A new Introduction, List of Variant Readings and table of
Citations of Theorists have been prepared specially for the
present edition by Gustave Reese and Steven Ledbetter.
The publisher is grateful to the Music Division of the New
York Public Library for making the copies of these works in its
collections available for reproduction.

International Standard Book Number: 0–486–20912–1
Library of Congress Catalog Card Number: 71–132318

Manufactured in the United States of America
Dover Publications, Inc.
180 Varick Street
New York, N.Y. 10014

Contents

Introduction

TO THE DOVER EDITION

Very little has been ascertained about Andreas Ornithoparchus, the author of *Musice active micrologus*. His birth date is conjectural, his death date unknown; even his name is a mask that no one has yet penetrated. Such varied solutions to the Greek form of his name as Vogelsang, Vogelhofer, Vogelmaier, and Vogelstätter have been proposed, but no name has been attached to a historical figure. Most of our knowledge about him must be inferred from his own comments in his most important work.

A native of Meyningen, Ornithoparchus must have been born about 1490. He traveled extensively in his youth—through Germany, Austria, Bohemia, and Hungary—and gathered material that he later employed in his discussion of various local uses of many churches in the third book of his treatise. According to his own statement, his treatise began to take form at the University of Rostock, where he matriculated in 1512. In the ensuing years, he read it in public at the universities of Tübingen, Heidelberg, and Mainz. Nothing is known about Ornithoparchus after the publication of the *Micrologus* other than the fact that he was matriculated at Greifswald early in 1518.[1] At least one partial example of Ornithoparchus's activity as a composer survives in the superius part-book of a music collection printed by Christian Egenolff (Paris, Bibliothèque nationale, Rés. Vm⁷ 504).[2] The twenty-ninth composition in Volume III of this print is a piece for which the only identification is the attribution "Ornitoparchus." Unfortunately, only the superius part of this source survives, and no concordance has been located to provide the lower voices of the composition.

Musice active micrologus seems to have been a very successful work; at any rate, it was reprinted quite frequently for several decades. Not least important, it attracted the attention and admiration of John Dowland nearly a full

---

[1] The small total of our knowledge regarding the life of Ornithoparchus, consisting mostly of the dates of his matriculation at various universities, is summarized by K. W. Niemöller in his article on the theorist in *Die Musik in Geschichte und Gegenwart* X, col. 405–407.

[2] An inventory of this source by Nanie Bridgman appears in "Christian Egenolff, imprimeur de musique," *Annales musicologiques* III, pp. 77–177.

century after it was originally written. Dowland made it available to the English-speaking public in a charming translation. The various editions of the original Latin version, however, must claim prior attention.

The editions of the *Micrologus* fall into two families: one group published in Leipzig and one in Cologne. The following editions have been located (the mnemonic sigla in parenthesis will be used throughout the remainder of this discussion; they are constructed with abbreviations for author, place of publication [L = Leipzig, C = Cologne], and the last two digits of the year of publication; i and ii are employed to distinguish between the two editions that appeared in 1517; later in the discussion D will be used to signify Dowland's translation of 1609):

(OL17i) Leipzig: V. Schumann, January 1517. [Paris, Bibliothèque nationale; this copy lacks sheet A]

(OL17ii) Leipzig: V. Schumann, November 1517. [London, British Museum; Berlin, Deutsche Staatsbibliothek; Darmstadt, Hessische Landes- und Hochschulbibliothek; Bonn, Universitätsbibliothek; Venice, Biblioteca Marciana; New York, Public Library; Washington, D.C., Library of Congress]

(OL19) Leipzig: V. Schumann, 1519. [Berlin, Deutsche Staatsbibliothek; Munich, Staatsbibliothek; Göttingen, Universitätsbibliothek; Brussels, Bibliothèque royale; Rochester, Sibley Library (this copy published in facsimile on microcards)]

(OL21) Leipzig: V. Schumann, 1521. [Possibly a "ghost" edition; Fétis mentioned a copy of a 1521 edition in Paris, Bibliothèque nationale, but an inquiry from W. S. Rockstro and William Barclay Squire for the article "Micrologus" in *Grove's Dictionary* failed to turn it up; the only copy found there was that of January 1517; the colophon Fétis quotes is that of the 1519 edition, but he seems to have imagined that "undevigesimi" meant the twenty-first, rather than the nineteenth, year after 1500]

(OC24) Cologne: H. Alopecius, 1524. [Harvard University, Houghton Library; this copy lacks its last sheet]

(OC33) Cologne: I. Gymnicus, 1533. [Paris, Bibliothèque nationale (formerly in the Bibliothèque du Conservatoire); London, British Museum; Bologna, Civico Museo Bibliografico Musicale]

(OC35) Cologne: I. Gymnicus, 1535. [Munich, Staatsbibliothek]

(*OC40*) Cologne: I. Gymnicus, 1540. [This edition is listed in the *Musicus danicus* (1687) of Matthias Henrikson Schacht, but no copy is known today][3]

(*OL55*) Leipzig: V. Schumann, 1555. [Inserted into the collection *Libelli titulum inscriptionemque iocus*; Jena, Universitätsbibliothek]

Of the editions listed above, *OL21*, *OC40*, and *OL55* were not available for the present study. The four Cologne editions were printed under the title *De arte cantandi micrologus*.

Determining a chronological order for *OL17i* and *OL17ii* can be a serious problem, owing to the chaotic state of the calendar in Europe through the first half of the sixteenth century. The year could begin at different dates in different localities. December 25 ("Christmas style"), January 1 ("Circumcision style"), March 25 ("Annunciation style"), and Easter Sunday ("Easter style") were the most common possibilities. If Leipzig followed the Easter style, as did most of France, for example, the date of *OL17i* as it appears in the colophon (January 1517) would be January 1518 according to the modern calendar, with the result that *OL17ii* (November 1517) would actually be the first edition of the treatise. However, Giry[4] reports that the Christmas style was in general use in the Empire in Carolingian times (December 25 was, after all, the anniversary of Charlemagne's coronation) and that the practice was followed in most of Germany until the time of Ferdinand I (1556–1564), although a few towns maintained other traditions; during the course of the sixteenth century, January 1 gradually came to be recognized in most of continental Europe as the first day of the year. Grotefend[5] provides substantially the same information with some further detail regarding exceptions. Fortunately the printer's colophon at the end of *OL17i* and *OL17ii* indicates which style was used in Leipzig in 1517. The phrase "Anni virginei partus" certainly refers to the Christmas style, so that the year began one week earlier than it would on a modern calendar. Thus, "January 1517" preceded "November 1517" in Leipzig, and *OL17i* was printed some ten months before *OL17ii*.

The Leipzig family of editions differs from the Cologne group in ways extending to the very typography of the volume. The former is not uniform

---

[3] M. H. Schacht, *Musicus danicus, eller Danske Sangmester*, Latin and Danish manuscript dated 1 January 1687, published by Godtfred Skjerne (Copenhagen, 1928). The first section of the work, "Bibliotheca musica sive authorum musicorum catalogus qui vel in theoria vel praxi musices scripto inclaruerunt," contains the entry (on p. 19) for Ornithoparchus.

[4] A. Giry, *Manuel de diplomatique* (Paris, 1894), pp. 109, 123.

[5] H. Grotefend, *Taschenbuch der Zeitrechnung des deutschen Mittelalters und der Neuzeit* (10th enlarged edition, ed. by T. Ulrich, Hanover, 1960), p. 12.

throughout. *OL17i* is an oblong quarto in roman type with Gothic headings; *OL17ii* and *OL19* are upright quartos with Gothic type throughout. The music examples and tables are made from wood blocks by a single impression (notes and staves cut into the same block); moreover, the same wood blocks are used throughout the three issues. Schumann saved the cuts that were made for *OL17i* and used them in his later editions. The Cologne editions, on the other hand, are all oblong quartos with the body of the text in italics and the headings in roman capitals. Here again there appears to be a continuity of the wood blocks used for the examples; most, if not all, are the same (although they differ from those of the Leipzig group).

There are remarkably few textual variants between the editions; no revisions appeared to complicate the issue, and the few differences between editions can be attributed almost entirely to typographical errors. The music examples, however, are another matter. The Cologne group of prints shows a number of major variants from the earlier Leipzig group: a few music examples are abridged; one or two are extended. In the discussion of the various church tones, the nature of some of them is changed by the addition of a flat to the signature. The significance of this observation becomes apparent only when one compares the music examples of the Cologne family with those in Dowland's translation of 1609: the major variants are identical. In addition, Dowland's title, *Andreas Ornithoparcus His Micrologus . . . : Containing the Art of Singing*, appears to be a free translation of the title under which the work was published in Cologne: *De arte cantandi micrologus*. It thus seems tolerably certain that Dowland was working with one or another of this second family of *Micrologus* editions, that he accepted the music examples as they stood in this edition, and that the numerous deviations from and abridgments of the original text in the translation were made by Dowland himself, and not by some earlier publisher of a Latin edition. It is not possible to determine, on the basis of variant readings, which Cologne edition Dowland had at hand (see, for example, No. 24 in the appended list of variant readings).

Dowland obviously entertained a high regard for the century-old treatise, a fact which may indicate that his own musical point of view—theoretically at least—tended to look backward to the Renaissance rather than forward to the Baroque. He pays tribute to Ornithoparchus in his preface to the reader:

> Excellent men have at all times in all Arts delivered to Posteritie their observations, thereby bringing Arts to a certainty and perfection. Among which there is no Writer more worthy in the Art of *Musicke*, than this Author *Ornithoparcus* . . . .

A careful examination of the English text against the original Latin, however, will reveal that, despite Dowland's wholehearted admiration for Ornithoparchus, he has made several lengthy abridgments and a number of shorter deletions in the text of the translation. These rarely occur in the course of musical discussion. Some of them consist of the omission of dedicatory material that Dowland probably felt would be of comparatively little interest to English readers of 1609, to whom the names of the persons receiving the dedications would be unknown. One deletion—following what is undoubtedly a typographical error in the Cologne family of prints—makes musical nonsense of one of the rules of counterpoint (Book IV, chapter 6, rule 8). The English reads, "If the *Discantus* be in a fourth above the *Tenor*, the *Base* requires a fift below, & the *Altus* a third or sixt above." If this arrangement is followed with the first option of the Altus, Discantus and Altus would be but a second apart, an unacceptable dissonance. Reference to the corresponding passage in the original treatise reveals that the word *infra* has been omitted in the Cologne group and in the Dowland print: the Altus should be "a third *below* or sixt above" the Tenor.

Other excisions reflect Dowland's rather sensitive political position in England. In 1594 he had failed to get a court appointment because he was a convert to Catholicism. He traveled on the Continent, beginning at the court of the Duke of Brunswick and intending to continue to Rome for study with Marenzio. In 1595 he wrote that he had given up the Catholic faith, a decision that may have facilitated his subsequent return to England. He left England again in 1598, having been appointed lutenist to King Christian IV of Denmark. Dismissed in 1606, he returned home for the last time; there he prepared his translation of *Musice active micrologus*. But he apparently felt that his religious sentiments were under suspicion, for he cut from the treatise several passages that were highly laudatory of prominent Catholic musicians (especially monks) and, in one case, of Pope Leo X. In this latter instance, Ornithoparchus speaks of the pontiff as "Sanctissimus in Christo pater: ac dominus." Dowland omits the entire phrase and contents himself with "Leo the Tenth." The abridgments are mentioned in the list of variant readings on pages xiii–xxiii below; see especially Nos. 29, 33, and 40.

In *Musice active micrologus*, Ornithoparchus has provided a broad survey of many aspects of musical practice. His own travels provided much information for his discussion of the practice of various churches and for his comments—usually caustic—on the quality of musical performance that he had heard. His theoretical background is based solidly on the works of theorists and writers on music listed early in the book, although he frequently refers to writers not included in the list. Upon examination of his many citations, however, one discovers that Ornithoparchus bases definitions and musical speculation on statements by other writers, but for the technical aspects of mensural music and the rules of counterpoint, his own authority usually suffices.

The treatise opens with the traditional general discussion of the nature and categories of music, derived principally from the *De institutione musica* of Boethius and other medieval works on music, including some by Guido and others attributed to Pope John XXII, St. Bernard, and St. Gregory. But in keeping with the emphasis on "musica activa" proclaimed in his title, Ornithoparchus keeps this speculative section quite short. The title of one paragraph in Book I, "De Musici et Cantoris distancia," is certainly a paraphrase of Guido's famous *Regulae rhythmicae*. Ornithoparchus quotes five lines from this work in the section "Qui dicantur Cantores."

Franchinus Gaffurius and Johannes Tinctoris are the best-known Renaissance theorists cited. Gaffurius is clearly Ornithoparchus's favorite source; he quotes frequently from both the *Theorica musicae* and the *Practica musicae*, although he places Gaffurius among the "theoretical," rather than the "practical" or "active," musicians in his list at the beginning of the book.

Writers known in fields other than music theory appear in the treatise as well. Jacobus Faber Stapulensis (Jacques Lefèvre d'Etaples, *c.* 1455–1537) was a prominent humanist philosopher, theologian, and mathematician at the University of Paris. His mathematical treatise on music, *Elementa musicalia*, published with *Arithmetica decem libris demonstrata* in 1496, was popular into the seventeenth century; Morley referred to it in *A Plaine and Easie Introduction to Practicall Musicke* (1597).

Giorgio Valla of Piacenza (1447–1500; often referred to by Ornithoparchus as "Placentinus") prepared the earliest Latin translation in modern times of Aristotle's *Poetics* and lectured at Venice, using the Aristotelian work as an authority for aesthetic judgments.[6] He was the first Italian scholar to study Greek music theory extensively. His writings on the subject, compiled as *De Harmonica*, chapters 5–9 of his posthumously published work, *De expetendis et fugiendis rebus opus* (Venice, 1501), is based on a thorough acquaintance with Aristoxenus, Cleonides, Aristides Quintilianus, and others.

Ludovicus Celius Rodiginus (Ludovico Ricchieri of Rovigo, 1469–1525) published the sixteen books of *Antiquae lectiones* in Milan in 1516. Ornithoparchus certainly had a copy of this work while preparing his own treatise, because he gives frequent exact citations for his quotations from this source.

Robert Stevenson has pointed out[7] that Ornithoparchus quotes the famous passage from Gaffurius (*Practica musicae*, Book III, chapter 3, rule 7) regarding imperfect consonances proceeding to perfect consonances, so useful in the application of *musica ficta*. However, Ornithoparchus states the case more strongly than Gaffurius. He does not limit his recommendation to the "end

---

[6] E. N. Tigerstedt, "Den Första Nyaristoteliska Renässanspoetiken," *Lychnos* (Uppsala, 1959), pp. 55–69.

[7] R. Stevenson, *Juan Bermudo* (The Hague, 1960), p. 34.

of a *cantilena* or other place in the composition," as does the Italian writer. Ornithoparchus specifies "always": "Imperfectas concordantias *semper sequatur proximior perfecta* . . ." (Book IV, chapter 3, rule 3). This innovation is taken over by Bermudo, who cites Ornithoparchus almost as frequently as he does Gaffurius.

Michael Collins considers the *Micrologus* the earliest treatise "to document the resolution of trochaic figures notated in color into dotted figures"[8] (Book II, chapter 11).

One further interesting feature of the work is that Ornithoparchus recommends the use of a score for the beginner in composition. His model (folio Liii) consists of a 10-line staff with two voice parts on it—one in white and one in black notation. This colored notation does not have any rhythmical significance; it merely serves to distinguish the parts from one another, a procedure also employed in the "medius" parts of some early English organ compositions.

But beyond these individual details, the *Micrologus* is especially significant in that it surpasses all other treatises of its time in breadth of material included. The discussion of mensural music in the second book contains an uncommon wealth of tables and musical examples. The unprecedented discussion of the formulas for the recitation of Biblical lessons, in Book III, provides important information for the study of the dramatic passion and its history.[9] The directness and practicality of Ornithoparchus's approach recommended itself to later writers, such as Claudius Sebastiani, whose *Bellum musicale inter plani et mensuralis cantus* . . . (Strasbourg, 1563) borrows from Ornithoparchus material on the *accentus*, counterpoint, and the ten rules for singing. This same directness and practicality should prove useful today as a guide to the essential features of musical thought in the early sixteenth century.

LIST OF VARIANT READINGS

The readings in the various editions of Ornithoparchus's treatise are remarkably uncomplicated: no more than two versions occur at any point. Since the study of the variants was undertaken in order to determine the extent of Dowland's fidelity to the original Latin version and to discover, if possible, which edition Dowland used for his translation, all variants in this

---

[8] M. Collins, "The Performance of Sesquialtera and Hemiolia in the 16th Century," *Journal of the American Musicological Society* XVII (1964), p. 23.

[9] See, for example, Rudolf Gerber, *Das Passionsrezitativ bei Heinrich Schütz und seine stilgeschichtlichen Grundlagen* (Gütersloh, 1929).

list are based on comparisons between the earliest *complete* Latin edition, *OL17ii* (the reading here abbreviated O), and the Dowland translation (here abbreviated D). Occasional minor typographical errors, which could have had no effect on the English translation, are not reported. The reference numbers in parenthesis for each entry are folio numbers in *OL17ii* and page numbers in D, respectively.

1. (title pages) *OL17i:* lacking.

OL17ii: Musice Active / Microlog[us] Andree Orni- / toparchi Ostro-franci Meyningensis, Artiu[m] / M[a]g[ist]ri, Libris Quattuor digest[us]. O[mn]ib[us] Mu- / sicae studiosis no[n] ta[m] utilis q[uam] necessarius. /

(This is followed by a six-line poem headed "Laurentius Thurschen-reutinus Ad studio- / sum Musices Lectorem." The poem appears in no other edition. The decorative border includes, at the bottom, two figures labeled "Orpheus" and "Euridice" and a short piece of music in two parts.)

OL19: title is the same through "necessarius," but is then followed by a different poem, in eight lines, headed "IN LIBELLI TITULUM INSCRIP- / TIONEMQUE IOCUS." The woodcut of Orpheus and Eurydice and the musical composition at the bottom of the page is the same as that for the earlier edition, but the decorative floral borders at the top and sides are different.

OC24: ANDREAE / ORNITHOPARCHI MEYNINGENSIS / de arte cantandi micrologus, libris / quatuor digestus, omnibus musicae / studiosis non tam utilis quam / necessarius. / Coloniae apud Heronem Alopecium / Anno. M. D. XXIIII. /

(Decorative border of figures playing musical intruments.)

The title pages of the later Cologne editions are much simpler, containing neither decorative borders nor encomiastic poetry.

OC33: ANDREAE OR- / NITOPARCHI MEYNINGENSIS DE / arte cantandi micrologus, libris quatuor / digestus, omnibus musicae studio- / sis non ta[m] utilis quam necessa- / rius, diligenter reco- / gnitus. / Coloniae apud Ioannem Gymnicum / Anno. M. D. XXXIII.

OC35: ANDREAE OR- / NITOPARCHI MEYNINGENSIS DE / arte cantandi micrologus, libris quatuor / digestus, omnibus musicae studio- / sis non tam utilis quam neces- / sarius, diligenter reco- / gnitus. / Coloniae apud Ioannem Gymnicum. / Anno. M. D. XXXV.

D: ANDREAS / ORNITHOPARCUS / HIS *MICROLOGUS,* / OR / INTRODUCTION: / Containing the Art of / *Singing.* / Digested into Foure Bookes. / NOT ONELY PROFITABLE, BUT / also necessary for all that are studious / *of Musicke.* / *ALSO THE DIMENSION AND PER-* / *fect Use of the* MONOCHORD, *according to* / Guido Aretinus. / BY *IOHN DOVLAND* LUTENIST, / Lute-player, and Bachelor of

Musicke in both | *the Uniuersities.* | 1609. | *LONDON:* | Printed for *Thomas Adams,* dwelling in *Paules* | Church-yard, at the Signe of the | white Lion. |

(Dowland's title page appears to be a translation of the title of one of the Cologne editions; the translator follows *OC24* most exactly, since his title contains no rendering of the phrase "diligenter recognitus," which appears in both the later editions (*OC33* and *OC35*).

2. (Ai^v; no equivalent in D)   In *OL17ii*, the verso of the title page contains two encomiastic poems, one by Nicolaus Marescalchus Thurius and one by Philippus Surus Miltenburge[n]sis, to whom Book III is dedicated. *OL19* contains the same poems. *OC24, OC33,* and *OC35* each contain two poems on the page in question, but the first of these is the one headed "IN LIBELLI TITULUM INSCRIP- | TIONEMQUE IOCUS" that had previously appeared only on the title page of *OL19*. The poem of Nicolaus Marescalchus is relegated to second place on the page and that of Philippus Surus is omitted. It would appear on the basis of these poems that *OC24* is based on *OL19*; the two later Cologne editions are probably based on *OC24*. None of the encomiastic poetry appears in D.

3. (Aiii; [page before 1])   O: A couplet by "Henricus Cotherus Bruno- politanus" (i.e., of Brunico, a town in the province of Bolzano in the Italian Tyrol) summarizes the contents of Book I;   D: Omitted.

4. (Aiii^v; 1)   O: The section entitled "De musica Mundana" ends with "quoniam immensus aurium sensum excedit sonitus";   D: Dowland adds one more sentence after his translation of this passage.

5. (Aiv^v; 4)   O: In "Quis vere musicus dicatur," Ornithoparchus refers to a chapter number in Boethius: "xxxiiii";   D: "35."

6. (Av; 5)   O: In "De Musice inventoribus," the words "Fabio teste" appear;   D: Omitted. Read: "...(both borne of Gods *as Fabius witnesses*)...."

7. (Bii; 11)   O: In "De ambitibus Tonorum," after the words "ac nota[n]di necessitas," Ornithoparchus continues: "Has dece[m] voces aliter ordina[n]t Aute[n]ti: et aliter Plagales. Aute[n]ti e[ni]m una[m] finali supponunt, octo supraponu[n]t. Plagales vero finem in medio locantes, quattuor supponu[n]t, et qui[n]q[ue] supraponu[n]t." D: This passage omitted. Read: "The authentic modes arrange these ten notes one way, and the plagal modes another. For the authentic modes place one note below the final and eight above. The plagal modes, however, locating the final in the middle, place four notes below and five above."

8. (Bii; 12) O: In diagram, column 1 includes the figures 8, 9, and 10; column 4 includes the figure 7; column 6 includes the figures 6 and 7; D: These figures omitted.

9. (C; 18) O: In "De numero modorum" there is a reference to "Joannes pontifex. 22."; D: "Ioannes Pontifex 12."

10. (Cᵛ; 18) O: Third of the three possible intervals of a fourth (diatesseron) in the hexachord is "mi ad la"; D: "*mi* to *fa*."

11. (Ciiᵛ; 20) O: In music example, fourth staff, the fourth note is *d*; D: This note omitted.

12. (Cvᵛ; 25) O: Second staff of music example ends with *b♮, c′, b♮*; D: Last nine notes of example omitted; *e♮* inserted to conclude example.

13. (Cviᵛ; 27) O: The last clause of "De clavibus affinalibus tonorum" contains the words "sub chorali Tenore"; D: These words not translated. Read: ". . . that the Base may have place to descend *below the chorale melody in the Tenor.*"

14. (Dᵛ; 29) O: In "De Tono primo," the third sentence ends with the words "octavam, nonam, et decima[m]"; D: "Nonam" omitted in translation. Read: "Now an *authenticall* progression, is the ascending beyond the *Finall Key* to an eight, *a ninth*, & a tenth."

15. (*Ibid.*) O: Music example "Gaudeamus" ends with *c′, e′, c′*; D: Example extended several notes.

16. (Dii; 30) O: In "De vero psallendi modo," the reference to Michael Galliculus concludes "apud vetere[m] Cella[m] Cistertii ordinis Celeberrimu[m] Cenobium"; D: This passage not translated. Read: ". . . unlesse I had found them both copiously and learnedly written by maister *Michael Galliculo de Muris* [i.e., Michael Meurer of Hainichen; see *MGG* IV, col. 1293–94], a most learned man *at the very famous Altzelle monastery of the Cistercian order.*" Note that in other references to the monastery (e.g., on page 70) Dowland translates "apud veterem Cellam . . . Cenobium" as "at the old Cell a Monastery." He was clearly unaware of the vernacular name of the place.

17. (*Ibid.*) O: Second staff of music example, the notes over "Meme[n]to domine da[vid]" are *a* (six times) and *g*; D: These notes are a third lower.

18. (Diii; 31) O: Music example, staff one, last three notes are all *d*; D: These three notes are a third higher.

19. (Div–Divᵛ; 33) O: No flat in signature for examples of the fifth tone; D: One flat in signature.

20. (Div^v–E; 34)   O: No flat in signature for sixth tone;   D: One flat in signature.

21. (Eii; 35)   O: "De Tono peregrino," music example, note 16 from end, no flat;   D: b♭.

22. (Eiii^v; 38)   O: A couplet by "Henricus Cotherus" summarizes the contents of Book II;   D: Omitted.

23. (Fii; 43)   O: Music example "TENOR in modo minori perfecto" begins with five *longae*;   D: The second, third, fourth, and fifth *longae* lack tails.

24. (Fvi^v; 51)   O: In "de Pausis," the word "indicialiter" appears twice; D: Dowland seems to misread this as "iudicialiter"—he translates it "judicially" instead of "indicatively." Since none of the Cologne editions reads "iudicialiter," it is not possible to determine, on the basis of such a misreading, which edition Dowland used for his translation.

25. (G; 52)   O: Flags appear on semiminima rests;   D: Flags omitted.

26. (G^v; 53)   O: In music example "BASSUS de pu[n]cto alterat[i]o[n]is" the prolation sign is ∅;   D: Prolation sign is ○.

27. (H; 60)   O: In "De genere multiplici" appears the sentence: "Horu[m] alterum destruit alterum, nec in suo esse perdurare sinit";   D: The clause "nec in suo ..." is not translated. Read: "The one of these [multiplex or submultiplex proportions] destroyeth the other, *and does not let it stand by itself.*"

28. (Hiv^v; 66)   O: The last paragraph of Book II contains the phrase "Tum propter illarum difficultatem proportionu[m], Tu[m] propter tenuitatem puerilium ingenioru[m]. Grandes enim materias, parva no[n] ferunt ingenia" and the phrase "maiore deniq[ue] reru[m] intuitu"; D: These passages not translated. Read: "Though there be many other kindes of *Proportions*, . . . yet have I omitted all these for briefenesse sake, least children ... should have their wits rather clogged than helped hereby, *first, on account of the difficulty of these proportions, then on account of the limitations of youthful ability. For small talents will not bear large subject matter.* ... Yet ... all that now for brevitie sake, or upon other occasions I now omit, shall be painefully set downe in a greater volume with more diligence and care, *and, finally, with a greater range of subjects considered.*"

29. (I–I^v; 67)   P: Lengthy passage appears in preface to Book III: "Que[m]admodu[m] e[ni]m militaris disciplina, imperatoru[m] decus existit: ita sacerdotu[m] ac clericoru[m] o[mn]i[u]m co[n]cinentia. Cuius ta[n]ta est dignitas, revere[n]tia, atq[ue] maiestas, ut o[mn]ia divina officia, non nisi per eam ordina[n]tur, regant[ur], co[m]pleant[ur]. Sed utina[m] b[e]n[e]: nam hac nostra tempestate: proh pudor, inter multos

vix pauci reperiu[n]t[ur] artis hui[us] periti, qui: ad que ordinati su[n]t officia: rite ac rationabiliter p[er]ficiu[n]t. Quod an fortune: que sepe promovet indignos, an prelatoru[m] incurie, ascribendu[m] sit, nescio. Nam ii sepius, et si in aliis paru[m] sapiant, ab ipsa modulationis disciplina: qua[m] ex patrum decreto scire tenentur: penit[us] sunt alieni. Quare retrusis doctis: quos ut ce[n]sores timent: si[mi]les sibi ceremoniis preficiu[n]t, prebe[n]dis onerant, dignitatib[us] cumula[n]t. Quo fit: ut alii ere, dolo, fraude, alii mu[n]ere, alii favore, alii aliis citra canonica[m] co[n]stitutione[m] viis: ad ecclesiasticas dignitates p[ro]-moti: no[n] se ecclesie: sed ecclesiam sibi servire credunt. In choro sta[n]tes, aut ut asini ad lyram omnino obmutescunt, aut absq[ue] lege, modo, ratione, velut boves ululando, concinnem cantu[m] co[n]fundunt: fideles a devotione impediu[n]t, in risum et cachi[n]natione[m] male canendo p[ro]voca[n]tes: Et sic ex oratorio spelu[n]ca[m] faciu[n]t Theatralem: dum concinentie disciplina[m], aut non didicerunt, aut: quia forte magni domini sunt: discere erubescu[n]t. Et hos tales Co[m]-me[n]tator Christiane religionis: licet emul[us]: his verbis increpat dicens. Ve vobis hominib[us] qui de numero bestiaru[m] co[m]putati estis: Bonu[m] quod in vobis est non cognoscentes: propter quod ad superiora ascenditis, et deo similes estis. Sed que sunt hec bona, que nos deo similes faciunt: Nisi ecclesiastici gradus ac sacerdotii dignitas, que omnem terrena[m] transilit dignitatem. Sacerdos enim, et regibus est celsior, et angelis sanctior. Quare propheta Psalmo 81 ipsis loquitur dice[n]s. Ego dixi dii estis, [et] filii excelsi omnes. Sed id gratia adoptante non natura generante apud divu[m] Augustinum conceditur. Bestiis autem co[n]numera[n]tur illi, dum neglecta ratione, qua cum angelis participamus, sensualitatem: que nos bestiis similimos efficit: sequuntur. Os suum, ad dei laudem non apperientes: Quibus et istud propheticum rite co[n]gruit: Os habent [et] non loquentur neq[ue] clamabunt in gutture suo. Insuper cum populus beatus dicatur: qui scit iubilationem. Constat tales a beatitudine longe alienos esse. Quonia[m], ut de iubila-tione a [OL19: ac] cantu sileam: Vix quidem legere possunt. Sed ut ipse verum fatear, facilius lege[n]do, q[uam] cantando, errores incurrimus. quia cum aliis canimus, soli autem legimus." D: This entire passage omitted. Read: "For just as military discipline becomes a source of glory for the emperor, so does the singing together of priests and clerics, of which the dignity, reverence, and majesty are so great that all divine offices are not regulated, guided, and completed except by means thereof. But would that this were done well, for in this our time (O shame!) among many there are scarcely a few to be found skilled in this art who carry out fitly and with respect those offices for which they have been ordained. I do not know whether this state of affairs should be ascribed to fortune (which often advances unworthy persons) or to the carelessness of prelates. For if these latter rather often know too little in other matters, they are complete strangers to the very discipline of modulating, which they are required to know by a decree of the church fathers. For this reason, having pushed back the learned, whom they fear as critics, they put persons similar to themselves in charge of the ceremonies, they load them down with prebends, and they overload them with dignities. Whereby it happens that some are promoted to ecclesiastical dignities by means of payment, deceit, or fraud, others through gifts, others through favors, and others by still other means outside the canonic regulations; they do not believe that they serve the church, but that the church serves them. Standing in the choir, they either remain wholly silent like donkeys to the lyre [cf. Phaedrus, *Fabulae*, app. 14: "Asinus ad lyram"] or else, howling like cattle without law, order, or reason, they confuse the euphonious song and impede the faithful in their devotions, provoking laughter and jeers by their bad singing. And thus they make a theater out of a place of prayer, since they either have not learned the discipline of singing together, or (because they may be great lords) they are ashamed to learn it. The Commentator of the Christian religion earnestly rebukes just such people with these words, saying: 'Woe to you men who are counted in the number of beasts, not knowing the good which is in you on account of which you ascend to higher things and are similar to God.' But what are these good things which make us similar to God if not the rank of churchmen and the dignity of priest, which transcends all earthly dignities? For a priest is both higher than kings and holier than angels. Wherefore the prophet says to them in Psalm 81[:6, in the Vulgate; Psalm 82:6 in the Protestant-Jewish numbering]: 'I say, "You are gods, sons of the Most High, all of you."' But according to St. Augustine this is granted by adopting grace, and is not inborn by nature. Those I have been talking about, however, are numbered among the beasts, since, having neglected reason, which we share with the angels, they pursue the things of the senses, which make us very similar to beasts: not opening their mouths in the praise of God. To this is consistent the prophecy [Psalm 113*:5, 7 in the Vulgate; Psalm 115:5, 7 in the Protestant-Jewish numbering]: 'They have mouths, but do not speak; [. . .] and they do not make a sound in their throat.' Moreover, since a people is called blessed that knows jubilation, it is clear that such people as these are very far from blessedness. For, to say no more about jubilation and song, they can scarcely even read. But to tell the truth, we run into errors more easily in reading than in singing; for we sing with others, but we read alone."

30. (Iᵛ; 68) O: A couplet by "Henricus Cotherus" summarizes the contents of Book III;   D: Dowland omits the couplet but, amusingly,

translates the heading: "The Argument of Master *Choterus* vpon the Third Booke."

31. (Iii; 69)   O: In Chapter 1, the following passage appears: "Neq[ue] e[ni]m sine Co[n]centu: neq[ue] sine Accentu: ecclesiastici regni: rite p[er]agu[n]t[ur] officia."   D: Dowland omits the phrase "neque sine Accentu"; read: "For the Functions of the Papale kingdome are not duely performed without Concent *nor without Accent* [i.e., Accentus, in the liturgical sense]."

32. (Iii–Iii^v; 69)   O: In reference to Pope Leo X, the phrase "Sanctissimus in Christo pater: ac d[omi]n[u]s" appears; in reference to Leo and Emperor Maximilian, the phrase "Ambo dii terreni; Ambo Christia[n]e reipublice culmina" appears;   D: Omitted from translation; read: "Which thing *our holiest father in Christ, and lord, Pope Leo* the Tenth, and *divine* Maximilian, the most famous Romane Emperour, *both terrestrial gods, both pinnacles of the Christian republic*, both chiefe lights of the good Arts, (and specially of Musicke). . . . ."

33. (Iiii; 70)   O: A lengthy passage appears in "De divisione Accentus" with the marginal note "Vetus Cella et laus eius": "In quo uno: que vere religionis sunt: invenio ornamenta, disciplinam, obedientiam, observantiam, vitam regularem, [et] sine qua monasteria tartara sunt: charitatem, bybliothecam preclarissimam, Cellam pigmentaria[m] preciosam, patru[m] m[u]ltitudinem et piam et devotam, illuminatissimoru[m] virorum turbam copiosam, Artiu[m] magistros duodecim, Sacre Theologie. Baccalaureos tres, Domi[n]o Martino de Lochen Abbate, Sacre pagine eximio doctore, Ac domino Michaele Geitano priore eiusdem pagine baccalaureo: rem ita administrantibus, ut et facultatum, et bonaru[m] disciplinarum copia: apud eos inveniatur, Nec inter ceteros artium diversarum professores desunt musici. Nec preter planum cantum: quem regulatissimu[m] habent: mensuralem aspernantur. Quippe Dominus prior imprimis: deinde frater Michael Galliculus utriusq[ue] musice studiosissimi sunt. Quorum alter organice, alter harmonice musice tantam peritia[m] assecutus est: ut summis musice principibus connumerari non i[m]merito possint. Transeo alios plerosq[ue] qui non minus mensuraliter, q[uam] si a cunabulis in sacellis principu[m] vixisse[n]t, canu[n]t. Tra[n]seo deniq[ue] preciosissimum ca[n]tilenarum thesaurum: quem tantum habent ut nec principi cuiq[ue] cedant."   D: This passage not translated. After "Yet the Monkes, and especially those of the Cistertian order, have the *Circumflex accent*, as at the old Cell [i.e., Altzelle; see no. 16 in this List] a Monastery of the same order my selfe have tried," read: "In this one monastery I find things which are of the true religion, among them ornaments, discipline,

obedience, observance, the regular life, and charity (without which monasteries are like Tartarus), a most excellent library, a painting room of great value, a multitude of fathers both pious and devoted, a large group of most illustrious men, twelve masters of arts, three bachelors of holy theology, in the abbot Martin de Lochen an exceptional doctor of holy writ, and in the prior Michael Geitanus, a bachelor of the same, these two administering affairs in such a way that there is found among them an abundance both of skills and of the worthy disciplines. Nor are musicians lacking among those professing the various arts. Nor, in addition to plainsong, which they have most regularly, do they spurn mensural music. Indeed the prior first of all and after him brother Michael Galliculus [Michael Meurer of Hainichen; see no. 16], are most zealous concerning both types of music, and have gained such skill, the one in instrumental, the other in harmonic music, that they can be numbered, not undeservedly, among the foremost in music. I pass over many others who sing mensurally just as if they had lived from the cradle in the chapels of princes. I pass over, finally, the treasury of most precious songs, which they have in such abundance that they are not inferior in this even to any prince." Dowland concludes the sentence that should have introduced the quotation with the following clause: "... and I my selfe have seene many of their bookes in the same place." It occurs in no Latin edition.

34. (Kii^v–Kiii; 76) O: Several brief passages appear in Ornithoparchus's dedicatory epistle to Schlick: "Est etenim omnibus nobis, ita naturaliter insitus scientaru[m] appetitus. ut nullus tam sapiens, nullus ta[m] insipiens. nullus tam equus, nullus tam iniquus reperiatur: i[n]terrogatus an hanc, vel illam artem scire vellet: quin vellem respondeat." "... Ab omnibus diliguntur, non discuntur ..." and "Validi enim carminis constitutio: ut ipse optime nosti: non tyronum: sed emeritorum militu[m] est opus. [et] non omnium: sed eoru[m] duxtaxat (quonia[m] poete nascimur) quos natura trahit ac allicit." D: These three passages not translated. After "which is proved by the natural desire hee hath to knowledge," read: "For indeed there is in each of us so strongly implanted a natural appetite for knowing, that no one can be found so wise, none so foolish, none so just, none so unjust, that, asked if he wished to know this or that art, he would reply, 'I do not wish to.'" Dowland continues, "For Arts are desired by all, though they be not bought by all; and are praised by all, though they be not searched after by all." Insert here: "They are prized by all, but not learned by all." Later, after "... not that hereby all men, to whom nature is not serviceable, should fall to composition, but that all men may iudge whether those things which be composed by others, be good or bad," read:

"For the composition of a good melody, as you know very well, is not work for beginners, but for 'veterans,' and not for everyone, but strictly for those whom nature draws and attracts (for poets are born)."

35. (Kiii^v; 77) O: A couplet by "Henricus Cotherus" summarizes the contents of Book IV; D: Omitted; Dowland translates only the heading: "The Argument of Master *Cotherus*."

36. (Kiv^v; 79) O: In the section "Quid sit Concordantia," the phrase ". . . Quaru[m] apud practicos duodecim in usu servant[ur] . . . ." D: Translates "duodecim" as "two"[!].

37. (L; 80) O: Imperfect consonances listed: 3, 6, 10, 13, 17, 20; D: 3, 6, and 10 omitted.

38. (Lii; 82) O: Rule 16 begins "Si bassus sexta[m] sub tenore . . ."; D: "Sextam" is translated "fift"[!].

39. (M^v; 87) O: Rule 8 places Altus "tertia[m] infra, vel sextam supra"; D: "Infra" omitted in translation.

40. (Mii^v; 89) O: In rule 4, two passages appear: "Tale[m] o pastores iis: q[uo]ru[m] b[e]n[e]ficio et vivitis et hoc habet[is] q[uo]d estis: p[ro] merit[is] mercede[m] redditis? Tale[s] p[ro] iis: quoru[m] largit[i]o[n]is ope[m] indies postulat[is], rogitat[is], extorq[ua]t[is]: p[re]ces fu[n]ditis?" and "Rixantes canes audiret satius su[m]mus omniu[m] parens, q[uam] hec v[est]ra murmura, nec lege nec modo prolata. Quid de privatis (bonoru[m] pace dictu[m] sit) orationibus dica[m]: cum publice: quas pro mortuis funditis: tales sint, ut hominibus displiceant, deu[m]: qui imperfecta dona odit: offendant, qua[m] vereor, illas, iis fore peiores. An non creditis, vos olim de villicatione vestra reddituros rationem? An non illud Ezechielis. 33. de manu vestra sanguine[m] eoru[m] requira[m]: attenditis? Hoc e[st] verbu[m] cunctis: quibus alioru[m] cura co[m]missa est: iugiter ruminandu[m], Hoc est Platonis ipsius speculum, in quo facie[m] sua[m] sepius conte[m]plari debent pastores, ut vita, subditis, sanctitatis prebea[n]t exemplu[m], et fidelibus defunctis oratio[n]e: prece, cantu pietatis prestent suffragiu[m] Justu[m] e[ni]m est, piu[m] est, sanctu[m] est pro defu[n]ctis orare ut a p[e]c[ca]tis solvant[ur]." D: These passages omitted. After "An impious fashion to be punished with the severest correction," read: "You pay back such a reward, o pastors, unto them by whose beneficence you both live and have this [post] which you occupy? You utter such prayers for them of whom you continually ask, demand, and extort the gift of largesse?" Dowland continues, "Think you that God is pleased with such howling, such noise, such mumbling, in which there is no devotion, no expressing of words, no articulating of syllables?", after which read: "The highest

parent of all would rather hear brawling dogs than these your rumblings, brought forth neither by rule nor by measure. What shall I say about private prayers (let it be said with the pardon of the worthy), when the public ones which you utter for the dead are such that they are displeasing to men and offend God, who hates imperfect gifts, and the latter, I fear, would be far worse than the former. Or do you not believe that you will have to give a reckoning of your stewardship at some time? Or do you not give heed to that saying of Ezekiel 33[:6]: 'I will require their blood at your hand'? This is the word to all those to whom is committed the care of others, to be ruminated continually; this is the mirror of Plato himself, in which pastors ought to contemplate their appearance more often, so that by their lives they may offer to the flock an example of holiness, and by means of supplication, prayer, and songs of piety, they may lend support to the deceased faithful. For it is a just, pious, and holy thing to pray for the dead that they may be released from their sins."

41. (Miiiᵛ–Miv; no equivalent in D)   O: The text of the treatise is followed by four poems, headed as follows: "Tetrastichon authoris ad Librum," "Libellus ad Lectorem," "Henrici Cotheri Brunopolitani Artium magistri, ad Andream Ornitoparchum Argutissimum artis modulatorie professorem, Epigramma," and "Tetrastichon Auctoris in invidum." These four poems appear in all Latin versions for which the appropriate pages are extant (the pages are lacking in *OC24*).   D: Poems omitted.

As stated above, the problem of variant readings is quite uncomplicated. With the exception of a few minor typographical errors not reported and the different title pages and encomiastic poems discussed above (nos. 1 and 2), *OL17i*, *OL17ii*, and *OL19* have identical readings. The three Cologne editions (*OC24*, *OC33*, and *OC35*) uniformly follow the O readings given above except in the case of the variants Nos. 12, 14, 15, 19, 20, 21, 26, 31, and 39, in which they uniformly follow the D readings.

CITATIONS OF THEORISTS BY ORNITHOPARCHUS

Ornithoparchus is often careful to provide full citations—work, book, and chapter—for his quotations. These are listed below along with numerous less specific references. Numbers in brackets have been supplied; all others are provided by Ornithoparchus.

Ornithoparchus remarks in his preface that he follows the works of the following twelve authors:

Theoretical:	Boetius Romanus
	Plutarchus Cheroneus
	Divus Augustinus
	Franchinus Gafforus
	Valla Placentinus
	Faber Stapulensis
Practical:	Guido Aretinus
	Joa[n]nes po[n]tifex ro. [XXII]
	Divus Bernardus
	Beatus Gregori[us]
	Berno Abbas
	Joa[n]nes Tinctoris

He does not limit himself to these writers, however; a number of others, ancient and contemporary, appear at least once in the work, as will be made clear in the list below, in which the spellings of authors' names are those of Ornithoparchus. The list includes composers mentioned by Ornithoparchus as well as some literary figures, especially those for whom he gives full citations.

BOOK I

CHAPTER I

Generalis musice descriptio: Gafforus, Theorica I, 3.

Musice divisio: Boetius, Musica I, 2.

De musica Mundana: Franchinus, Theorica I, 1.

Macrobius, Super So[m]nio Scipionis II.

Boetius, [Musica I, 2].

Cicero, De republica VI.

Lodovicus Celius Rodiginus, Lectionum antiquarum V, 25.

Dorilaus.

Plinius.

De musica Humana: Celius, [Lectionum antiquarum V, 25].

De Organica musica: Celius, [*ibid.*]

De musica Harmonica: Boetius.

Placentinus, Musica II, 3.

De Activa musica: Augustinus, Musica I, [2].

Guido, [Dialogus] doctrinalis.

Franchinus, Theorica I, 3.

De Plana musica: Bernhardus, Musica.

De utilitate huius artis: Joannes Papa xxii, Musica ch. 2.

De Musici et Cantoris distancia: Franchinus, Theorica I, 4.
  Boetius.
  Augustinus.
Quis vere musicus dicatur: Boetius, I, 34.
  Plutarchus, Musica.
Qui dicantur Cantores: Joannes papa 22, ch. 2.
  Guido Aretinus, [Regulae rhythmicae].
  Fabius Quintilianus, [I, 10].
De Musice inventoribus: Fabius Quintilianus, [*ibid.*].
  Celius, Lectionum antiquarum V, [28].

CHAPTER 2

De vocibus: Boetius, I, 3.
  Celius, Antiquaru[m] lec. X, 53.
Quis voces Musicas primo i[n]venit: Gafforus, Theorica V, 6, and Practica I, 2.
  Guido, Introductorium.
  Joannes 22 pontifex.

CHAPTER 3

De Clavibus: Guido Aretinus, Introductorium.
De Clavium numero ac differentia: Franchinus, Practica I, 1.
  Joa[n]nes papa 22.
  Guido, Introductorium.
De clavibus signandis: Franchinus, Practica I, 3.
  Berno.
De Clavibus regule, No. 4: Berno, Musica I.
  No. 5: Guido, Micrologus, ch. 5.

CHAPTER 4

De Tonis in genere: Guido.
De Tonorum numero: Guido, Micrologus, ch. 11.
  Joannes pontifex, ch. 10.
  Fra[n]chi[nus], Theorica V, [8], and Practica I, 7.
De finalibus Tonorum: Bernhardus, Musica.
  Guido, Dialogus doctrinalis.
De ambitibus Tonorum: Bernhardus, Musica, prologue.
De repercussionibus Tonorum: Guido.
Regule de Tonis: Pontifex, ch. 12.
Quot modis Toni cognoscantur: Bernhardus.
  Pontifex, ch. 12 and 16.

CHAPTER 5

De Solfizatione: Gafforus.
De Solfizatione regule, No. 6: Bernhardus, dyalogus [Tonale S. Bernardi].
  No. 8: Franchin[us], Practica I, 4.

CHAPTER 6

De Mutationibus: Georgi[us] Valla, Musica III, 4.

CHAPTER 7

De modis seu intervallis: Boetius, I, 8.
  Placentius, II, 8.
  Georgius Valla, II, 2.
De numero modorum: Boetius, I, 16.
  Faber Stapulensis.
  Macrobius.
  Joannes pontifex 22, ch. 8.
Semiditonus: Faber Stapulensis.
  Placentinus.
  Pontifex, ch. 8.
Ditonus: Placentinus.
  Pontifex.
Diatesseron: Boetius, I, 17, and IV, 13.
  Pontifex, ch. 8.
Diapente: Boetius, I, 18, and IV, 13.
  Pontifex.
Semitoniumdiapente: Georgius Valla, III, 21.
Tonusdiapente: Stapulensis.
Diapason: Guido, Micrologus, ch. 5 and 9.
  Franchinus, Practica I, 7.
  Plutarchus.
  Boetius.
  Guido.
De intervallis prohibitis: Stapulensis.
Semiditonusdiapente: Placentinus, III, 24.
Ditonusdiapente: Georgius Valla, III, 26.
Semiditonusdiapason: Valla, ch. 31.
Bisdiapason: Macrobius.
  Ambrosius Nolanus.
  Erasmus.
  Aristoteles.

CHAPTER 9

De diffinitione/utilitate, ac usu Monochordi:
  Guido, [Dialogus] doctrinalis.
  Joannes pontifex xxii, Musica, ch. 7.
De Monochordi usu: Berno Cluniacensis abbas, Musica II.

CHAPTER 10

De coniunctis: Bernhardus.

De proportione dupla: Franchinus, Practica II, 4.
De Sesquialtera: Fra[n]chinus.
Se [De] Sesquioctava: Aulus Gellius, XIX, 14.
   Franchi[nus].

BOOK III

CHAPTER 2

De diffinitione ac divisione Accentus: Isidor[us], Ethi. I, 17.
De divisione Accentus: Priscianus.
   Isidorus.
   Michael Galliculus.

CHAPTER 6

De accentu epistolarum: Michael Muris Galliculus.

BOOK IV

CHAPTER 1

De diffinitione, divisione ac nominum contrapuncti differe[n]tia: Nicomachus
   Musicus.
   Philippus Beroaldus, Apuleiani Commentarii, X.
   Joannes Okeken, mutetus 36 vocum [possibly the ninefold 4-part
   canon "Deo gratia(s)"; but see the Ockeghem bibliography by
   D. Plamenac in *MGG* IX, col. 1834, for a discussion of the problems
   regarding the identity of this renowned work; see also E. E.
   Lowinsky, "Ockeghem's Canon for Thirty-six Voices: An Essay
   in Music Iconography," in *Essays in Musicology in Honor of Dragan
   Plamenac on His 70th Birthday*, ed. by Gustave Reese and Robert J.
   Snow (Pittsburgh, 1969), pp. 155–180].
   Franchinus, III, [1].
   Bacheus.

CHAPTER 2

De consonantiis ac dissonantiis: Boetius.
   Celius, X, 53.
Quid sit Concordantia: Tinctor.
   Stapulensis, III.
De discordantiis: Boetius.
   Tinctor.

CHAPTER 3

Concordanciarum regule, No. 1: Franchinus, III, 3.
   No. 3: Gafforus, *ibid.*

GUSTAVE REESE
STEVEN LEDBETTER

To facilitate comparison of the Latin and English texts, numbers have been placed in the margins to indicate where corresponding pages in the other language begin. These marginal numbers represent the single consecutive page numeration added to the present edition.

Musice active micrologus

BY

ANDREAS ORNITHOPARCHUS

De proportione dupla: Franchinus, Practica II, 4.
De Sesquialtera: Fra[n]chinus.
Se [De] Sesquioctava: Aulus Gellius, XIX, 14.
  Franchi[nus].

BOOK III

CHAPTER 2

De diffinitione ac divisione Accentus: Isidor[us], Ethi. I, 17.
De divisione Accentus: Priscianus.
  Isidorus.
  Michael Galliculus.

CHAPTER 6

De accentu epistolarum: Michael Muris Galliculus.

BOOK IV

CHAPTER I

De diffinitione, divisione ac nominum contrapuncti differe[n]tia: Nicomachus
  Musicus.
  Philippus Beroaldus, Apuleiani Commentarii, X.
  Joannes Okeken, mutetus 36 vocum [possibly the ninefold 4-part
  canon "Deo gratia(s)"; but see the Ockeghem bibliography by
  D. Plamenac in *MGG* IX, col. 1834, for a discussion of the problems
  regarding the identity of this renowned work; see also E. E.
  Lowinsky, "Ockeghem's Canon for Thirty-six Voices: An Essay
  in Music Iconography," in *Essays in Musicology in Honor of Dragan
  Plamenac on His 70th Birthday,* ed. by Gustave Reese and Robert J.
  Snow (Pittsburgh, 1969), pp. 155–180].
  Franchinus, III, [1].
  Bacheus.

CHAPTER 2

De consonantiis ac dissonantiis: Boetius.
  Celius, X, 53.
Quid sit Concordantia: Tinctor.
  Stapulensis, III.
De discordantiis: Boetius.
  Tinctor.

CHAPTER 3

Concordanciarum regule, No. 1: Franchinus, III, 3.
  No. 3: Gafforus, *ibid.*

CHAPTER 4

De generalibus contrapuncti preceptis, No. 20: Franchinus.
No. 22: Franchinus.

CHAPTER 5

De Discantu: Tinctor.
De Tenore: Gafforus, III, 5.
De clausulis formalibus: Tinctor.

CHAPTER 8

De vario canentium ritu ac dece[m] canendi mandatis: Fra[n]chin[us].
De dece[m] ma[n]datis o[mn]i canenti necessariis, No. 3: Valerius, De
Cleobi [et] Bitone fratribus, V.
Macrobius, De So[m]nio Scipionis, II.
No. 10: Guido.

GUSTAVE REESE
STEVEN LEDBETTER

To facilitate comparison of the Latin and English texts, numbers have been placed in the margins to indicate where corresponding pages in the other language begin. These marginal numbers represent the single consecutive page numeration added to the present edition.

Musice active micrologus

BY

ANDREAS ORNITHOPARCHUS

Musice Actiue

Microlog' Andree Orni-

toparchi Oftrofranci Meyningenfis, Artiū
Mgři, Libris Quattuor digeft⁹. Oib⁹ Mu-
ficæ ftudiofis nō tā vtilis q̃ necelfarius.

Laurentius Thurfchenreutinus Ad ftudio-
fum Muficer Lectorem.

Mufica : quam rurfus mēdis purgauerit author:
    Iam redit ante oculos : lector amice : tuos .
Iā redit ante oculos, Lypfick excuſſa Schumām
    Arte Valentini : qui bene preſſit eam .
Arte Valentini facta eft nitidiſſima tota:
    Et tibi Arionios afferet illa fonos .

ORPHEVS   EVRIDICE

DISCANTVS

TENOR

Nicolaus Marescalcus Thurius.

Utriusq; Juris doctor, In Musicen Andree Ornithoparchi.

Attica si quid habet, vel si quid Romula musa,
  Si quid Jessee : sacra camena lyre.
Ingenio clarus dedit Ornitoparchus et arte,
  Connectens paruo : dogmata multa : libro.
Addiditille Typos : ne res obscura moretur,
  Auribus atq; oculis : vtilis vsq; placet.
Ergo age qui veras, facilesq; ad neumata leges
  Scire cupis, mox huc : empturienter ades.

Philippus Surus Miltenburgésis.

Artium Magister ad Lectorem Musice studiosum.

Si tua musarum, dignaris corpora cetu,
  Atq; scius Cytharis : semper adesse cupis,
hunc pete : prebebit studiosa Pallade cunctos
  Accessus, facilesq; illius artis opes.
Nempe hec tellurem, pontum, volucresq;, ferasq;
  Astra, deos, homines, Musica auerna rapit.
Aere quidem paruo venit hec charissime lector.
  Ergo Ανρασ satis neu videaris ονος

4

Spectabilibus preclarisꝗ viris Luneburgensis reipublice mo
deratoribus oculatissimis: Andreas Ornitoparchus
Meyningensis Liberalium disciplinarum
Magister. Salutem ·:·

Ocratem illum: quem Clarij oraculum dei sapientissi
mum predicauit: dicere solitum legimus. Pectora ho
minū fenestrata esse oportere: nec ocultos habere sen
sus. Quod si nobis hodie obtigisset: pꝝes ampliss. pro
fecto beneuolentiam erga vos, vestrosꝗ, palam vide
retis meam. Sed quū sermo animorū sit inder Nec ni
si aut verbis, aut scriptis homines: abstrusos hominū
conatus cognoscatis: Absentis scripta, non secus ac co
rã loquētis verba: equis animis suscipiatis queso. Nec mihi surgunt cri
ste: Nec crescentem tumidis inflo sermonibus vtrē, Sed integritas ve
stra facit, Comitas facit, religio facit (qua pꝝe ceterꝝ borealibus: qui Bal
tica accolunt littora: clari estis) ꝗ concinentie disciplinã: quã greci Musi
cen dicunt: Christiane religionis altricē, morū, probitatis, rerūpublicarū
deniꝗ: si Priscis fides vlla prestanda est: parentem, tractare tentauerim,
Uela insanis vndis crediderim. Zoilis atꝗ Thersitis in me seuiendi co
piam dederim. Uarias regiones: nõ citra rerum mearum iacturam: eius
rei inquirende gratia accesserim, pro quiete lassitudinem, pro solatio tri
bulationem, pro gloria contumeliã, pro abundantia inopiam sepe (vt fit)
sustinuerim. Sed hec omnia: viri maximates: leuia visa sunt. Ut dormitã
tibus ceteris: quos vestra respub. fouet: ipse inprimis vestre, et subinde
toti Germane iuuentuti hac in re prodessem, mores cõponerem, atꝗ per
honesta musice solatia, ab illicitis conatibus reuocatos: ad seria paulatim
studia adulescētes incitarē, Nã et Socrates, et Plato, Pythagoriciꝗ oēs
iuuenes iuuenculasꝗ in musicis erudiri: non ad lasciuie incitamenta: qui
bus ars ipsa vilescit: Sed ad motus animi sub regula, rationeꝗ moderã
dos communi lege sanxerūt. Cum enim inquieta sit iuuenum natura, ob
lectamentorumꝗ p oia cupida, et ob id seueriorem non suscipiat discipli
nam: sub honesta Musice voluptate, ad ea ducatur solatia: que honestam
valeant oblectare senectutem. Sed inter ea, quibꝰ se oblectare humanus
solet animus, Quod maius, quod salubri9, quod honestius musica sit: in
uenio nihil. Cuius tanta vis est: vt nec serum repellat, nec etatem, Et: vt
est apud Macrobiū reconditissime scientie virū: nullū tam immite, tãꝗ
asperū pectus sit, quod nõ oblectamentorū eius moueat affectu, Curas
enim abigit, clemētiam suadet, iras et repꝝimit et suggerit, arteis alit, con
cordiam nutrit, heroū mentes ad facta fortia accēdit, cohibet vitia. vir
tutes et gignit, et ornat genitas, mores cõponit. Inter oia eñ que sensum
patiuntur, id solū mores obtinet: quod auribus obuiū est: quēadmodū in
Musicis problematibus diffusius Aristotiles declarat. hic Agamēnon

A ij

Arro
gãtie
ac as
sctati
on'ex
cusa
tio.

Soc
tes.
Pla.
Py
tha
goris
a.

Ma.

Phi=
lelp. ꝑbi ipator,ad bellũ Troianũ itur⁹,auctoꝛe Philelpho, muficũdomi reliqt,
qui Clitemneſtrã coniugẽ per muliebꝛiũ virtutũ laudes,ad pudicitiam,

i cõui
ꝑuijs. ꝑbitatẽꝗ cõiugalẽ cãtu hoꝛtareꝓ.Quare nõ pꝛius illã ab Ægiſtho vicia
tũ ferunt:ꝗ̃ is e medio muſicũ:ꝙ adulteriũ impediebat:impie ſuſtuliſſet.

Qui=
tilia=
nus. Sed et Licurgus:ꝗ̃uis feueriſſimarũ legũ Lacedemonijs fuis Aucto ꝛ
eẽt:Muſices ſtudiũ egregie videꝓ amplexat⁹,ſcribit Quitilian⁹,Trãſeo
veteres illos philoſophos,ita eñ ꝗ̃ fapientes dici maluerunt:qui in hac
vna:tãꝗ Gazophilatio quodã:ſummã ſtudioꝛũ fuoꝛũ repoſuert.Trãſeo
Reges ꝛ pꝛincipes:qui ob mirandã artis hui⁹ dulcedinẽ,immẽfa auri põ
dera cõterunt.Trãſeo deniꝗ religioſiſſimos quoſꝗ:qui ꝛ ſi ab oibus ter

Arif.
Rof=
tochi=
um. renis voluptatibus ſint alieni:in hac tamen vna , tãꝗ diuino ꝗdã ob=
lectamẽto,iugiter pſilkũt.Que cũ pia ſit,iucunda ſit,celeſtis ſit:naturã ha
bens ꝛ diuinã,et pulchꝛã,et beatã,libellũ hunc:quo omnis actiue muſice
nodoſitas explicaꝓ:apud Roſtochiũ Baltice oꝛe celebꝛe Gymnaſiũ, pꝛi

Tu=
bin=
ga. ma fetura natũ:et iam in tribus pꝛeclaris Germanie Academijs:Tubin
genſi, heydelbergẽſi ac Moguntino:maioꝛũ cẽſura emendatũ,ac pu=

hey=
delb=
ga. blice lectum: veſtre vrbis ingenuis aduleſcentulis dicare ſtatui.Vt ho=
rũ meritis poſteritas adiuta,non mihi,ſed ipſis tãꝗ mouẽtibus cauſis:
iura gratiarũ ꝑſoluat.Quãobꝛẽ:patres oculatiſſimi : pꝛudẽtiã veſtrã oꝛo

Mo=
gun=
tia. (vos ſaltẽ, vt exoꝛatoꝛ ſiem ſinite)Vt ꝛ libellũ hũc,piũ magis ꝗ̃ iucũdũ,
non temeritate ſed pietate in lucẽ editũ,veſtriſꝗ filijs dicatũ:amicis ocu
lis inſpicere,ꝛ vt eũdẽ pie ac hũaniter fouere,dignemini.Styli hũilitatẽ,
ac libꝛi paruitatẽ nõ dedignantes:ieiunis eñ,nõ delicatis (licet ꝛ iꝑi ꝙ
ſuo cõducat ſtomacho,in eo inueniãꝓ)ſcript⁹eſt.Inſup cũ paruos parua,
ac magnos magna deceant:paruus ſum,parua do:maioꝛa polliceoꝛ,quũ
factus fuero maioꝛ.Ualete felices viri tum ornatiſſ.tum pꝛudentiſſimi.

Pꝛefatio in opcris diuiſionem.

Iuſti
nian⁹
hoꝛa
tius. ¶ Quom ſit vtilius multo,pauca idonea effundere, ꝗ̃ multis inutilibus
pꝛegrauari,vt imperatoꝛia ſcribit maieſtas hoc Flacci Uenuſini carmie
cõmonefacta,Quicquid pꝛecipies eſto bꝛeuis,vt cito dicta,Percipiãt ai
dociles,teneãtꝗ fideles. hinc bꝛeuiſſimis qbuſdã regulis, actiue muſice
pꝛecepta:ꝛ ſi nõ oñia,potiſſima tamẽ:ex varijs autoꝛũ libꝛis:in vnũ col
ligere decreuimus.Omniũ eñ habere notitiã ac in nullo penitus pecca
re,diuinitatis potius, ꝗ̃ humanitatis eſt indiciũ,Quos aũt hac in re du=
ces ſectatus ſum,et quoꝛum patrocinio fꝛetus potiſſimum, ij ſunt.

Theoꝛici
{
Boetius Romanus
Plutarchus Cheroneus
Diuus Auguſtinus
Franchinus Gaffoꝛus
Ualla Placentinus
Faber ſtapuleuſis
}

¶ Pꝛactici
{
Guido Aretinus
Ioãnes põtifer ꝛo.
Diuus Bernardus
Beatus Gꝛegoꝛi⁹
Berno Abbas
Ioãnes Tinctoꝛis
}

Uerborꝝ igitꝰ ambage poſtergata, breuitati ſtudentes, que certitudinis eſt mater ⱥ mnem actiuam muſicam libris quattuoꝛ (tot enim conſtat par tibus) duximus enodandam. Quoꝛū pꝛimus plani cantus pꝛincipia de- clarabit, Menſuralem alter, Tertius accentum: At cōtra punctum (ceu partium aliarum moderatoꝛem ac parentem) loco poſtremo liber quar- tus enodabit. Singuloꝛum inſuper capita libꝛoꝛum, pꝛout oꝛdo dederit: ſuis queꝗ locis explicabuntur.

Muſice Oꝛnitoparchiane liber Pꝛimus

Plani cantus pꝛincipia declarans.

Henrici Cotheri Grunopolitani.

Argumentum libri Pꝛimi.

Carmina pontificum monſtrat: ſua munera: pꝛimus.
Fac animum haud lateant lectoꝛ amice tuum,

De Muſice diffinitiōe / diuiſiōe.

vtilitate ac eius inuentoꝛibus.

Caput Pꝛimum.

Rtem modulatoꝛiam: qua nil dulcius in terris: ſcripturi: Ne btꝰ ex paruo erroꝛe magnus conſurgat, a diffinitione (qua omni- Tho um rerum natura cognoſcitur) ſumamus exoꝛdiū, a facilioꝛi- mas. bus, vt conuenientioꝛ diſciplina fiat, incipientes. Unde ⁊ a ge nere: poteſtate eius explicata, ad ſpeciuoca magis pꝛogredia- mur. Gñaliter pꝛimū: inde facta diuiſione: ſingulū eoꝝ ſpe̅alꝭ deſcribēdo.

Generalis muſice deſcriptio.

❡ Eſt autē muſica (vt Frangin⁹ Gaffoꝛus Laudenſis: li. i. ca. iij. Theo- Frā rice ſue ſcribit) Modulationis peritia in ſono cantuꝗ conſiſtens. Sono chin⁹ dico: pꝛopter eam: quā celeſtium oꝛbium motus efficiunt, muſicam. Can- tu vero, ne eam: qua nos vtimur, diffinitione ſecludam.

Muſice diuiſio

❡ Muſicam tripartitam eſſe, Boetius: cui inter latinos Muſice ſcripto Boe- res pꝛimi honoꝛes debentur: libꝛo pꝛimo Muſice ſue, ca. ij. oſtendit: Mū tius. danam ſcilicet, humanam: ac Inſtrumentalem.

A ij

De musica Mundana.

Plu. ⸿ Cū ercogitaſſet deus:quē cūcta ad harmoniā fabricaſſe Plutarchus
contendit:mundum hunc conſtituere mobilem : neceſſum fuit:vt anima
agentē ac mouentē ſupadderet,non enim a ſeipſie,niſi animata mouent
Frā⸗ corpa:inquit Franchinus li.primo.Theo.ca.i. Motus autē ille,quoniā
chi⸗ velociſſimus eſt,ac regulariſſimus,ſine ſono non fit. Er ipſo enim circū⸗
nus. ductu orbium:ſonū fieri neceſſe eſt, ſcribit Macrobius li.z.ſuper Sōnio
Ma⸗ Scipionis:Nec obmiſit Boetius cū dirit. Qui fieri poteſt, vt tam velor
crobi mundi machina,tacito ſilentiæ curſu moueatur. Non pōt ab hac celi ver
us. tigine ratus ordo modulatiōs abſiſtere. Natura etiā fert:inquit Romane
Boe⸗ eloquentie princeps Cicero li.6.de repub. Ut extrema er altera parte
tius. grauiter:er altera vero acute ſonent. Eſt igitur Muſica mundana har⸗
Cice monia,ſyderū motu,atæ ſperarū impulſu, cauſata. hanc er celorum con
ro. centu,elemētorū neru,atæ temporum varietate,deprehenſam eſſe : Lo⸗
Celi douicus Celius Rodiginus,lectionum antiquarum lib.5.c.z5. ſcribit.
us Recte igitur Dorilaus philoſophus mundum eſſe organum dei direrit.
Rodi Cur autem ad aures noſtras non perueniat ſonus illius . ſcdm Plinium
gin?. cauſa eſt:quoniam immenſus aurium ſenſum ercedit ſonitus.
Dori
laus.
Pli⸗
nius.

De musica Humana.

⸿ humana muſica eſt:diuerſorū in vno cōpoſito elementorū concordan⸗
tia, qua ſpūalis natura corporee iungitur:ac rationalis cū irrationali con
cordia copulatur, que er corporis et anime conneru procedit . Non enim
ea,qua anima corpori iungitur amicitia,corporeis ligatur vinculis: ſed
virtualibus:er humorū proportiōe cauſatis. Quid em anime poteſtates,
Celi⸗ inquit Celius:tam diſſentaneas ac compugnantes ſepe conſpirare facit:
us. Quid corporis elementa conciliat, Que alia vis, ſpiritalem vigorē men⸗
tis cōpotem:mortali ac terrene cōpagi fermentat atæ cōglutinat:ꝗ mu⸗
ſica illa:quā vnuſquiſæ in ſeipſum deſcendens deprehendit, Simile em
ſuo ſimili ſaluatur:diſſimili vero perturbatur. hic eſt cur diſſonos ſonos
perhorreſcimus : concordem autem concentum audientes delectamur,
quia ſimilem in nobis concordiam eſſe cognoſcimus.

De musica Instrumentali.

⸿ Muſica inſtrumētalis eſt harmonia,inſtrumentorum preſidio cauſa⸗
ta.Et quoniam inſtrumenta aut artificialia ſunt,aut naturalia: erit vna,
que artificialib? inſtrumētis perficitur:alia que naturalibus. hanc har
monicam, illam vero Organicam,philoſophi nominant.

De Organica musica.

¶ Organica musica, scribit Celius: ea est, que ad instrumenta spectat. Ut est peritia, concentum pulsu, manu, flatu, perficiens. Pulsu, vt Cymbala, sistra, 7 huiusmodi. Flatu, vt organa, tube, tibie, cornua. Manu vero, his ea comprehenduntur instrumenta: que, vel digitorum discapedinatiõe, vel clauium articulatione, gubernantur. Ea tamẽ que voluptatibus des fluunt instrumenta, a Celio Rodigino deiciuntur. *Discapedinatio.*

De musica Harmonica.

¶ harmonica musica est facultas: differentias acutorũ, grauiũꝗ sonorũ, sensu ac ratione perpendẽs: Boetius, Uel est peritia, hũana voce sonos, naturaliũ instrumentorũ presidio, pducens, productos dijudicãs. hecut Placentinᵒlib.z.ca.z. musice sue scribit, duplex est: Inspectiua et actiua. *Boetius. Placentiᵒ*

De musica Inspectiua.

¶ Inspectiua musica est sciẽtia: sonos naturalibus instrumẽtꝝ formatos: nõ auribᵒ, quarũ sunt obtusa iudicia: sed ingenio rationeꝗ perpendens.

De Actiua musica.

¶ Actiua musica quã et practicam dicimus, vt diuus Aug. lib .I. musice sue refert, Est bene modulandi scientia. Uel scõm Guidonẽ in pincipio doctrinalis sui: est ars liberalis, veraciter canendi principia administrãs. hanc Franchinus li.I.ca.z. Theorice sic diffinit, Est sciẽtia perfecte modulationis: sonis, verbis, ac numeris consistens, que pariformiter duplex est, scilicet Mensuralis ac Plana. *Augustinus. Guido. Frãchinᵒ*

De musica Mensurali.

¶ Mensuralis musica est notarum diuersa quantitas, figurarum inequalitas. Quoniam augentur ac minuuntur iuxta modi, temporis, ac prolationis exigentiam, de qua latius in secundo huius.

De Plana musica.

¶ Plana musica (vt diuus Bernhardus regularis ac vere concinentie singularis inquisitor: in principio Musice sue scribit) est regula, naturã ac formã cantuũ regulariũ determinans. Natura quidem in dispositione, forma autem in progressione ac compositione consistit. Uel plana musica dus. est: notarũ simplex et vniformis prolatio: que nec augeri, nec minui põt, *Ber-bar-dus.*

De vtilitate huius artis.

Joannes papa xxij.

¶ Tanta est hui⁹ artis vtilitas: scribit Joannes eius nominis Papa xxij. ca.ij. musice sue, Ut si quis operā illi dederit: de cantus qualitate an vulgaris sit, an vrban⁹, an verus, an falsus, iudicabit, Scit et falsum corrigere, et nouū componere. Nō est igit (inquit idem) parua laus, nō modica vtilitas, nō vilipēdendus musice labor. Que sui cognitore compositi cantus facit iudicem, falsi emendatorem, ac noui inuentorem.

De Musici et Cantoris distancia.

Triplex gñs musicorū.

¶ Cōcinnē facultate, pfitentiū, triplex est genus, inquit Franchinus lib. i.ca.iiij. Theorice sue. Unū qd instrumentis agit: Aliud fingit carmina. Tertiū instrumentorum opus, carmenq̃ dijudicat. Et primum quidem quod instrumentis agit, totam ibi consumit operam, vt Cytharedi, Organiste, et ceteri omnes, qui instrumentis artificiū probāt. A musice nāq̃ sciētie intellectu seiuncti sunt: quoniā famulanf, nihil ratiōis afferentes: cum sint totius speculationis expertes, sensum sequuti. Etsi multa perite ac docte facere videanf: constat tamen eos non habere scientiā, Quoniā rem quā pfitef, intellectus puritate non teneant. et ob hoc eis Musicen bene modulandi negamus scientiā. Est etenim scientia sine vsu, et maior plerūq̃, q̃ in eis q̃ vsu precellunt. Celeriore em digitorū mobilitate non scientie, que soli animo insistit, attribuimus, sed vsui. Nam si aliter esset, vnusquisq̃ quo esset artis peritior: eo esset digitis celerior, Nec tñ oibus qui instrumentis concinunt, musices scientiā negam⁹. Quippe organista et qui in cytharis canit: musices scientiā habere poterit, Quod si sit, optimos tales artifices iudicamus. ¶ Secundū genus poetarū est: Quod naturali instinctu potius: q̃ speculatione ducitur ad carmē. hoc Boeti⁹ a musices speculatione segregat: Augustinus aūt cōnumerat. ¶ Tertiū genus musicorum est, quod iudicandi peritiam assumit, et cantilenas bonas a malis discernit. Quod cum totum in speculatione ac ratione sit positum, musice arti proprie conuenit.

Boetius. Augustinus.

Quis vere musicus dicatur.

Boetius.

¶ Is igitur vere musicus est: cui adest speculationis rationisq̃ facultas: non cui cantandi tantū practicabilis adest modus, dicente Boetio lib.i. ca.xxxiiij. Musicus is dicitur: qui ratione perpensa, canendi scientiā, nō operis seruitio, sed imperio speculationis assumit, et cui nihil et speculationis et operationis desit. Quare vsum consentaneum esse viro docto. Cheroneus ille Plutarchus in musica sua, Meonij Uatis auctoritate cōpulsus: ostendit, persuasione hac, Quoniam speculatio cognitionem solū gignit: vsus autem eandem ad opus reducit.

Qui dicantur Cantores.

¶ Practicus huius discipline cantor dicif. Qui ea ppnunciat ac canit: que musicus dictante ratione pponit. Unde inutilis est concentus, qué cãtor abiecta ratione pnúciare tentauerit: si idipsum quod pnúciat, intellectus puritate non tenuerit. Recte igif Joannes papa.zz.ca.z.inquit. Cui cã tore melius cõparauero ĝ ebrio: qui domú quidem repetit, sed quo calle reuertatur, penitus ignorat. Est pfecto Musicus ad cãtorê, sicut ptor ad preconê, Quod Guidonis Aretini, ista probat sententia. Musicorum ac cantorú magna est distantia: Isti sciunt, illi dicunt que componit musica: Nam qui facit quod non sapit, diffinif bestia: Uerú si tonantis vocis lau dent acumina: superabit philomena vl' vocalis asina. Speculatiuus itaĝ musicus practicú antecellit. Est eñ prestantius multo, scire, quod quisĝ facit: ĝ id ipsum facere, quod scit. Inde edificiorum opera, ac triumphos cernimus attribui ijs: quorum imperio ac ratione constituta sunt: non quorum opere seruitioĝ sunt perfecta. Plurimú igitur interest, Music⁹ ne quis dicatur, an cantor. Nam et Fabius Quintilianus, inter claros sa pientia viros: Musicos vsĝ adeo celebratos cõmemorat, Ut ijdem mu sici et vates et sapientes iudicarentur. Cantores autem: qui musicam nec a limine salutauerint: Guido bestijs connumerat.

(margin:) Joã. papa
(margin:) Gui do. Are tin⁹.
(margin:) Quit ilian⁹

De Musice inuentoribus.

¶ Musicam antiquissimã esse, clarissimi scriptores testimonio sunt: Nam et Orpheus et Linus, ambo dijs geniti: Fabio teste: ea claruerunt. Cui⁹ inuentionê alij, alijs attribuerunt. Tum, ĝ ob vetustissimã antiquitatem, biiane inuentionis auctor incertior sit, Tum ĝ tante rei dignitas, tot tan tosĝ in amorem sui trahit: Ut singuli (si fieri possit) auctores se dici ve lint. Quare ⁊ alij Linum Thebeum, alij Orpheum Treiciú, alij Amphio nem Dirceum, alij Pythagoram Samiú, artem hãc reperisse arbitranf, Insuper Eusebius Dionysium, Diodorus Mercuriú, Polybius arcadú maiores. Apud quos tanta est musice celebritas: Ut eius imperitiam illic fateri turpissimú sit. Nec id lasciuie causa vel delitiarú: Sed vt labores as siduos: preterea asperitatem: duriciem, ac austeriores mores: er celi qua dã tristicia peruenientes: hac: quasi dulcedine, remolliant atĝ contempe rent: inquit Celius lectionú antiquarú lib.ſ. Si tñ Josepho ac sacrĝ lris: fides vlla prestanda est: Tubal filius Lamech, eius inuentor precipuus, ⁊ antiquitate primus: ante diluuiú duabus tabulis, lateritia scilicet et mar morea, posteris eam reliquit inscriptã, Quarú alterã: marmorea scilicet: vsĝ hodie in Syria esse: quidã prodiderunt. Sed ne er inuentorú plurali tate error consurgat: Constat Tubal ante diluuium, Mosen apud he breos, Orpheú, Amphionê, et ceteros tales apud gentiles, Pythagoram apud grecos: Boetiú vero apud latinos: musica primum claruisse.

(margin:) Fabi us. Qui tilia nus. Lin⁹. Am phi. Py tha. Euse bius. Dio dor⁹. Arca des. Jose phus. Tu bal. Celi us.

II

Caput Secundum de vocibus.

Mo
ses.
Boe.

COnsonantia, que omnē musice regit modulationem, sine voce non fit, nec vox sine sono: inquit Boetius lib.1.ca.3. Vocis igitur descriptionem inuestigantes: Necessario duximus inquirendum: qui soni proprie voces dicantur. Notandū ergo est, ꝙ solius animātis sonus, vox proprie dicitur. Inanimata eni voca-

Celi
us.

lia non sunt: scribit Celius antiquarii lec. lib.10.ca.53. Et si fistulas aut fidiculas dicamus vocales: translaticiū est, atꝙ nois abusio. Neꝙ animātibus omnibus vox est: sanguine enim carentia, non vociferant. Neꝙ pisces vocem emittunt: quia vox est aeris motus: ꝙ aūt aerē non recipiūt. Cum igitur animal tantum vocem emittat: et non omne, neꝙ omni corporis parte: Manus enim attrite stridunt non vocem faciunt. Est igitur vox sonus ab ore animalis perfecti, consilio vel significatione prolatus. Consilio dico propter tussim: que vox non est. Significatione vero propter dentium stridorem. Sed quū hec vocis descriptio, voci viue tantum, non surde musicali (que imprimis cū sola syllaba sit, nisi exprimatur actualiter, surda est) conueniat: oportet aliam ipsi magis conuenientem inuestigare. Est igiᵗ vox musicalis quedam syllaba, notarū tenores exprimens. Nota vero, Est figura qua cantus intensio vel remissio designatur.

Quis voces Musicas primo iuenit.

Gaf-
forus
Gui.

¶ Quom autem omnis modulatio vocibus perficiatur: et voces scribi non possunt, sed memoria teneantur: vt Gafforus lib .5. Theorice. ca.6. et primi practice.2.ca. refert, Quo ergo facilius memorie mandarentur, Guido ille monachus Aretinus, diuina inspiratione ductus: hymnū diui Joannis baptiste deuote examinans: rythmorū sex capitales syllabas, scilicet. vt.re.mi.fa.sol.la. musicis consonantijs coueuire perpendit. Qua re eas introductorij sui chordis applicauit: Quod Joannes .22. Roma-

Joā.
papa

ne vrbis pontifex approbauit.

De vocum diuisione.

¶ Vocum diuisionem, qua in vnisonas, equisonas, consonas, emmeles et sic deinceps diuiduntur, in quarto huius discutiam, hic solum quod ad presens sufficit ponderando. Vocum ergo.

| Alie | ⎰ bmolles ⎱ Naturales ⎰ Hdurales | ⎱ dicūtur ⎰ scilicet. | ⎰ vt fa ⎱ re sol ⎰ mi la | ⎱ quia. | ⎰ mollem ⎱ mediocre ⎰ durum | ⎱ causant ⎰ sonum. |

¶ Vocū insuper alie supiores, scilicet fa.sol.la. alie iferiores scᵹ vt.re. mi.

Regule de Vocibus.

¶ Prima: vt in harmonico concentu, aliaru vocu caput est et principiu.
¶ Secunda: voces superiores in descensu, Inferiores in ascensu rite proferuntur. huic tamen regule loci contra ire quattuor inueniuntur.
¶ Primus in ffaut nunq̃ canitur vt, nisi sit cantandum fa. in bfa♮mi.
¶ Secundus, in bfa♮mi oportet sp ea, quã Schala requirit canere vocẽ
¶ Tertius, vna et eadem vox non debet repeti in secundis, licet idipsum in quartis, quintis, et octauis optime fieri possit.
¶ Quartus, nec superiores in descensu, nec inferiores in ascensu cantentur: quando mutationem causant non necessariam.

¶ Progressio sex musicalium vocu secundum
Arsim z Thesun.

Caput tertium de Clauibus.

LAtinorum prudentia musicorum: grecam sollertiam imitata (cũ **Lati** antea difficillimis quibusdam signis, chordas signarent cãtores) **musi**musicale introductorium, primitus litteris insigniuit. Quibus po **ci.** stea Guido Aretinus, quas repperit voces, coniũxit: clauesq̃ mu **Gui.** sicales per lineas ac spatia: vt in introductorio claret suo : primus omniũ ordinauit, Est igitur Clauis: aggregatum ex littera et voce. Principium enim cuiusq̃ clauis littera est, finis vero vox, Uoce dico, non vocibus, Tum q̃ omnes claues vocum pluralitatem non habeant, Tum q̃ generum, specierum, ac differentiarum: ex quibus diffinitio constituitur: nomi na, pluraliter exprimi nequeant: animal enim, nõ animalia genus est: ho mo species, non homines, Rationale differentia non rationales. Uel for maltus: Clauis est reseratio cantus, eo q̃ similitudine clauis realis tans tum aperiat ⸪

De Clauium nume-
ro ac differentia.

¶ Claues: vt Franchin9. lib. p̃mo practice ca. I. scribit: sunt due z viginti **Frã** numero. Licet Ioãnes papa. zz. et Guido (quẽ ipse post Boetiũ in musi **chin9** ca plurimũ valuisse ca. quinto fatet) viginti tantũ ponãt. Hec aũt viginti

due claues, triplici cōpzehendunt oxdine. Quoxū pximus capitalium est,
secundus minutarū, tertius geminatarum. Et iste claues omnes diffe-
runt inter se positione, figuratione, appellatione, quia vna aliter ponitur,
figuratur, appellatur q̃ alia. Capitalium sunt octo scilicet. Γ.A.H.C.D.
E.F.G. Minutarū item octo scilicet. a.b.c.d.e.f.g.. bfa♮mi cm̄ non vna
clauis est, sed due, Quod ex mutationibus, vocibus: ac instrumentis pxo-
batur. Jdem de octaua eius superioze bbfa ♮♮mi, sentiendum est. Geminatarum vero sex sunt, scilicet aa. bb. ♮♮. cc. dd. et ee. harū autem omnium
seriem: decem lineis: ac spacijs totidem: subscripta declarat figura.

¶ Guidonis Aretini: ozdinis sancti Benedicti mo-
nachi, Musici acutissimi introductoxiū sequitur: qui
post Boetium solus, apud latinos Musicam illustra-
uit, voces reperit: claues ozdinauit, ac ex diuina quadam industria facillimum quendam pxacticandi modum inuenit, vt in sequenti pictasmate videre licet.

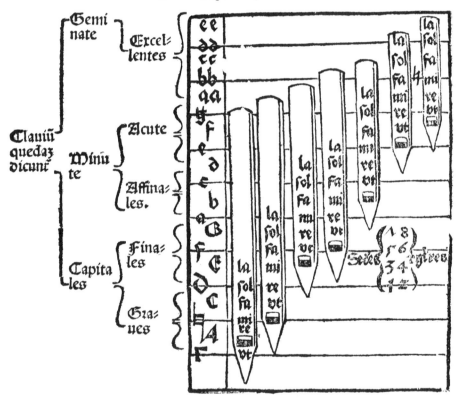

De clauibus signandis.

¶ Clauium quedam signande, siue vt alij volunt signate, quedam ve=
ro non signate dicuntur, Signataru quinqʒ sunt principales, scilicet, Гut,
Ffaut: csolfaut: gsolreut, et ddlasol. Quas Ambrosiani: vt Franchinus

Am=
brosi
ani.

li.i.practice ca.iij
refert: coloribus
signabant. Ffaut
rubro, csolfaut gl
auco. bb vero ge
minatã celesti co=
lore pingentes.
Gregoriani autē:
quos Rõana imi
tatur ecclesia:om
nes lineas eodeʒ
colore signantes:
quamlibet signa=
tarum, initiali sua
littera, aut alio
quouis signo fi=
gurant hoc mõ.

Gre=
goria
ni.

dd ddlasol	dd
♮ gsolreũt	♮
c csolfaut	
Fзⱦ ffaũt	
Г Гut	Г

Signa clauiũ signata=
rum in cantu Plano.

Signa earundem
in mensurali.

¶ Sed que minus principaliter signantur due sunt, scilicet b rotundum,
et ♮ quadratum. Primum quidem vocem fa: secundum vero mi:eo in qʒ
reperiⱦ loco:cantandũ demõstrat. Et nisi quis caute b a ♮ discernat, can=
tui confusionem facere videtur:inquit Berno, sicut vinum et aquam cõ=
fundens:neutrum deinde discernere potest.

Ad Lectores.

¶ Quom peccatũ sit fieri per plura, quod paucioribꝰfieri põt:Cãdidiss.
lectores:Neglecta igiⱦ manu:qua tyronũ ingenia impediũⱦ,seducunⱦ,
distrahunⱦ,Schalam hanc suprascriptã,numerando ediscite. hac eñ co=
gnita, voces,claues,oẽs deniqʒ mutatiões facillie cognoscetʒ ex intuitu.

De Clauibus regule.

¶ Prima. Clauiũ signataru,altera distat ab altera p quintã:dẽpta Гut:
que ab ffaut p septimã seiungiⱦ. ¶ Secunda, Claues de numero impari
in lineis: pares vero in spacijs continenⱦ. ¶ Tertia, Ɵẽs signate:a qbꝰ

B

allarū iudiciū sumitur: in linea ponunt. ¶ Quarta, Græca littera in gra=
uiori introductorij parte locat, ob grecorū reuerentiam, a quibus musica
defluxit ad nos: inquit enim Berno abbas lib. I. musice sue. Grecã litterã
maluerūt ponere moderni cp latinam, vt greci innuant hui⁹ artis aucto=
res. ¶ Quinta, Ōmes claues ab eadē lra incipientes, distant per octauã:
inquit Guido micrologi sui. ſ. ca. ¶ Sexta, De octauis idē est iudiciū.
¶ Septima, non licet musico plano vltra ſ ut descendere, nec supra ecla
ascēdere. hic tres supreme claues, nõ habēt voces inferiores: ꝗa vlt eas
nõ fit ascēsus, Nec tres infime superiores, quia infra eas nõ fit descensus.
¶ Octaua, Quoties in cantu fracto, vltra extremas claues proceditur
(quod sepius fieri solet) sumantur voces ab octauis.

Caput quartum de Tonis in genere.

Gui. Tonus: vt Guido refert: est regula in fine cantum dijudicans:
vel ē cognitio principū, medij, ac finis cuiuslibet cantus: ascen
sum et descensum indicans.

De Tonorum numero.

¶ Grecorū quattuor tantū tonos obseruat auctoritas: inquit Guido mi=
crologi. II. ca. Prothū scꝫ, Deutherū, Tritū ꞇ Tetrardū. Latini aūt ascēsū
et descensū cõsiderātes, atꝗ quēuis grecorū in autentū et plagalē ptien=
tes: octo tonis omne quod canit concludūt, instar octo partiuorationis.
Joã. Nam non incongruum videtur, scribit Joannes pontifex ca. Io. Ut octo
papa tonis omne quod canit moderet: queadmodū octo ꝑtibusorationis omne
Frã ꝗð ðr, hij aūt octo Tõi: vt Frãchi. li. ſ. Theor. ca. vlti. ꞇ ꝓmo practice. ꞇ
chī⁹ ca. declarat: hijs apð auctores noibꝰ appellant. Prim⁹ Dorius, secundus
Hypodori⁹, terti⁹ Phrygi⁹: que barbarū appellat Porphyrio: ꝗrt⁹ hypo
phrigi⁹, ꝗnt⁹ Lydi⁹, sextus hypolydius, septimus Mixolydius . octaui
aūt quidã hypermixolydiū dixerunt, alij proprium illi nomen denegauert.

[131]

De finalibus Tonorum.

Ber= ¶ Finales (vt diuus Bernhardus in musica sua non minus vere cp bre=
har= uiter expressit) sunt littere Cantuum terminatiue. In his enim omis cã=
dus tus regularis et non transpositus terminari debet, et sunt numero quat=
tuor: vt scribit dominus Guido in Dialogo doctrinalis sui.

Sci= { Dsolre / Elami / Ffaut / Gsolreut } in qua fi=nit omis=cantus . { Primi / Tertij / Quinti / Septimi } et { Secundi / Quarti / Serti / Octaui } tonorum re=
licet. gularium.

16

De ambitibus Tonorum.

¶Unde ambitus est nihil aliud, q̃ circuit⁹, seu spaciũ tonis, ṗ ascensu ac
descensu, musicorũ auctoritate, concessum. Concedũtur aũt cuiq̃ tonorũ
non plusq̃ decē note seu voces, in q̃bus cursum suũ habeat: inquit diuus
Bernhardus in ṗlogo musice sue. Cui⁹ triplex ibidē ratio assignaf scilic̓ **Ber.**
psalterij decachordi auctoritas, equalitat̓ dignitas, ac notãdi necessitas.
Has decē voces aliter ordinãt Autētr̃: et aliter Plagales. Autēti ẽm vnã
finali supponunt, octo supraponũt. Plagales vero finem in medio locan
tes, quattuor supponũt, et quiq̃ supraponũt, Licet nũc neotericorũ luxu-
rians licētia, vndecimã cuilibet superaddat, vt ĩ subscripta figura claret.

	1	2		3	4		5	6		7	8	
								10		10 9 8	10	
		10		10 9 8			10 9 8	8		7 6	9 8 7	
		9 8 7 6	7 6	7 6	7 6		7 6	7 6		5 4	6 5	
	Ambi:	5 4	5 4	Ambi:	5	7 6 5	Ambi:	5 4	5 4	Ambi:	4 3	4 3	**Am.**
	autē:	3 2 1	3 2	autēn:	4 3 2 1	4 3 2 1	autēn	3 2 1	3 2 1	Autēn:	2 1	2 1	**Plag.**
		1 2	1 2 3 4 5		1 2 3 4 5			1 2 3 4			3 4 5		
	Prothus.		Deuter⁹			Tritus.			Tetrardus			

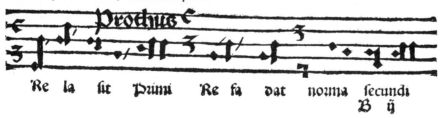

De repercussionibus Tonorum.

¶Unde repercussio: que et Trop⁹ a Guidone dicitur: est cuiuslibet toni
propria et adequata melodia. Uel est proprium cuiusq̃ toni interuallum.
vt in sequentibus patet exemplis.

Prothus

Re   la   sit   Primi   Re   fa   dat   norma   secundi

deūterūs

Mi mi dat ternus   Mi la poscit   si   bi   quartus

Critūs

Ut sol   qnt⁹ petit   Sextus   fa la si   bi   querit

Tetrardus

Ut sol impar tetrardus   Ut fa postremus   habebit

Regule de Tonis.

¶ Prima. omnes toni impares autenti sunt, pares vero plagales, hij, q̄
plus descendunt:isti vero:quia supra finalem plus ascendunt :sic dicti.
¶ Secunda regula. Omnis cantus in principio vltra notam finalē mox
scandens ad quintam, autenti est toni. Qui vero ad tertiã, vel quartam:
infra finalem mox ceciderit:plagalis . ¶ Tertia. Cant⁹ in medio vltra fi
nem ad octauam non scandens, etiam si in principio quintam habuerit,
plagalis est toni, nisi repercussio autenti, ibi reperta, eū preseruet. vt An-
tiphona Erortum est:que octaui toni iudicatur:quia in medio ascensum
autenti non habet, Sed repercussio septimi in principio mox apparens,
eam vt autenti maneat, preseruat. Uide pontificem. 12. ca.

Quot modis Toni cognoscantur.

¶ Tonos tripliciter cognoscimus:principio scilicet, medio, et fine. Prin
cipio, nam cantus in principio, vltra finem mox scandens ad quintam, est
autenti toni. vt supra in secunda regula dictum est . Medio, et quidē pri
mo, penes ascensum, Nam cant⁹ qui in medio octauam tetigerit, autenti est toni, qui vero non, plagalis. Secundo, penes repercussionem , quã
quisq̃ tonorum habet propriam, vt supra:ex qua, solo auditu , cuius toni
sit cantus, quinis dinoscitur. Fine, vt supra de finalibus claruit. ¶ Cer-

ta insuper reperiuntur cantica, que vt autentus ascendunt, et vt plagalis descendit, et illa neutralia dicunt: siue mixta: licet diuo Bernhardo minus probata: Inquit enim. Et que est illa execrabilis licentia, que opposita coniungit: metas naturales transgrediens, vt discontinuitatem iuncture, ita iniuriam irrogat nature. Plane igitur insaniunt qui et plagalem eleuare: et autentum deprimere: presumunt. hec tamen cantica (me iudice) in fine diligenter sunt consideranda, ad quem tonum plus declinet: dum enim ex quinta in finale descendunt, autentica sunt: Sin aute ex tertia vel quarta in fine scandut, plagalia dicent. Uide Pontifice. 12. et. 16. caplis. *Bernbar. Joã. papa*

Caput quintum de Solfizatione.

Unde Solfizatio est cuiuslibet cantus, per voces musicales, iuxta exigentiam mi et fa, regulata modulatio. Est enim solfizare (teste Gafforo) sillabas ac nomina vocu. exprimere. *Gafforus*

De triplici canendi modo.

¶ Omnis cantus tripliciter cantari pot, scilicet Solfizando: qd tyronum est, vt canere assuescant. Sonos tantu emittedo: qd instrumentistaru est, vt audientium atqz consentietu animis, curas vel immittant, vel adimat. Textum applicando, quod Cantoru est, vt laudes deo depromant.

De Schalis.

¶ Quoniam tonoru diuersitas, solfizandi diuersitatem causet, potissimu circa mi et fa. in bfa♮mi: qua superius no vnam, sed duas claues esse conclusum? Ideo musicoru sollertia duas schalas: sub quibus omnis cantus regulat, atqz decurrit: excogitauit. Et primam quidem a ♮ duro, ♮ duralem. Secundam vero a b molli, b mollem nominari precepit.

Schale generalis descriptio.

¶ Est itaqz Schala in genere, nihil aliud, nisi cognitio mi et fa, in bfa♮mi, et octauis eius.

Quid sit schala ♮ duralis.

¶ Schala ♮ duralis est vocum musicalium progressio, scandens ex a in ♮ duriter, id est per vocem mi.

B ij

Quid sit schala ♭ mollis.

¶ Schala vero bmollis est vocum musicaliũ progressio, scandens et a in bmolliter, id est per vocem fa. bmollis igit̃ schala in bfa♮mi fa : ♮duralis vero sp mi, requirit, vt in sequenti Paragraphia ad oculum licet videre.

x

¶ Tertia. Cantū sub schala ♮durali decurrere, est nihil aliud, q̃ in bfa♮
♮mi mi canere, Sub schala autem bmolli, fa. ¶ Quarta, Cantu currēte
sub schala ♮durali, cantande sunt voces infime, clauium sui generis,
Sub schala vero bmolli supreme. ¶ Quinta. Ō mi solfizanti videre erit
necessarium, an cantus regularis existat, nec ne. Cantus enun transposi=
tio, mutationis schale plerumq̃ est occasio. ¶ Sexta. Ō mis cantus in fi=
nalibus terminatus, est regularis ꞇ non transpositus, inquit diuus Bern

hardus in dyalogo suo. ¶ Septima. Quoties cantus ascendit ex Dsolre
ad alamire per quintam mediate vel immediate, et vltra tantum ad secū
dam, cantandum est fa in bfa♮mi in omni tono, quo ad cantus iterū dsol=
re tetigerit, siue signet̃ siue nō Cassatur aūt hec regula quotiens cantꝰ ad
ffaut mor nō reciderit vt in hymno Aue maris stella licz videre. ¶ Octa=
ua. In bfa♮mi et octauis eius, non licet canere mi pro fa, nec ecōtra, quia
sunt voces dissone et repugnātes, Inquit Franchinꝰ lib.I.practice ca.4.
¶ Nona. b in locis: vbi preter naturam signatur: respectus est mutatiōis
¶ Decima. Uariata schala, variantur ꞇ mutatiōes cum ea, ꞇ in toto ꞇ in
parte. In toto, vt in transpositis canticis, In parte vt in coniunctosis.
¶ Undecima. Quoties signatur̃ fa vel mi, preter naturam, oportet solfi=
zantem signaturam sequi, quo ad durauerit. ¶ Duodecima, Cum de
octauis idem sit iudicium: quare in eis eadem fiat solfizatio vocum.

Caput sextum de Mu-
tationibus ·:·

Vnde mutatio (vt Georgiꝰ Ualla lib.3.cap.4.musice sue de=
clarat) Est alterius pro altero positio, Sed hec diffinitio:
quoniam generalis est: Musico proprie non conuenit. Est
igitur Mutatio (prout nostro conuenit proposito) vocis
consone pro voce consona, in eadem claue positio. Et q̃a omnes voce
consone non sunt, omnes mutatiōe inter se non recipiunt. Necessarium
erit igitur videre: quibus mutatio vocibus: et quibus non conueniat:
quoniam nec ♮durales in bmolles mutantur, nec ediuerso: hoc autem
licet videre in pictasmate subscripto.

Directorium mu-
tationū Se-
quitur.

21

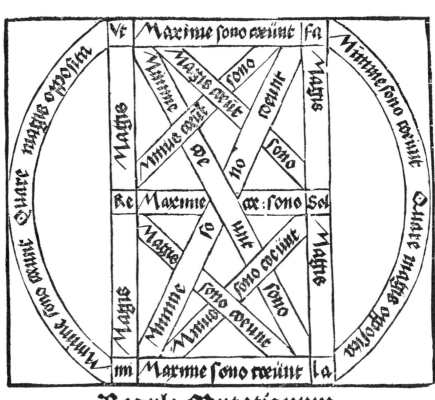

Regule Mutationum.

¶ Prima. Quoties defecerit ſex muſicalium vocum progreſſio, neceſſa=
rio fit mutatio. ¶ Secunda. In claue vnam vocem habente: mutatio
nulla fieri poteſt. qa vnica vox ibi in ſeipſam nõ mutatur, licet bñ repeta=
tur. Tertia. In clauibus duas vocesbabentibus, due mutationes fiunt,
prima de inferiore in ſuperiorem, ſecunda ediuerſo. Ab hac regula excipi=
unf claues, vnius generɜ voces habétes. vt ccſolfa, et ddlaſol. ¶ Quar
ta. Clauis tres habens voces, mutationes ſex admittit, licet ibi ſchalam
variari neceſſe ſit. ¶ Quinta. Nulla fiat mutatio, niſi neceſſitas ad eam
nos impellat. ¶ Sexta. Uoces bmolles in ♮durales mutari non poſſũt,
nec econtra, quia diſſonant. ¶ Septima. Uoces naturales, et in ♮dura=
les, et in bmolles mutantur, quia ancipites ſunt, preter mi et ſol, re et fa,
que inter ſe non mutantur, quia in eadem claue habitare non inueniunf.
¶ Octaua. In cantus deſcenſu inferior in ſuperiorem vertatur, in aſcen
ſu autem ediuerſo. ¶ Nona. In claue vnam vocem habente, mutatio=
nes tot fieri poſſunt, quot in eius octaua, quoniã de hijs idem eſt iuditiũ.

¶ Decima, Mentalis, non vocalis mutatio facienda est, nisi due vl' tres note ponantur in eodem loco mutabili.

Caput septimum de mo-
dis seu interuallis.

Nteruallum (vt Boetius: cuius ingenium in musica nemo attigit vnq̃: lib.i.ca.8.scribit) Est soni acuti grauisq̃ distantia.
Uel: vt Placentius lib.z.ca.8.refert:est via a grauitate in acu-
men, et ediuerso. Uel est distantia vocis a voce, penes ascensu̅
et decensum considerata, Et quo liquet vnisonum no̅ esse modum, licet
sit modo:u̅ principiu̅, quéadmodu̅ vnitas numero:u̅, dicente Boetio:
quemadmodum vnitas pluralitatis numeriq̃ principium est, ita equali-
tas pportionu̅. ¶ Est autem vnisonus: scdm Georgiu̅ Uallam. lib.z.ca.
.z. Status vocis, neq̃ in acutu̅, neq̃ in graue tendens. Uel est duarum
vel plurium notarum, in eodem loco coniunctio: vt patet in exercitio.

Boetius.
Placentinus.
Boetius.
Ualla.

De numero modorum.

¶ Sunt autem vsitata interualla nonem numero, scilicet Semitonium.
et est saltus de voce in vocem, per secundam imperfectam, molliter sonans et fit solum inter mi et fa voces. Et dicitur Semitonium, non q̃ di
midium sit toni: Tonus enim in duo equa diuidi non potest: sed dicitur.
Semitonium, quasi imperfectus tonus: Semum em̅ dici solet, quod per-
fectu̅ non est: inquit Boetius. lib.i.ca.16. Quottuplex autem sit semitoni
um, in Theoricis olim discutiam. ¶ Tonus: vt Faber Stapulensis scri
bit: est consonantiarum principium. Uel est consonantia, Epogdoo nu̅e-
ro causata. Inquit enim Macrobius Epogdous est nu̅erus, ex quo sym-
phonia generatur, quã Greci tonon dicunt. Uel est vocis a voce, per secundam perfectã distantia, potéter sonans. dictus a tonando. ¶ Tonare enim: scribit Joannes pontifer.zz.ca.8.est potenter sonare. Et fit to
nus inter omnes voces preter mi et fa, co̅stans ex duobus semitonijs mi'
noribus et vno commate.

Boetius.
Macrobius.
Joa. papa

Semiditonus.

¶ Quem Faber Stapulensis sesquitonium nominat, Est interuallum
vocis a voce, per tertiam imperfectam, Tono et hemitonio constans se
cundum Placentinu̅. Species duas habet apud pontificem.ca.8. Prima est de re ad fa: secunda de mi ad sol: vt in exercitio clarebit.   ₵

Stapulé.
Placen.

[138]

23

Ditonus.

¶ Est perfecta tertia : sic dictus : quasi duos tonos in se habeat, Placentino ac pontifice testibus : Species habet pariformiter duas, Prima est de vt ad mi. Secunda de fa ad la.

Diatesseron.

Boetius.

¶ Apud Boetium li.1.ca.17. Est consonātia quattuor vocū, et triū interualloꝛū. Uel est saltus de voce in vocem per quartam : Constans duobꝰ tonis et minoꝛe semitonio. Species habet tres, apud Boetiū li.4.ca.13. et apud pōtif.c.8. Pꝛia est de vt ad fa: scda de re ad sol: tertia de mi ad la.

Diapente.

Ioā. papa

¶ Est consonantia quinꝗ vocum et quattuoꝛ interuallorum: habet Boetius li.1.ca.18. Uel est saltus vocis a voce per quintam, constans tribus tonis et semitonio. Species habet quattuoꝛ apud Boetium li. quarto. ca.13. Quaꝛe pontifex ipsam Quadrimodum esse dicit. Pꝛima est de vt ad sol: secunda de re ad la: tertia de mi ad mi: quarta de fa ad fa.

Semitoniumdiapente.

[139]

¶ Est interuallum vocis a voce per sextam imperfectam, scdm Georgium Uallam li.3.ca.21. tonis tribus ac duobus semitonijs constitutum.

Tonusdiapente.

Sta-pul.

¶ Est vocis a voce per sextam pfctāꝫ distantia. Quam Stapulensis ex quattuoꝛ tonis ac minoꝛe semitonio constare testatur.

Diapason.

Gui.

¶ Que sola a Guidone micrologi.9.ca.perfecta consonantia dicitur: secundum eundem ca.5. Est interuallum in quo Diatesseron et Diapente iunguntur. Uel vt Franchinus li.1.pꝛact.ca.7. scribit Est consonantia octo sonoꝛum et septem interualloꝛum. Uel est consonantia: auctoꝛe Plutarcho ꝺupla ratione perpensa. Conficient autem imaginis gratia, ꝺuplam rationem.6.et 12. Sed quibus hee descriptiones obscure videbuntur: hanc saltem capiant, Est vocis a voce per octauā digressio : Tonis quinꝗ et duobus minoꝛibus Semitonijs constituta. Species apud Boetium et Guidonem celeberrimos musice scriptoꝛes: septē habet. A quaꝫ

Frā-chi. Boetius.

libet enim littera ad sibi similem, diapason est. Omnis insuper modus, tot Gul.
species habet vna minus: quot voces

Directorium modorum sequitur.

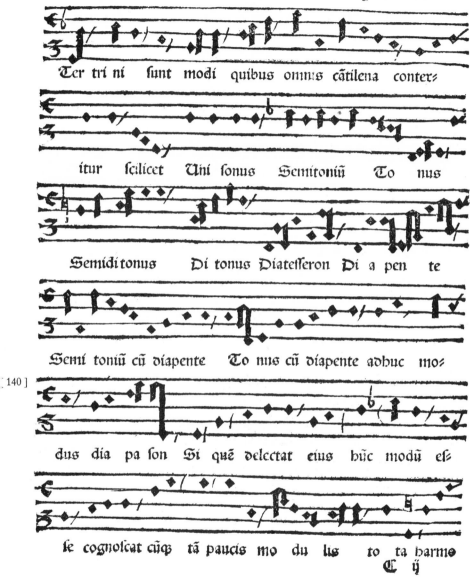

Ter tri ni   sunt modi   quibus omnis cãtilena   conter=

itur   scilicet   Uni sonus   Semitoniũ   To   nus

Semiditonus   Di tonus Diatesseron Di a pen   te

Semi toniũ cũ diapente   To nus cũ diapente adhuc   mo=

dus dia pa son Si quẽ delectat eius   hũc modũ es=

le cognoscat cũ<del>q</del> tã paucis mo du lis   to ta harmo

C ij

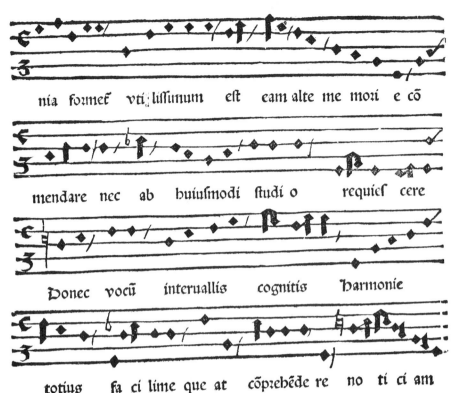

nia formet vtiliſſunum eſt eam alte me moꝛi e cõ

mendare nec ab huiuſmodi ſtudi o requieſ cere

Donec vocũ interuallis cognitis harmonie

totius fa ci lime que at cõpꝛehẽde re no ti ci am

De interuallis pꝛohibitis.

⁋ Sunt alia quedam interualla admodum rara, ac Tyꝛonibus poni pꝛo hibita. Ut enim poetarum atꝗ oꝛatoꝛũ docta licentia, quedam emeritis ſuis militibus concedit: Tyꝛonibus pꝛohibet, ita et muſicoꝛum . hoꝛum autem nomina ſunt hec. ⁋ Tritonus.

Sta- ⁋ Et eſt ſaltus de voce in vocem per quartam duram, tres integros to-
pulẽ- nos complectens abſꝗ ſemitonio, quare et Diateſſeron maioꝛ eſt. dicente
ſis Stapulenſe, Diateſſeron conſonantiam Tritonus tranſcendit, Et habetur hic modus in reſponſoꝛio, Iſti ſunt dies, dominica iudica, et in ꝛeſpon
ſoꝛio: Uoꝛ tonitrui, in dictione euangeliſta, vt ſic.

Joan nes eſt e uange li ſta

Semidiapente.

¶ Eſt interuall̄ ī per quintam imperfectam:duos tonos cū duobus ſemi
tonijs concludens.Quod licet in plano non reperiatur cantu:conditori
bus tamen:qui idipſum vitare tenentur:noticia eius confert plurimum.

Semiditonuſdiapente.

¶ Eſt per ſeptimā imperfectā interuallum. hoc apud Placentinū lib.3.Geor
ca.24.ton⁹ quatuor,ac ſemitonia duo comprehendit.huius exemplum gius
babet in Antipbona.Cū inducerent puerū ieſum,in dictione,Accepit. Placen.

**Ditonuſ=
diapente.**

Parentes   ei   us   accepit

¶ Eſt per ſeptimā perfectā,vocis a voce diſtantia,Tonis quinqꝫ et vno Ual
ſemitonio conſtās:ſecundū Georgiū Uallam li.3.ca.26.offendit autem la.
in reſponſorio.Sancta legio,de ſancto Mauritio,i dictione Aganenſiū.

Sancta   le   gio   Aganenſiū

Semidiapaſon.

¶ Eſt imperfecta octaua,Tonis quattuor ac trib⁹ ſemitonijs cōſtituta,
ab omni cantu plano reiecta,componiſtis tamen cognitu digna.

Semitoniumdiapaſon.

¶ Eſt ſaltus per nonam imperfectam,quinqꝫ tonis ac tribus ſemitonijs
conſtitutus Tonus autem cum diapaſon perfecta nona eſt,Tonis ſex,ſe-
mitonijs vero duobus,cauſata.

Semiditonuſdiapaſon.

¶ Interuallum eſt per decimam imperfectam,teſte Ualla.ca.31.ſex tonis ac tribus ſemitonijs creatum.Ditonus cum Diapaſon vero,perfecta
decima eſt,ſeptem tonis ac duobus ſemitonijs conflata.

C iij

141]

Diapaſondiapente.

¶ Conſonantia eſt duodecim ſonorum, interuallorū vndecim, conſtans tonis octo, Semitonijs autem tribus. horum modorum exempla in muſica plana admodum ſunt rara, in menſurali vero frequentiora.

Biſdiapaſon.

Am=
broſi=
us
Nola
nus.
Eraſ
mus
Ari=
ſto.

¶Eſt per quindecimā interuallū, ſecundū Macrobiū quadrupla propor tione cauſatū. Jn quo antiquitas cōſiſtendū, nec vltra progrediendū eſſe cenſuit. vt Ambroſius Nolanus apud Eraſmū alterū Germanie noſtre Nola lumen in Adagio Biſdiapaſon declarat. Tum ꝙ humane vocis terminꝰ naturalis (que vltra quindecim voces ſcandens gannitus: infra vero procedens ſcreatus magis ꝙ vox eſſe videtur) exiſtat. Tum ꝙ Ariſtote= les muſicam mere mathematicam eſſe neget. Jta enim temperatam eſſe oportet muſicam, vt nec ſenſui ratio, nec ſenſus rationi reclamet.

[142]

Caput octauum de dimen= ſione Monochordi.

Monocordū, vnius chorde inſtrumentū, tali induſtria rite cō ficiſ. Recipe lignū duarū vlnarū, vel placite longitudinis: duorū digitorū latitudinē: et totidem ſpiſſitudinē habens, atꝗ idipſum caua per mediū, extremitatibus omnibus ma nentibus illeſis, et cooperiaſ aſſere tenui leuigato ac feneſtrato, ad modū lutine: per cuiꝰ mediū linea vna occulta trahaſ. et in illius principio pun= ctus vnius lra F ſigneſ. Erit enim prima inſtrumenti magada. Poſt totā lineam a puncto F, in nouem partes equas diuide, atꝗ in primo diuiſio= nis puncto Γ vt pone, in ſecundo nihil, in tertio Cfaut, in quarto nihil, in quinto Gſolreut, in ſexto cſolfaut, in ſeptimo gſolreut minutam, in octa= uo nihil, vltumo autem Cifram, que tenebit locū ſecunde magade. hoc facto, ſpatium quod a Γut, vſꝗ ad ſecundam magadam eſt: iterū in par= tes nouem diſtingue. Jn quarum prima, A graue pone, in tertia Dſolre, in quita alamire, in ſexta dlaſolre, in ſeptima aalamire. Deinde ab Are in ſecundam magadam iterum fac partes nouem, ꞇ in prima pone ♮ graue, in tertia Elami, in quinta ♮mi in minutis, in ſexta elami acutam, in ſepti= ma ♮mi, in geminatis. Quo facto, ſpacium hoc totū a prima magada i ſe= cundam per partes quattuor diſtingue, et in prima pone Bfa in grauibꝰ, in ſecunda Ffaut finalem, i tertia ffaut acutam. Deinde incipe in Bfa gra ui et totam lineam conū verſus, in quatuor partes partire, et in prima po

ne ♭ ſemitonium inter D et E capitales, in ſecunda ♭ſa in minutis, inter
tia ♭♭fa in excellentib⁹. Hoc facto, incipe in Semitonio, quod inter D et
E eſt, et totam lineã in quattuoꝛ partes equas ſcinde, Et in pꝛima ſigna-
bis ♭ ſemitonium inter G capitalem et minutam, in ſecunda ♭ ſemitonium inter d et e acutas, in tertia ♭fa inter dd et ee, excellentes. Et ſi tertiam in duas equas vlterius diuiſeris, habebis ſemitoniũ inter g acutã
et aa excellens. Poſtea fige pedem circini in cſolfaut, et ſpacium verſus ſe
cundã magadã in duas partes diſtingue, i cui⁹ medio ccſolfa ponito. Si-
militer a dlaſolre ſpacium verſus conum in duo equalia partire, et in me
dio loca ddlaſol. Poſtremũ ab e acuta ꝯſus ſecundã magadã ſpaciũ diuide, ꝛ in medio habebis eela cũ vera monochoꝛdi dimenſione. His ſic factis, in extremis magadarum punctis, pone parua ipſius choꝛde ſuſtenta
cula: ne choꝛde ſonus lignoꝛum contactu obtundatur. Quibus paratis,
affigatur atꝗ ſuperducatur vna chorda enea ſatis foꝛtis, groſſa, atꝗ bene extenſa, vt ſonum audibilé reddat, et habebis monochoꝛdũ perfectũ.
Cuius foꝛma hec erit.

Caput nonum de diffinitione /
vtilitate, ac vſu Monochoꝛdi.

MOnochoꝛdum (vt dominus Guido in pꝛincipio ſui doctrinalis oſtendit) Eſt lignũ lõgũ quadratũ, intus concauũ, ſu-
perducta choꝛda, cuius ſonitu, vocum varietates appꝛeben
dimus. Uel eſt rudis magiſter, atꝗ indoctus, doctos diſci-
pulos faciens. Alijs enim oſtendit: quod ipſe nõ ſapit, vera dicit, menti-
ri neſcit, diligenter inſtruit, ac de ſenſus tarditate neminem coꝛripit. Dici
tum autem eſt Monochoꝛdum: a choꝛda vna ſicut Tetrachoꝛdũ a quattuoꝛ. Et decachoꝛdum a decem, Inquit Joannes pontifex. xxij. ca. vij.
muſice ſue.

Gui-

Tet-
choꝛ-
dum

Deca
choꝛ-
dum

De Monochordi vtilitate.

¶ Ad hoc imprimis ercogitatũ Monochordum eristit: vt iudex sit mu﹣
sicalium vocum atqɜ interuallorum. Tum cantus verus ne sit an falsus,
prebeat experimentum. Deinde vt Ceruicosis, ac falsis musicis, erroris
semitam recludat, ac veritatis viam aperiat. Postremum, vt pueris ad
musicam aspirantibus iter facile prebeat, Incipientes alliciat, progrediē﹣
tes dirigat, atqɜ ita ex indoctis doctos faciat.

De Monochordi vsu.

¶ Monochordi vsus est: inquit Berno Cluniacensis abbas, li. z. mu﹣
Ber﹣sice sue: vt quantum vnaquɜqɜ vox altera sit grauior, subtilior ve cogno﹣
no. scamus. Cum igitur cantum et quidem grauissimum: te magistro, duce
monochordo: discere volueris, Pone monochordum ante te ad mēsam:
Et i qua claue, prima nota illius cantus: quem scire desideras: posita sit,
attende. Qua inuenta: eandem in monochordo cum plectro tange, ꝗ qui
erit sonus, is erit quem queris. hoc modo deinceps per singulas notas
ipsius cantus discurre, et sic te magistro cantum grauissimum quemqɜ fa﹣
cile et inuenies et addisces.

[144]

Caput decimum de musica ficta.

St autem musica ficta: quam greci Sinemenon vocant: cantus
preter regularem schalarum exigentiam editus. Uel est cantus
coniunctosus.

De coniunctis.

Ber﹣¶ Coniunctas veteres adiunctas dixere, eo ꝗ preter naturam canticis,
nbar vel euphonie, vel pficiendorũ modorũ causa, adantur, dicēte diuo Bern﹣
dus. hardo, in qualibet maneria, vbi molliore sonũ fieri expedit, pro dura vo﹣
ce mollis ponatur: fartum tamen, ne cantus similitudinē alterius toni as﹣
sumere videaɫ. Est autē coniuncta, canere vocē in claue, que nō est in ea.
Uel est toni i semitoniũ aut semitonij in tonũ subita et iprouisa mutatio.

De coniunctarum diuisione ac numero.

¶ Sunt itaqɜ duplices coniũcte: Tollerabiles scilicet, qñ canɨ vox in cla﹣
ue que in ea non est, reperɨ tamen in eius octaua, vt cātando mi in Are,
la in Dsolre. Intollerabiles: quando canitur vox in claue, que in ea non
est, neqɜ in ei9 octaua, vt cantando fa in Elami, mi in Ffaut. harum auɫ

30

tem coniunctarū ouo sunt signa, scilicet ♭ rotundum et ♮ quadratū. Pri
mum in locis ♮ duralibus. Secundum in ♭ mollibus coniunctam fieri de
monstrat. ⸿ Sunt autem octo coniuncte magis vsitate, licet et vbilibet
plures fieri possint, Prima in A graui, ♭ rotundo designatur. Scōa in E
finali eodem quo et precedens signo denotatur. Tertia in Ffaut conspi
citur, q et ♮ duro ibi notato oinoscitur. Quarta in a minuta fit, quā ♭ mol
le cognoscibilem reddit. Quinta in c affinali ♮ duro notaf. Sexta in e acu
ta ♭ orbiculari deprehenditur. Septima in f acuta ♮ quadrato indicatur.
Octaua in aa geminata locum sibi vendicat, quā et ♭ rotundum ibi signa
tum demonstrat. harum autem omnium exempla tum in plano, tum in
mensurali copiosa inueniuntur.

Sequitur schala ficta.

⸿ Schala ficta priores et in acumine et i grauitate excedit. Infra Γ graue
enim (quoniam in A fa canit) oitonum addit. Ultra eela etiam (in ea
enim fa profert) per ouos gradus excrescit. Quare ad eius formationē,
ouodecim linee necessario requiruntur, vt claret in figura subscripta.

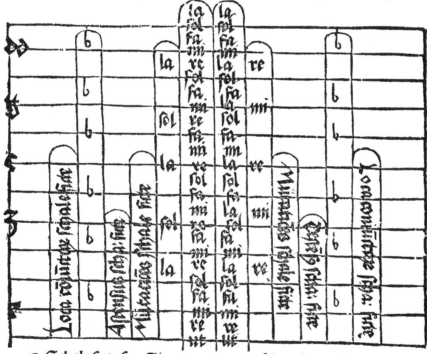

[145]

☞ Schala ficta seu Sinemenon et que sub ea fiunt Mutationes.

Regule musices ficte.

¶ Prima, Melius ac suauius est canere per tollerabiles coniunctas, ῷ proprias clauium voces. ¶ Secunda, Tollerabiles coniuncte cantũ non viciant sed intollerabiles. ¶ Tertia, Musica ficta fingit in quacũꝗ claue quãcunꝗ voce psonãtie causa. ¶ Quarta, Signato fa in bfa♮mi vt quouis alio loco, si cantus er ea saltum immediatum fecerit ad quartam, quintam, vel octauam, ꞇ ibi fa necessario venit signandum, propter vitare Tritonum. Semidiapente ac Semidiapason modos inusitatos ac prohibitos, vt in infrascripto claret exemplo.

Musices Ficte exercitium.

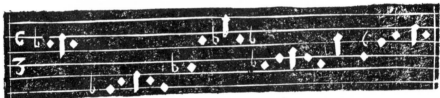

Caput vndecimum de cantu ac transpositione.

Vnde cãtus, Est melodia er sono, modo, tono, per voce viuã formata. Sono dico propter notarum scripturam, quam improprie cantum dicimus. per modum, ascensum et descensum intelligo, propter preces nocturnas atꝗ defunctorum, que in vnisono leguntur, Tono: propter auium garritũ, qui nullo comprehenditur tono. Quod enim in sylogismo modus et figura, hoc in cantu tonus facit ac scbala. Uocem viuam dico, propter musica instrumenta. Uel aliter, Cantus est viue vocis secundum arsim ac thesim coaptatio. Uel vt Gafforus in Theoricis lib. 5. ca. 6. scribit, Est plurium vocum ab eodem principio deductio. Et hec descriptio proprie buic syllabarum progressioni (qm̃ cantus non est) conuenit.

Gaf‐
fo.

32

De deductionum Numero.

¶ Tres igitur sũt huiusmodi deductiões: Prima ♮ duralis dicitur, duriter modulanda. quia in bfa♮mi et octauis eius mi requirit. ¶ Secunda bmollis ẽ, que blando ac suaui concentu discurrit, in bfa♮mi nãncꝗ fa poscit. ¶ Tertia naturalis quasi neutralis dicitur. In bfa♮mi enim nec mi, nec fa cupit: quia locum talẽ non attingit.

Deductionum Regule.

¶ Prima, vbicunꝗ ponitur vt, in schala, ibi est alicuius deductionis principium, vbi fa, ibi mediũ, et vbi la, ibi finis, vt in subscripta claret figura.

$$\text{In} \left\{\begin{array}{c} G \\ F \\ a \end{array}\right\} \text{natura} \left\{\begin{array}{c} F \\ b \\ d \end{array}\right\} \text{bmol.} \left\{\begin{array}{c} g \\ c \\ e \end{array}\right\} ♉ ♮ \text{dura} \left\{\begin{array}{c} \text{Principiũ} \\ \text{Medium} \\ \text{Finis} \end{array}\right.$$

¶ Scõa regula. Cuius deductionis hec vel illa nota existat, sic facile dinosces. Considera vocem ibi cantandam, cum qua descende vsꝗ ad suũ fundamentum, puta vt, et vbi tale repertum fuerit, videatur, que deductio ibi habeat initium Nam de tali erit nota de qua queris.

De Transpositione.

¶ Vnde transpositio Est cantus vel clauis a propria sede remotio. Est enim transponere cantum vel clauem a loco proprio remouere, et est duplex transpositio, scilicet cantus et clauis.

[147]

De transpositione Cantus.

¶ Est coniunctarum euitatio. Dum enim coniunctas (quoniã viciosum reddunt cantum) vitare intendimus, cantũ ex loco proprio sui finis sursum ad quintam eleuamus. vt in responsorio, Jte in orbem, lucide claret.

Regulariter ♦ Jrregulariter

J te in or bem   J te in or bem

De clauibus affinalibus tonorum.

¶ Claues:quas affinales dicim9:sunt littere cantuum irregularium terminatiue.Quarum secundum Guidonem,Bernonem,ac diuum Grego
rium,tres sunt.Licet Ambrosiani plures ponant.

Scz { Alamire } Jn qua fi { Primi } et { Secundi } tonorum
{ bfa♮mi } nit omis { Tertij } { Quarti } transpo
{ csolfaut } cantus. { Quinti } { Sexti } sitorum.

¶ Fit autem ista cantuum illegalitas,vt scribit Pontifex .14.ca. musice
siue,interdum venialiter,cantorum ignauia interdum, er irrefutabili anti
quitate nonnunq̃ , pleramq̃ etiam contrapunctandi causa,vt Baritonus sub chorali Tenore locum descendendi habeat.

De transpositione regule.

¶ Prima.Cantus septimi et octaui tonorum non transponitur.Non sur
sum ad dlasolre, vt Ambrosiani arbitrantur:quia tonus autentus nõ ha
bet locum iurgendi ad decimam,Nec infra ad Cfaut,quoniã plagalis nõ
habet locum cadendi ad quintã neq̃ enim vltra eela scandendũ : neq̃ infra Ґut descendendum est: vt supra claruit,Quare inquit Joannes pontifer.Oportet eum qui vicarium habere non potest,ipse suum per se officium administret. ¶ Secunda regula,Cantus in dlasolre aut in Cfaut terminatus , aut Ambrosianus est, aut cantorum inscitia corruptus.
dicéte Pontifice,Quoties in cantu Tetrardi vlla euenit aberratio , dica
mus eam ex cantorum procedere inscitia,et corrigendam esse musicorum
peritia,Gregorianorum enim, talem non admittit cantum, auctoritas.
¶ Tertia, Uni9 vocis errauee in aliqua claue locatio, causa est cur toti
us cantus fiat transpositio. ¶ Quarta,Trãspositio est coniunctarum remedium atq̃ excusatio. ¶ Quinta,Omnis transpositio er finali, ad quin
tam propriam affinalem fiat,nisi necessitate ad quartam fieri cogaƭ. Tũc
autem ad quartam transponere compellimur : quando post quintariam
transpositionem plures coniũcte, q̃ ante fuerant oriuntur: vt in responso
rio Que est ista, sub tertio tonn licet videre hoc modo.

[148]

Que est ista regulariter   Transpositio quin   Trãspositio q̃rtaria
               taria nõ valens   bene valens

¶ Serta Eede voces post transpositioñe cantande sunt, que canebantur
ante. ¶ Septima. Jn canticis irregularib⁹ ad quintam transpositis, cantandum est mi in bfa♮mi in omi tono, nisi fa specialiter signetur. ¶ Octaua, Jn cãticis ad quartam trãpositis, in bfa♮emi sem̄per fa, p̃ofertur, nisi
mi specialiter notetur. ¶ Nona Transpositio ad quartã cognoscitur quã
do cantus per vocem sue scbale non conuenientem terminatur. Ul'quã-
do in p̃incipio cantus transpositi fa signatũ reperitur. Cui transpositio-
ni diuus Bernbardus omnio reclamare videtur: cum inquit: dignũ qui- **Ber-**
dem est vt qui regulariter viuere p̃oposuerunt, etiã recte canendi scien- **bar.**
tiam babeãt: repudiatis eorum licentijs: qui similitudinem magis q̃ naturam in cantibus attendentes: cobereñtia disiungũt, coniungunt opposita, cantum: vt libet: non vt licet: incipiunt et termiant, deponũt, eleuãt,
cõponunt et ordinant. Per inconsultam enim huiusmodi transpositionem tanta in cantibus orta est confusio: vt plures alterius manerıeı esse
credantur. ¶ Decima regula. Cantus in Gsolreut terminatus: signato fa
ın bfa♮mi, est p̃imı vel secũdi toni ad quartam transpositi. Et qui in ala
mire tertij vel quarti, vt Que est ista, et sic de alijs.

De Transpositio-
ne clauium.

¶ Clauium transpositio est Clauis signate ob defectum linearũ, vel eleuatio, vel depressio. de qua tales dantur regule. ¶ P̃ima, Clauũ trãspositio cantũ non irregularisat, quia regularē finē non variat. ¶ Secun
da. Quanto clauis trãposita descendit a p̃oria p̃ecedente: tanto nota se
quens clauem illam transpositam ascendit, et ediuerso. vt in infrascriptis
claret exemplis.

bec sunt cõuiuia   que tibi placēt   o patris   sapien tia

Caput.xij.de to-
nis in specie.

Q Uom innat⁹ sit nobis a generalioribus ad specialia magis **Arī.**
  p̃ocessus: vt summ⁹ ille philosopborum omnıũ p̃ınceps,
                                   D

ac naturalis intelligentie lumen Aristoteles, primo de phisico auditu declarat. Congruo igitur ordine post generalem tonorum explanationem, ad speciuoca transeamus: vnuscuiuscp naturam latius ac clarius enodando. Et primum quidem primi.

De Tono primo.

Ber-
nbar-
dus.

¶ Primus tonus: vt diuus Bernhardus scribit: est regula autentũ prime manerie determinans. Uel est Prothi autentica progressio. Est autẽ progressio autentica, ascensⁱ vltra finem ad octauam, nonam, et decimã.

Fra.

Et formatur primi toni progressio ex ea diapenthes specie, que est ex D in a, et ea diatesseron specie: que ab a in D acutam est, inquit Franchinus. li. 1. pratice, ca. 8. Finalem sedem habet in Dsolre regularem, vt in alamire irregularẽ. Principia eiⁱ apd Guidonem sunt. C.D.E.F.G. et a, cuiⁱ forma capitalis est hec.

Capitale Primi toni.   Sacerdos   in eternũ   Gaudea mus

De Tonorum differentijs.

¶ Differentie de tonorum essentia non sunt: sed pro indoctis tantum: vt in diuersis tonorum initijs facilius ordiantur, reperte. Inquit enim
Joã.
papa

pontifex. 23. c. musice sue. Ego nullam huius rei causam: nisi vsum: inuenio: nec ab vllo musicorum scripta reperi. Necp diuus Bernhardus multum approbare videtur. Multarum enim confusionum errorumcp occasionem dant differentie. Cum igitur obsequium nostrũ: quod deo prestamus: rationabile esse debeat: relictis differentijs (quas nulla probat ratio) solum de capitalibus tonorũ Tenoribus solliciti sint studiosi lectores: ne iutilibus superuacaneiscp preceptis se inuoluant: noctis caliginẽ induant, ac rem facilem, obscurissimam reddant ac difficillimam, necp enim irrationabilibⁱ flasciis: sed bene moratis ac regulatis canticis gaudet deus, qui omnia ordine regulatissimo constituit. Quare et Psalmista dicit.
Psal.
Laudate dominũ in cymbalis bonesonantibus. Non enim bene sonantibus dixisset, si deus quouis boatu, screatu, ac strepitu laudari voluisset.

De diuisionibus Psalmorum.

¶ Psalmos: quibus i diuinis vtimur laudibⁱ: duplices inuenio. Maiores scilicet et minores. Minores omnes psalmi dicuntur, preter duo can-

tica, ſcilicet diue virginis et Zacharie. Canticum etiã Symeonis, in qui⸗
buſdam dyoceſibus pro maioꝛe, in quibuſdam pro minoꝛe pſalmo reputa⸗
tur, Ut ipſe oꝛbeṁ terrarum luſtrando expertuſſum.

De vero pſallendi modo.

¶ Quom pſalmi concentu, magnũ, magno in myſterio: prophetã vſum   Quʒ
eſſe: tum Celij Rodigini, tũ Theologoꝛũ omniũ teſtetur auctoꝛitas, pla   id ſit
cuit non nihil de vero pſallendi modo, ſcriptis noſtris inſerere. Uñ pſal⸗   pſal⸗
lere, eſt cũ quodã iubilo laudes deo opti. max, decãtare, Qua in re tanta   lere.
eſt: Proh pudoꝛ: diuerſitas, vt ſinguli ſinguloꝛ pſallendi modos habere   Joã.
videãt̃, Nec ſtatuta nec ꝓcepta patrũ ſuãtes, ſed quiſꝗ vt vult ⁊ pſallit ⁊   papa
canit. Uñ tanta in eccleſia orta eſt diſſenſio, tanta diſcoꝛdia, tãta confuſio,
vt vix duo eundẽ pſallendi ritũ teneant. Hoc grauiter repꝛehendit pon⸗
tifex ca. zz. muſice ſue: et quidẽ digne: cum inquit. Cum vnus dñs, vna
fide, vno baptiſmate, et omnino moꝛũ vnitate oblectet̃: quis non credat
illumipſum cantoꝛum multiplici diſcoꝛdia grauiſſime offendi? Quare nõ
nullas, de vero pſallendi modo regulas tradidiſſem: Niſi eas iam a dño   Mi⸗
Michaele Galliculo de muris viro ſane doctiſſimo, apud veterẽ Cellã   chael
Ciſtertij ordinis celeberrimũ Cenobium: et copioſe et erudite conſcrip⸗   gallis
tas offendiſſem. Omnes igitur eius rei cupidos ad hunc remitto, ſolũ me   culꝰ
ijs, qne intonationes pſalmoꝛum concernunt: intromittendo.

De intonationibꝰ pſalmoꝛũ regule.

¶ Prima. Omnes pſalmi maioꝛes cũ aſcenſu: minoꝛes vero abſꝗ aſceſu
ſunt intonãdi. ¶ Scda. Dictiones indeclinabiles, hebꝛaice, ac barbare,
in medio accentu acuto ſunt pꝛoferende. ¶ Tertia. Intonatio pſalmoꝛũ
minoꝛũ primi toni ex alamire: maioꝛum vero ex F faut eſt hoc modo.

Laudate   pueri   dñm   laudate   nomẽ   domini

Memẽto   domine   dauid   Magnificat   anima   mea   dñm

¶ Melodia verſuũ ĩ rñſoꝛijs, a muſicis receutioꝛibus iam ad placitũ foꝛ

D ij

matur, Introitum autem vsque hodie inuiolabiter seruatur, secundum
Priscorum decreta hoc modo.

Melodia versuum in responsorijs primi toni

Melodia versuum in introitibus primi toni

De Tono secundo.

¶ Secundus tonus: vt diuus Bernhardus inquit: Est regula plagalem
prime manerie determinans. Uel est plagalis Prothi progressio. Est
autem plagalis progressio, descensus vltra finem ad quintam, vel saltem
quartā. Initia eius scdm Guidonē sunt A.C.D.F. ꝛ G. octaui auten=
ti fines rite occupat, quia miles Sui ducis castra iure gentium licite inha
bitat. Formula autem secundi toni hec est.

Capitale secūdi toni   Miserator dominus   hec mūdū spernes

¶ Intonatio psalmorum minorum et
Ffaut: maiorū vero et Cfaut habe=
tur hoc modo.

Laudate pueri   dominū Laudate nomē   domi   ni

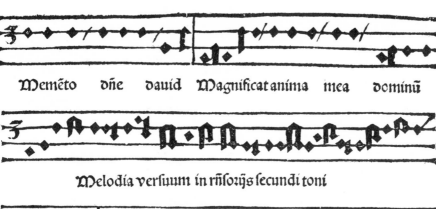

Memẽto   dñe   dauid   Magnificat anima   mea   dominũ

Melodia verſuum in rñſorijs ſecundi toni

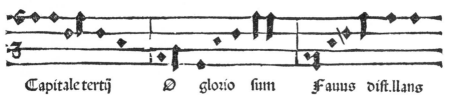

Melodia verſuũ in introitibus ſecũdi toni

De tertio Tono.

¶ Tertius tonus eſt Regula autentum ſecunde manerie determinans.
Uľ eſt autentica Deuteri progreſſio, ſedem habens finalem in Elami re⸗
gularem, Uel in ♮mi irregularem: Initia eius ſecundum Guidoné ſunt
E.F.G.et c.Cuius formula capitalis eſt hec.

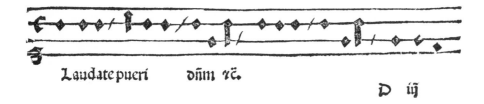

Capitale tertij   Ø   glorio   ſum   Fauus diſt.llans

¶ Intonatio pſalmorum minorum ex cſolfaut, maiorum vero ex Gſol⸗
reut eſt: huius modi.

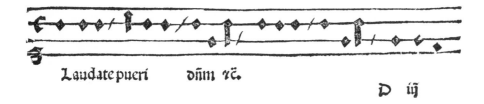

Laudate pueri   dñm ꝛc.

                                        D iij

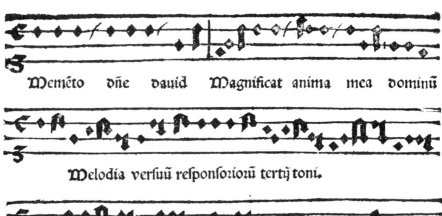

Meméto   dñe   dauid   Magnificat anima   mea   dominũ

Melodia verſuũ reſponſoꝛioꝛũ tertij toni.

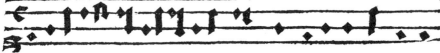

Melodia verſuũ introitualiũ tertij toni

De Tono quarto.

⁋ Quartꝰ tonus, teſte Bernhardo, Eſt regula plaga=
lem ſecunde manerie, determinans, vel eſt plagalis
deuteri pꝛogreſſio, eoſdem quos ſuꝑ autentus finem
occupás. Initia illi accidũt ſex, ſcilicet C.D.E.F.G.
et a. Cuius tenoꝛ pꝛincipalis eſt hic, vt ſequitur.

Capitale quarti   Tota pulchꝛa es hec   eſt dies

⁋ Intonatio pſalmoꝛum minoꝛum ex alamire, maio
rum vero ex Elami eſt hoc modo.

Laudate   pue ri   dominũ laudate noīe   domi ni

Meméto domine dauid   Magnificat anima mea domi   num

Melodia versuũ rũsoriorũ quarti toni

Melodia versuũ in officijs diuinis, Quarti toni

De Tono quinto.

¶ Quintus tonus est regula, autentum tertie mane=
rie determinans, Uel est autentica Triti progressio.
Cuius finis regularis in Ffaut est, irregularis autẽ
in csolfaut. Principia eius (teste Franchino) quat=
tuor sunt, scilicet F.a.c.et G. Cuius formula capita=
lis est hec.

Capitale quinti   Gaude dei genitrix   Gau   di   a

Intonatio psalmorum minorum ex csolfaut, maiorũ
vero ex Ffaut, et habetur et intonatur hoc modo.

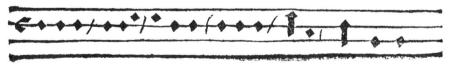

Laudate pueri domiñu rc.

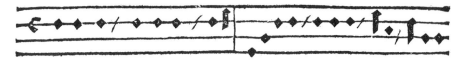

Memento domine dauid Magnificat anima mea dñm

harmonia versuū responsoriorū, quinti toni.

Progressio versiū introitualiū quinti toni

De Tono sexto.

¶ Sextus tonus est regula, plagalē tertie manerie determinens. Uel est plaʒ lis Triti ꝑgresso, cum suo autento in finalibus uste participans. Cui initia quattuor accidunt scilicet C. D. F, et a: Inquit Franchinus. 13. ca. practice sue. Et Guido in dialogo doctrinali. Cuius formula capitalis est hec.

Capitale Ueni electa mea Diligebat eam

¶ Intonatio psalmorum minorum ex alamire, maiorum ex ffaut procedit hoc modo.

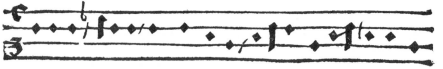

Laudate pueri domi num Laudate nomē domi ni

Memento domine dauid Magnificat ani ma mea dñm

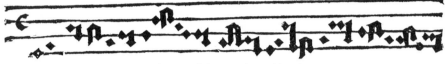

Melodia verſuũ in rñſoꝛijs Sexti ioni

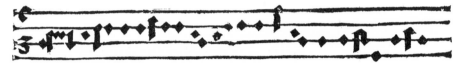

Melodia verſuũ in introicibus Sexti

De To:IIII ſeptimo.

¶ Septimus tonus eſt regula, autentum quarte manerie determinans, Uel eſt autentica Tetrardi pꝛogreſſio. Finem habet in Gſolreut regulariter tantũ.
Cui initia quicꝗ accidunt ſcilicet G, a, ♮, c et d. Cui⁹
formula capitalis eſt hec.

Capitale ſeptimi   Exoꝛtum eſt   Clamauerunt

¶ Jntonatio pſalmoꝛum minoꝛum ex dlaſolre, maioꝛum autem ex bfa♮mi foꝛmatur
hoc modo.

Laudate pueri dominũ   Laudate nomē   domi ni
                                         Œ

Meméto domine dauid   Magnificat anima mea dominū

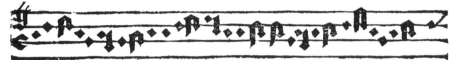

Melodia versuũ rñsoriorũ Septimi toni

Melodia versuũ iutroitualiũ Septimi toni

De Tono octauo.

¶ Octauus tonus est regula, plagalem quarte ma=
nerie determinans. Uel est plagalis Tetrardi pro=
gressio, eundem cum suo autento, finem possidens.
Cuius initia sunt D. F. G. a et c. Formula aũt princi
palis hec que sequitur.

Capitale octaui Dum ortus   Justi   con fi te bun tur

¶ Intonatio psalmorum minorum ex csol=
faut habetur, maiorum autem ex Gsolreut
procedit modo quo sequitur.

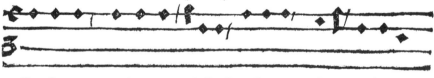

Laudate   pueri   dominũ Laudate nomē   domi ni

44

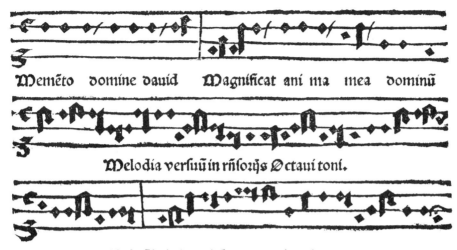

Meméto domine dauid   Magnificat ani ma mea dominũ

Melodia verfuũ in rñſozÿs Octaui toni.

Melodia in introitibus octaui toni.

De Tono peregrino.

¶ Eſt alius tonus: quem nonnulli Peregrinum nominant,
Non ⱷ peregrinozum:ſed ⱷ in noſtra concinnentia rarus admodum ac peregrinus ſit,ſic dictus.Nam nõ niſi ad vnam an-
tiphonam.Nos qui viuimus,ſcilicet, τ ad pſalmos duos,puta.
Jn exitu, et Benedicite,tenoz eius,decantatur. Jn finali quoⱷ
ſeptimi vltima eius terminatur,vt Franchinus oſtendit. Cuius tenoz eſt qui ſequitur.

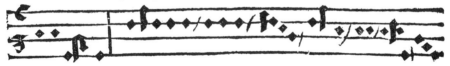

Peregrin⁹ ton⁹ Jn exitu iſrael de egypto dom⁹ Jacobde pplo barbaro

Qȝ diuerſi diuerſis delectentur modis.
Caput Tredecimum.

Q Uom non omnium oza eodem cibo capiantur, vt ſcribit Joʒ:
Pontifex.16.capi.muſice ſue, ſed ille quidem acriozib⁹, iſte pa:
vero leniozibus eſcis iuuetur.Jdeo nõ omniũ aures eiuſdẽ
modi ſono oblectãt . Alios nãⱷ mozoſa ac curialis þmi va-

E ij

gatio delectat. Alios rauca scdi grauitas capit. Alios seuera ac quasi in
dignitas tertij insultatio iuuat. Alios adulatorius quarti sonus attrahit.
Alij modesta quinti petulātia mouentur. Alij lachrymosa sexti voce mul=
Gui. centur. Alij inimicos septimi saltus libenter audiūt. Alij decētem et qua=
si matronalem octaui canorem diligunt. Nec mirum: inquit Guido. **13.**
micrologi capi: si varietate sonorum delectatur auditus, cum varietate
colorum gratuletur visus, odorum varietate foueatur olfactus, ac muta
tis saporibus lingua congaudeat. Quapropter bene cautus sit musicus,
vt cantum in eo tono disponat, in quo plurimum delectari auditores cog
noscit. Ut si iuuenum rogatu cantum componere voluerit: iuuenilis sit
ille et lasciuus. Si vero senum, morosus sit, et seueritatē exprimens. Quē=
admodum enim comediarum scriptor: si partes iuuenis, seni: z luxuriosi,
auaro mandauerit, derisui habet. Ita et modulator, si i tristi re salientem
modum adduxerit, et in leta lachrymabilem. Qua autem id fiat industria
Cassi modorum proprietas declarat. Quoniam (vt scribit Cassiodorus in epi=
odo= stola ad Boetium, et resumit Celius antiquarum lectionū. lib. 5. ca. 22)
rus. Dorius prudentie largitor est, ac castitatis effector. Phrygius pugnas ex=
citat, et votum furoris inflammat. Eolius animi tempestates trāquillat,
somnumqp iam placatis tribuit. Lydius intellectum obtusis acuit: terre=
no desyderio grauatis, celestium appetētiam inducit, bonorum operator
eximius. Lydium tamen; Plato lib. de rep. tertio: plurimum reprobat: tū
qp flebilis: tum qp femineus sit. Dorium autem probat : tum qp virilis: tū
qp viros fortes et delectet, et rei bellice repertor exiscat. Nostri autem cul=
tioris seculi homines: modo Dorio, modo Phrygio, modo Lydio, modo
alijs vtuntur modis. Quoniam in alio et alio negotio: alium sibi modum
conuenire perpenduut. Nec mirum: omnis etenim animi habitus canti=
Ma= bus gubernatur: scribit Macrobius: nā dat cantꝰ somnos, adimitqp : nec
crobi non curas et immittit et retrahit, iram suggerit, clementiam suadet, mor
us. bis medetur, et effectus supra fidem varios producit: inquit Franciscus
Frā Petraca. hos ad leticiam inanem: hos ad deuotum z sanctum gaudiū,
cisc. piasqp nonnunqp lachrymas, mouet. De quibus omnibus malo tacere, qp
Pe= aliquid inconsulte determinare, ne puerorum ingenia inutilibus potius
trar= qp necessarijs preceptis videar grauare. Quoniam qui in exponendo plu
cha. ra qp necesse est superfundit, addit tenebras, non tollit densitatem : inquit
Macrobius lib. 2. super Somnio Scipiōis. Dent igitur ijs paucis ope=
ram studiosi: atqp ediscant precepta hec : quoniā ad sequētem tractatū ne=
cessario requiruntur intelligendum.

Libri Primi finis.
Sequitur Secundus.

Uenerabili ac multe bñuolentie viro, domío Georgio Brac-
chio Musico peritissimo, ac Ducalis cantorie Wir-
tenbergensis ductori primario, Andreas Or-
nitoparchus Meyningēsis Salutē.

Um Platonis illā: qua non nobísmetipsis, sed et patrie, et amicis, nos natos dicit: accuratius ruminassem senten tiam, Georgi colendissime: quasi viribus destitutus, ac horrore tremefactus elangui. Et vt primus ille Romani imperij monarcha: cū Alexandri statuam ad Gades pri mum cōspexisset: q̄ nil memoria dignum gessisset, inge muit: ita et ipse (quoniā omnia quibus homo letatur, veluti forma, vo- luptates, etas, valitudo, delitie, pretereūt, sed famā extendere factis, hoc virtutis opus) q̄ nil tale fecerim, ingemui. Quare post multa suspiria, re sumpto tandem spiritu (licet multis curarū fluctibus, aduersitatum tur- binibus, ac variarū perturbationum procellis, agitarer) quid nam poste- ritati: quod me vixisse testetur: relinquerem, cogitaui. Et cum huc atq̄ il luc animus deflecteretur, tandem concinentie disciplinam: tum q̄ mo- ralitati coniuncta, tum q̄ laudis dei ministra sit: e mltis delegi. Inter om nes enim scholasticas disciplinas: quas vulgo liberales nominant: nulla moralior, nulla iucundior, nulla diuinior: vt ipse optime nosti: ipsa musica reperitur. Cuius licet: multi sint professores: paucissim tamen (odio ne an ignauia id fiat nescio) formales eius artis reperiuntur scriptores. Quo fit, vt preter eos, qui in sacellis principū aut sunt, aut olim fuert: nulli, aut admodum pauci veri musici inueniantur. Unde et ars ipsa: quasi sub mo dio lumen: occulta vilescit, laus summi omnium conditoris decrescit, et emulorum turba, quasi iam victrix ullo prohibente, per omnē fere Ger maniā, in artis huius excidium c— : plus z pius indies inualescit. his igitur causis concitatus: vir pre— issime, ac humanitate tua (quā mi- hi ex florentissimo Tubingensi g_mnasio venienti, et ad edes tuas: quas dono principis tui possides amenissimas: diuertenti, ostēdisti maximam) confisus, cū antea planam musicam scripsissem: tuis auspicijs ad mensura lem etiā stilū me verti. Et quiccūquid floris longa aliorū in se habuere volumina: velut apis: breuissimis preceptis, et eisdem facilimis, in hunc secundum practice nostre librum, comportauimus. Quem nomini tuo di catū, etiam censure tue subijcimus, vt et a mendis expurges: et ab emulo rū (quis bonorū fama iugiter laceratur) latratu redimas, protegas, de- fendas. Cū etenim eorū: que quis nouit: bonus iudex existat: merito cen soriā illi in me comitto potestatem, quē iampridem pium, equū, doctum: apud me: que non fallitur: docuit experientia. doctorum parens fatetur Sueuia, ac tota superior veneratur Germania. Uale igitur felix: vir eru- ditissime: et Andream tuum ab emulorum morsu defende.

E ij

[marginal notes:] Pla-to. Juli⁹ Alex- āder- i sta- tua Tu- bigē se gy- mna- sium. Sue- uia doc- toruz pa- rēs.

Musice Omitoparchiane Liber secūdus Mēsuralis catilene rudimēta declarās.

henrici Cotheri Brunopolitani Artium magistri.
Argumentum Libri secundi.

Alter habet varie discrimina dulcia vocis
Quis curas lenit mens, abigitꝗ suas.

Caput Primum de artis huius Utilitate ac laudibus.

Boe.
BOetius ille romanus, Cuius ingenium in musica nemo superauit uno nec attigit vnꝗ, in primo sue musice, tātam (iquit) musicis concentibus inesse efficatiā: vt etiam homo si vellet eis carere nō possit. Musica enim curas abigit insomnes, infantes cōpescit vagietes, laborantum mitigat labores, fessos reparat artus, ac perturbatos reformat animos. Omnis etiam in hac vita anima, ita

Ma.
musicis sonis capitur: vt nō solum, qui sunt habitu cultiores: iquit Macrobius: verū vniuerse quoꝗ barbare nationes, cantus: quibus vel ad ardorem virtutis animentur: vel ad mollitiem voluptatis resoluantur: exerceant, Et ita delinimentis canticis occupantur: vt et ad bellum progressui, et item receptui canatur: cantu et excitante et rursus sedante vir-

Isidor.
tutem. Ea autem precipue id efficit musica: quā mensuralē nomināt. hec

Arió
enim non modo homines: inquit Isidorus: sed et bestias, serpentes, vo-

Am-
lucres, atꝗ delphines ad auditum sue modulatiōis, prouocat. Qua vna

phió
vel maxime Arion in medijs vndis vitam preseruauit, Amphyon Dirce-

Or-
us lapides ac saxa in Thebarum muros congregauit, Orpheus traxit Eu-

phe⁹
ridicen coniugem ab inferis reuocauit. Tymothe⁹ vir Phrygius. Alex-

Ty-
andrū magnum, totius orbis domitorem, ab epulis ad arma capescenda

mo.
inflammauit: et mox: mutato modulationis instrumento: eundem ab ar-

Alex
mis rursus ad conuiuiū reuocauit, Regius quoꝗ psaltes Dauid. Saulē

āder.
Israelis regem: cum a spiritu vexaretur immundo, liberauit: hec etiam

mag-
est: qua non solum summus ille rerum opifex deus, verū et Stygij Iouis

nus.
furiales anime placantur, mitigantur, refocillantur, Ipsa enim est cete-

Da-
rarum disciplinarū domina, que et Stigia arua, Neptunia regna, Iouis

uid
quoꝗ etheri loca, eterna luce corusca, pmulcere potest. Que et sola, relic-

tis terris, volat ante tribunal summi iudicis, vbi sonant iugiter organa

sanctorum: vbi angeli et archangeli hymnum deo infatigabiliter decantant, vbi Cherubin et Seraphin, sanct⁹, incessabili voce proclamāt. Adde ꝙ nulla disciplina sine musica possit esse perfecta. Quare et Pythago-

ras difcipulis:vt in melodijs et obdoꝛmirent et a fomno refurgerent:pꝛe
cepit.Moꝛes pꝛeterea hominum,mufica et regit et componit.Nã et Ne
ro quoad muficã coluit,Seneca tefte,mitiffimus extitit.Sed vbi relicta
mufica:ad necromantie diabolicas artes animum vertit:tum pꝛimũ fe-
uire cepit:ex agno lupus factus,atꝙ ex manfuetiffimo pꝛincipe,in feuiffi-
mam beftiam eft transfoꝛmatus.Sed ne longioꝛ folito digreffio fiat,Ne-
ue et ignotis pꝛocedatur,bꝛeuiffimis verbis,quid mufica fit,aperiã.Eft
igiꝛ mufica menfuralis,peritia modulatiõis,in figuris,foꝛma difcretis:
modo,tempoꝛe,ac pꝛolatione quantificatis:confiftens.Uel eft ars cuius
harmonia,et figurarum et vocum varietate,perficitur.

Caput fecundum de figuris.

Vnde figura eft quoddam fignum:vocis,filentijꝙ repꝛefen-
tatiuum.Uocis dico,pꝛopter fpecies notarum:que pꝛoferun-
tur.Silentij vero pꝛopter paufas notis equiualentes,que ar-
tificiofo filentio menfurantur.

De figurarum numero.

¶ Quinꝙ tantũ figuras Pꝛifci obferuauere:tanꝙ pꝛincipales,ac tribus
mufice gradibus quãtificabiles.Ex quibus alias quafdã deduxit pofte-
ritas agilitatis caufa:iuxta illud Ouidij.Ex alijs alias reparat natura fi-
guras.Quarum coꝛpoꝛa figurarum,foꝛmantur modo quo fequitur.
¶ Maxima eft figura cuius longitudo latitudinem triplicat:filũ habens
in dextra parte furfum vel deoꝛfum.¶ Longa eft nota cuius longitudo
duplicat latitudinem:filum habens inftar maxime.¶ Bꝛeuis eft figura
qnadrato coꝛpoꝛe foꝛmata,filo carens.¶ Semibꝛeuis eft nota rotunda
ad modum oui,Uel:vt Franchino placet:Trianguli.¶ Minima.Eft
figura vt Semibꝛeuis,cũ virgula afcedente vel defcendéte.¶ Semiminima,Eft nota vt minima,coloꝛe variata.¶ Fufa,eft nota inftar femi-
minime,habens vncum in dextra parte.¶ Semifufa,eft figura inftar fu-
fe foꝛmata,fed fecundo vnco ab ea difcreta,vt fic.

Octo figu-
rarũ coꝛpa
{
Maxima
Longa
Bꝛeuis
Semibꝛeuis

Minima
Semiminima
Fufa
Semifufa
}

¶ Est alia quedam figura vt minima formata, sed numero ternario copulata, que sesquialterata dicitur, quoniã tres pro duabus decantãtur. Figura insuper duabus caudis descripta, nullam reputatur habere, quia altera alteram impedit.

Caput tertium de
Ligaturis.

Vnde ligatura, vt Gafforus lib. z. ca. ſ. scribit, Est simpliciũ
figurarum, per tractus debitos coniunctio. Uel est cõdepen-
dentia principalium figurarum secũdum tractus sursum vl'
deorsum in rectitudine vel obliquitate.

De Ligaturis regule generales.

Gaf-
forus

¶ Prima, Quattuor sunt note ligabiles scilicet maxima, longa, breuis, z
semibreuis. ¶ Secunda, Omnis nota ligabilis: preter maximam: dupli-
ci corpore: quadrato scilicet et obliquo figurari potest. ¶ Tertia, Oñis
nota ligabilis, secundum ascensum et descensum vel suĩpsius, vel proxie
sequentis, venit iudicãda. ¶ Quarta, Omnis nota ligabilis aut erit initialis, aut media, aut finalis. ¶ Quinta, simplicium notarum accidentia
puta alteratio, imperfectio, et huiusmodi (Franchino teste) ipsis quoqɜ

Frã-
chin⁹

ligatis solent accidere.

De initialibus regule.

¶ Prima, Oñis initialis: siue quadrata, siue obliqua: carẽs cauda, secũda descente, est longa. ¶ Secunda, omnis initialis sine cauda, secunda
ascendente, breuis est. ¶ Tertia, omnis initialis habens caudam deorsum in sinistra eius parte, breuis est. ¶ Quarta, Oñis initialis qualitercunqɜ formata, habens caudam in sinistra parte sursum, Semibreuis est
vna cum proxima sequente, non curando, an ascendat siue descendat.

De Medijs regule.

¶ Prima, Omnis nota inter primam et vltimam dicitur media. Secũda, Omnis nota media, qualitercunqɜ formata aut posita: breuis est.
¶ Tertia, Longa principium et finẽ ligature intrare potest, mediũ nũq̃.
¶ Quarta, Breuis principio, medio, et fine ligatur q̃ aptissime. ¶ Quinta, Semibreuis principio, medio, et fine ligari potest: mediãte caude in sinistra parte sursum tracta.

De Vltimis regule.

¶ Prima. Omnis vltima quadrata descendens est longa. ¶ Secunda, Omnis vltima quadrata ascendens breuis est. ¶ Tertia, Omnis obliqua finalis siue ascendat siue descendat est breuis. ¶ Quarta, Maxima vbicunḡ posita fuerit semper manet maxima. harum autem regularum exempla, sequens tenor declarat.

TENOR exercitij ligaturarum

Baritonus exercitij.

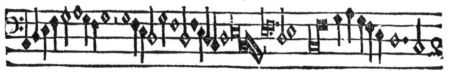

Ligaturarū.

De modo tempo re ac prolatiōe.

Caput Quartum.

Usice gradus, quis principalium figurarum cognoscimus valorem, tres sunt, scilicet mod⁹, tempus, ac prolatio. Nec quiuis eorum agit in quasḡ, sed suas tantum. Ut, modus in maximas, ac longas, Tempus in breues, ac prolatio in semibreues.

F

De Modo.

¶ Modus:teſte Franchino lib.z.ca.7.pract.Eſt menſura longarum in Franchino maximis,aut breuium in longis.Uel eſt principium quátitatʒ maximarũ et longarum formale,ipſas aut ternario aut binario numero menſurans. Omnis nanʠ figura,duplici menſuratur valore.

Scʒ ⎰Ternario⎱ Et ſic dr̃ ⎰Perfecta⎱ qa ⎰Perfctm̃ ſup tria ponim⁹
    ⎰Binario ⎱   ⎰Impfecta⎱   ⎰Imperfectum ad duo li⁻
                                     ⎱mitamus.

De Modi diuiſione.

¶ Modus vt hic ſumitur duplex eſt,Maior ſcilicet,qui ineſt maximis et longis,Ac minor qui in longis ac breuib⁹ eſt,Et horũ quiuis penes per⁻ fectum atʠ imperfectum ſcinditur.

De Modo maiore.

¶ Modus maior pfectus,Eſt maxima tris habens in ſe longas.Uel eſt triũ longarum in vna maxima dimenſio.Cuius ſignũ eſt Circul⁹ perfec⁻ tus ternario numero ſociatus ſic.O3.Sed maior imperfectus eſt maxima duas in ſe longas concludens,Qui et circulo imperfecto,ternario nume⁻ ro iuncto,dinoſcitur ſic.C3.

De Modo minore.

¶ Modus minor pfect⁹,eſt lõga tris habens in ſe breues.Uel eſt triũ bre⁻ uium i vna longa dimenſio.Cuius ſignũ Circulus eſt perfectus,binario numero ſociatus.ſic.O2.Sed minor imperfectus,eſt longa duab⁹ tantũ breuibus menſuranda.Cuius ſignũ eſt numeri binarii abſentia.Uel Se⁻ micirculus binario nũero iũctus,ſic.Cz.O.C.vt in ſubiecto quadrato.

De Tempore.

¶ Eſt aũt tp̃s Breuis duas l' tris i ſe ſemibreues ɔcludẽs.Ut̃ duarũ aut triũ ſemibreuiũ in vna breui dimenſio,Et eſt duplex,ſcilicet Perfectũ,Et eſt breuis tribus ſemibreuibus menſuranda.Cui⁹ ſignũ eſt nũerus terna rius circulo vel ſemicirculo coniunctus,aut circulus pfectus abſʠ nũe⁻

ro posita z, sic Oz.Cz.O. Imperfectū est quo breuis duabus semibreui=
bus tantum mensuratur. Quod et binario numero, perfecto circulo con=
iuncto, aut semicirculo sine numero posito dinoscitur sic: Oz.C.Cz,

De Prolatione.

¶ Uñ .platio est essentialis Semibreuiū quātitas. Uel est duaꝝ aut triū
minimarū cōtra vnā semibreuē positio. Et est dupler, scilicet Maior, Et
est Semibreuis trib⁹ minimis mēsurata. Uel est triū minimarū i vna se
mibreui cōclusio. Cuius signū est punctus signo temporali inscriptus sic.
⊙. C. Minor prolatio est Semibreuis duabus tantum minimis dimē=
sa Cuius signum est puncti absentia: Jnquit enim Franchious, Jmperfe
ctionem figure secum deferunt. deficientibus signis, hoc modo

Frã=
chin⁹

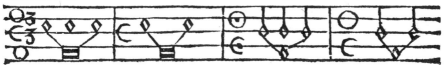

Tempus pfectū   Jmperfectum   Prolatio maior   Minor

¶ Doꝛū autem triū graduū: quidā musice peritus, satis docte ac compen
diose: pro tyronum institutione: infrascriptum cōdidit exemplum. Quod
saluo suo honoꝛe non dedignamur nostris scriptis apponere.

TENOR in modo minoꝛi perfecto.   ¶ DISCANTUS in pꝛ

latione maioꝛe.   BASSU Sin tempoꝛe pfecto.

Caput quintum de signis.

L Jcet tanta musicoꝛum de signis sit dissensio: regularum atꝗ er=
emploꝛum confusio: vt etiam consumato musico ambiguitatem
generare videāt, ita: vt Plutarchus Cheroneus, vir vndeciūꝗ Plu=
doctissimus, in eo libꝛo: quē de musica scripsit: dicat. Nostris tpꝛ tar=
bus, tantos auctus differentie foꝛma ercepit, et vsꝗ adeo discessit a moꝛe chus
maioꝛū: vt nulla sit amplius discipline mentio, nulla ꝑceptio, nulla certi=
                                        F ij

tudo. Quãuis etiã in dubijs diffiniendũ nõ ſit, ſed ſuſpenſa ſentẽtia tenẽ-
da, tamen ne Tyrunculi, artis huius cupidi, ab inſtituti ſui propoſito, aut
reuocentur, aut male inſtituantur, relictis rarioribus, ea que crebriori mu
ſicorum: quos nunc probat auctoritas: vſu celebrantur, paucis aperiem9:
eam. que de circulo et numero eſt, ambiguitatem: olim in Theoricis era
dicando. Eſt igitur ſignum, quedam figura cantui prepoſita, modum,
tempus, ac prolationem indicans.

De ſignorum diuiſione.

¶ Signorum alia principalia, alia minus principalia dicuntur. Principalia ſunt: que ad cognitiõem modi, temporis ac prolationis conducũt. Et
illa quidem bipartita ſunt, Extrinſeca ſcilicet, et Intrinſeca. Extrinſeca
dicuntur illa: que pro cognoſcendis muſice gradibus extrinſecus ſe offe-
runt: vt numerus, circulus, ac punctus.

De ſignis extrin-
ſecis regule.

¶ Prima, Circulus ſe ſolo poſitus tempus indicat. Et hoc ſi perfectus
ſit, perfectum. Sin autẽ imperfectus, imperfectum. Cum autem numero
iungitur, modum declarat. ¶ Secunda, Circulus numero ternario iunctus modum maiorem, Binario vero ſociatus minorem repreſentat.
¶ Tertia, Ubicunq eſt modus maior, ibi eſt et minor, ſed non econtra.
¶ Quarta, Ternarius numerus circulo iunctus, temporis perfecti eſt in
dicium: Binarius vero imperfecti. ¶ Quinta, Punctus in ſigno temporali clauſus, prolationem deſignat maiorem, hoc modo.

Signo-
rũ aliud
{
  O3 / C3 } modi maioris { Perfecti / Impfecti } tpis perfecti
  Oz / Cz } modi minoris { Perfecti / Impfecti } Tpis imperfecti
  ⊙ / ₵ } plationis maioris { Perfecti / Impfecti } Temporis
  O / C } Temporis { Perfecti / Impfecti } prolationis minoris
}

¶ Tum autem ex trium principalium signorum, numeri scilicet, circuli ac puncti, commixtione, diuersa formetur signa: quo facilius eorundem elucescat noticia: et suus cuiusq figure valor tribuatur: placuit resolutoriam tabulam, cuiusq figure: in quocunq etiam signo posite, valorem ex intuitu indicantem: modo quo sequitur, subijcere.

Minima											
	z	z	z	z	z	z	z	z	z	z	z
Seibre:	o	o	o	o	o	o	o	o	o	o	o
	z	z	z		z	z	z	z	z	z	z
Breuis	=	=	=	=	=	=	=	=	=	=	=
	z	z	z	z	z	z	z	z	z	z	z
Longa	=	=	=	=	=	=	=	=	=	=	=
	z	z	z	z	z	z	z	z	z	z	z
Maxia	=	=	=	=	=	=	=	=	=	=	=
Signa	⊙	⊙	⊙	⊙	⊙	○	○	ℂ	ℂ	ℂ	ℂ

Tabula signorum resolutoria valorem cuiusq figure ex intuitu demonstrans.

De signis intrinsecis.

¶ Signa intrinseca sunt, quibus graduu musicalium perfectio in figuris denotatur, citra extrinsecorum signorum appositionem. Quorum tria sunt: Trium scilicet temporu pause inuentio. Quando enim in cantu reperitur pausa tria tangens spatia, modum indicat minorem perfectum, Si due, maiorem perfectum, Inquit enim Franchinus: non incongruu esse maio Frā ri modo duas trium temporum pausas apponi, si minori vna apponatur. chin⁹ ¶ Notarum denigratio, Quoties enim inueniuntur tres longe coloraste, modus minor perfectus denotatur. Quando tres breues, tempus per

F iij

fectum. Tribus autē semibreuibus coloratis, prolatio maior demonstraf.
¶ Tertium est quarundam paularū geminatio. Quoties enim due pau
se semibreues, cū semibreui nota collocanf, temp⁹ perfectū designaf. Per
duas aūt minimas cū nota minima, prolatio maior declaratur, hoc mō.

Modus   Modus   Tempus pfectū   prolatio maior
maior   minor

De signis minus principalibus

¶Signa minus principalia sunt, que ad cognitionē
modi, temporis ac prolationis non conducunt. ⁊ hec
varia sunt, vt i sequēti quadrato licet ad sēsū videre.

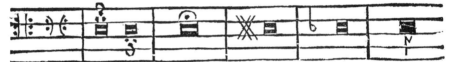

Repetitiōis   Conue: Cōcordātie   Aspira   bmollitatis   dealba:
             nientie   cardinalis   tionis   tionis

V Caput sextum de Tactu.

Nde Tactus est motio successiua in cantu, mensure equalita
tem dirigens. Uel est quidā motus, manu pcentoris signorū
indicio formatus, cantum dirigens mensuraliter.

De tactus diuisione.

¶ Tactus tripartitus est: maior scilicet, minor et pportionatus. Maior
est mensura, tardo ac motu quasi reciproco facta. hunc tactum et integrū
et totalem nominant auctores. Et qm verus est omnium cātilenarum ta
ctus: Semibreuem non diminutam suo motu comprehendit: vel breuē,
in duplo diminutam. ¶ Minor, est maioris medium: quem Semitactū
dicunt. Qm semibreuem in duplo diminutam suo motu mensurat, indoc
tis tantum probatus. ¶ Proportionatus, est quo tres semibreues con
tra vnam, vt in Tripla: aut contra duas, vt in Sesquialtera: proferūtur.
de quo, capitulo de proportionibus, latius dicetur.

Regula de Tactu.

¶ Semibꝛeuis in omibus signis (diminutionis, augmentationis, ac proportionum demptis) tactu mensuratur integro, vt in sequenti paragraphia claret.

⊙3	24	9	3	1				
O3	24	9	3	1	𝄋			
₵3	12	6	3	1	𝄋			
⊙2	12	6	2	1				
⊙	12	6	3	1				
₵	8	4	2	1				
O	12	6	3	1	1			
₵	8	4	2	1	1			
						4ᵒʳ tacti vni…	8 tactibus mi…	16 tactibus mini…

Tabula Tactuum resolutoꝛia.

167]

Caput septimum de Augmentatione.

Quoniam in pꝛecedente capitulo augmétationis ac diminutionis métio facta existit. Quare ne ex ignotis pꝛocedat: qd
vtrūꝗ sit libet discutere. ¶ Est itaꝗ augmentatio alicui⁹
cantus in suis notis plurificatio. Uel est alicui⁹ note excre-
mentum. In ea etenim minima pꝛo semibꝛeui, Semibꝛeuis pꝛo bꝛeuí, ac
bꝛeuis pꝛo longa ponitur.

Quibus augmentatio signis cognoscat.

¶ Augmétationis tria sunt signa, Pꝛimū est paucitas notarū, in vna can
tilene parte. ¶ Secundu est canonis inscriptio, dicendo bꝛeuis sit maxima, Semibꝛeuis longa, ac minia bꝛeuis. Uel crescit in duplo, triplo, hexa

gio numero rc. ¶ Tertium est punctus in signo temporali, circa vnam
duntaxat catilene partem repertus. Unam dico, nam si apud omnes of=
fenditur, non augmentationis: sed maioris prolationis: erit indicium.

De augmētatione regule.

¶ Prima. Augmentatio est diminutionis contradictio. ¶ Secunda, In
augmentatione minima figura, tactu mensuratur integro. ¶ Tertia, In
ter prolationem et augmentationem hoc interest. q̄ augmētatio minimā
tactu profert vno, prolatio autem tres, hoc est Semibreuem perfec=
tam, que tunc proportionato metitur tactu. ¶ Quarta, Pause non secus
ac note augētur et minuūtur. ¶ Quinta. Augmentatio raro preterq̄ in te
nore fieri debet. ¶ Sexta, Maxima non augmentatur: quia maiorem se:
cuius valorem assumat: non habet. Errant igitur qui in maxima sub tali.
⊙ 3. signo posita, octuaginta vnum tactus concludūt, quoniam nec vl=
tra .27. tactus maxima excrescit, nec maiorem se (quia maximū est, quo
nihil existit maius) admittit. Insuper cum: vt in natura, ita et in arte fru=
stra positum sit nihil: frustra maxima augmentaretur, quoniam in nullo
vnq̄ cantu tantus status: vt 81. tactus in vnisono canantur, reperitur.
¶ Septima. Augmentatio, preter maximam, alias om̄es notarū species
sub se comprehendit: de qua sequens videatur exemplum.

[168]

Augmentatio.   Prolatio maior.   Baritonus sub

signo Semiditatis.   Prolatio maior.

Quid sit Canon.

¶ Quom de Canone mentio habita sit: ne studiosos
hac in re suspendam, quid canon sit aperiam. Est igi=
tur Canon, imaginaria preceptio: et positis, non po=
sitam, catilene partem eliciens. Uel est regula argute
cantus secreta reuelans. Canonibus autem vtimur
subtilitatis, breuitatȝ. ac tentatiõis grā, hoc modo.

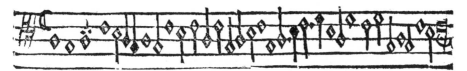

CANØN.
BASSUS er tenoze in Diapente post tempus vnum

Caput octauum de diminutione.

Iminutio:que verius Sincopatio dicitur: Est pzimarie quã **Frã.** titatis notularũ variatio,scribit Franchinus li. 2.pzact.14. **chi.** Uel est quedã mesure pzescisio. Ut enim i Grammatica secla pzo secula per Sincopen dicimus:ita in Musica figurarũ cõ= natam atqʒ cozriuatã mensurã sincopa pzescindimus. Gene= raliter ergo Syncopatio nõ diminutio:qm species est fyncopatiõis:dicet.

De speciebus Syncopationis.

¶ Syncopationis due sunt species.Semiditas scilicet et diminutio.
¶ Semiditas est pzimarie notarum mensure medietas,in imperfecto tẽ= pe tantũ locabilis,Cuius bec sunt signa. O ʒ. C ʒ. ₵ . ₵ . ₵ , in omnibus enim istis. medietas mensure pzescinditur,per virgulã pzopzie: per numerũ autem,inquantũ vim babeat pzopoztionis duple.'Recte igit Erasmus Lapicida in omnibus istis signis numerum numero supponit boc modo.O ʒ.C ʒ.Pzopoztio enim,non vnius, sed duarum quantita= **Eras** tum est relatio,vt alibi latius declarabimus, **mus lapici da.**

De diminutione.

¶ Diminutio, vt veteres sensere: est tertie partis ab ipsa mesura abstra= ctio.Sed recentiozum laudabilio: est opinio ac verioz, qui diminutionẽ a semiditate non disternant. vt Joannes Tinctozis,omniũ:qui in musica claruerunt:scriptoz pzeclarissimus:z Franchinus Gaffozus: lib.2.ca.14 sanrerunt·Est itaqʒ diminutio medie partis in mensura pzescisio, nil dis= crepans a Semiditate:nisi qʒ i signis perfectis,ac figuris ternario nume= ro metiẽdis reperitur.Quare nõ possũ nõ deridere quosdam cõponistas: ita enim dici volunt:musice monstra: qui cum artis nec pzima elementa viderint, se musicos musicozum pzoclamant: omnia ignozantes,de om= nibus se iactitant, atqʒ artem bãc:plurib⁹ antea seculis a doctissimis qui=

Quis basꝗ, ꝝ vt Quintiliani verbis vtar: claris sapientia viris celebzatã: inep
tilia tꝗs suis:citra artis maiestatẽ, vsu potius ꝗ igenio fabzicatis:dehonestãt,
nus. coꝛrumpunt, defedant, quibusꝗ signis pzo libitu vtentes, nec valoꝛẽ nec
mensuram pensitantes:carminis suauitate, stultoꝛū auribus potius, ꝗ ar
tis maiestate, doctoꝛū iudicio, parere student. Qualem quendã arcis Pza
gensis organistam conducticiū, noui. Qui cum: vt de altioꝛibus sileã: nec
perfectum tempus ab imperfecto discernat, se et musicam scribere recon-
ditissimã, vulgo coꝛã dicit, et Franchinū celeberrimū musice scriptoꝛem:
quem nec a limine salutauit:moꝛdere, vilipendere, nec lectu quidem dig
num iudicare, nõ erubescit. O stulta iactantia:o temeritas ridicula : o gra
dis insania:que haud alia ratione doctissimos quosꝗ rodit:ꝗ ꝗ eiusdem
muse emula nõ existit. Dij faxint: vt in laqueos lupus cadat, ne facinus tã
callidum, tam pzauum, tanꝗ nefarium deinceps cõmittat , nec coꝛnicula
alienis plumis glozietur. Delyrus enim censetur : qui id ipsum alijs pze-
scribit:cuius ipse elementa nec dum viderit. Quemadmodum Phoꝛmio
Gꝛecus oꝛatoꝛ:vt est apud Ci.scdo de oꝛatoꝛe : qui dum apud Antiochū

Cice Asie regem, hannibale coꝛam,de imperatoꝛis officio copiosius peroꝛas-
ro. set:nec ipse castra vnꝗ vidisset, nec arma:mirantibus cunctis qui tū ade-
Han rant:tandem quesitus et ipse hannibal, quid de tali philosopho iudica-
nibal ret:respondisse fertur:multos se delyros senes sepe vidisse:sed qui magꝫ-
ꝗ Phoꝛmio deliraret neminẽ. Nunc ad rem redeo et Amusos illos atꝗ
ridiculos Phoꝛmiones(quoꝛū plures musice pzouintiam:pzohpudoꝛ:in-
uasere) harmoniaꝛū non compositoꝛes:ymmo coꝛruptoꝛes,non musaꝝ,
sed furiaꝛū alumnos: vir minimo digoꝛ honoꝛe. Ridenda enim sunt can
tica in ipsis musice fontibus non radicata.licet quantumuis consona sint.
Quoniã non artifex artem,sed ars artificem decoꝛat. Nullū ergo compo-
nista musice confert decoꝛẽ,sed ediuerso.Quippe non ex industria,sed diu
turna quadam consuetudine pleriꝗ (quia foꝛte a cunabulis in cantoꝛijs
virerunt) cantica etiam consona condunt:sed quid sit quod condiderūt,
non intelligunt.quia est cognoscentes,sed quid est non intelligẽtes. Quti-
bus saluatoꝛis nostri dictū in cruce rite conuenit.Pater ignosce illis,quia
nesciunt quid faciunt. Fides itaꝗ nec vlla pzestetur componistis , nisi inueniantur arte pzobati.Quoꝛū aut pzobata est auctoꝛitas, ꝗ sunt. Joã̄nes

Oke Okekẽ, Joãnes Tinctoꝛis, Loyset, Uerbonet, Alexãder agricola, Jacob⁹
ken. Obꝛecht, Josquin, Petꝝ de larue, henric⁹ Jsaack henric⁹ Fynck. An-
Tin. tonius Bꝛūmel, Matheus Pipilare, Georgius Bꝛack, Erasmus Lapi-
Loy- cida, Caspar Czeys, Conradus Reyn, et similes:quoꝛū poemata ex artis
set, radicibus emanare ꝑspiciunt . Sed ne ex derisiõe ira consurgat, et ex ira
Alex odium,missum faciamus hec,ad diminutionem redeuntes:quã võ tertiã
ãder. partem vt olim (eam enim inuenire difficile est) sed alteram abstrahere
Jos- cum Franchino et Tinctoꝛe concludamus,Ut enim hoc signum ₵ ,hu-
quin. ius C.duplum est:ita et istud ₵ illius O .Quamobzem errant condi-
Pe.

to:es, etiam probati: dum in circulo perfecto virgula scisso, vltra figura:
rum: quoniã perfecti temporis sunt: ternariam numerositatem, binariam
mensure progressionem non attendunt, semibreuem ad tactum proferen:
tes, cum due cantande sint. In eo enim signo, ita constituendus est cãtus:
vt perfectiõe ternarij seruata: in binaria mensura, clausulas recipiat ac fi
nem. Nam hoc in signo $\emptyset$ eundem note valorem quem in illo O, ha:
bent, seruant: sed sola mensura binari$\bullet$ numero metienda est. hoc modo.

Bru
mel.
Ma
the⁹.
Ge:
org.
Eras
mus.
Hen:
ricus
Ysac.
h.
Fick
Cal.
Czeil
Cō.
Rein

Tabula
de Tac:
tu dimi:
nuto.

Quibus signis diminutio signetur.

¶ Designat aut diminutio tripliciter, scz Canonice, nũeraliter, virgula:
riter. ¶ Canonice, dicendo. Decrescit in duplo, in triplo. quadruplo et
hui⁹mōi. ¶ Nũeralit, $\emptyset$ is eni nũerus circulo vel semicirculo cõiunct⁹,
vltra hoc qð essentialiter indicat, etiã minuit iuxta sue figure denomina:
tionẽ. Ut binarius circulo integro sociatus: vltra tp̃s: quod in tali signo
imperfectũ esse declarat: duplam etiam denotat diminutionem. Ternari
us triplã. Quaternarius quadruplam, et sic deinceps. Uirgulariter, qñ
scilicet per virgulam signũ tp̃is scinditur: hoc modo. $\emptyset$. $\mathcal{C}$. $\emptyset$. $\mathcal{C}$.

De Syncopatione regule.

¶ P:ia, Syncopatio tp̃ali cõpetit mẽsure, nõ ip̃is figuris. ¶ Scða. Syn
copatio vt notas, ita z pausas respicit. ¶ Tertia, Syncopatõ ñ notap aut
pausap valorẽ aufert, ß mẽsurã. ¶ Quarta, Nũer⁹ plationẽ nõ minuit, q̃a
vi suã in pũctũ custodiente circulo dirigere neq̃t. ¶ Quita, Inter diminu
tionẽ ac semiditatẽ: nulla est differentia tact⁹ seu mensure. sed soli⁹ nature.
¶ Serta, Diminutio ẽ augmẽtatiõis cõtradictio. ¶ Septia, Nõ ẽ incõue
niens vt eidẽ signo dupler: Uirgularis scz ac nũeralis accidat diminutio,
hoc mõ. $\mathcal{C}$ z. ¶ Octaua, Uirgularis syncopatio frequens est: nũeralis
rara, canonica rarissima. quare de prima sequens est exemplũ atq̃ secũda.

171]

Diminutio Uirgularis Semiditas

Syncopatio numeralis

Caput nonum
de Pausis.

Tin-
cto.
Gaf-
fo29.

PAusa, vt Tinctoris scribit, Est taciturnitatis signum. Uel (vt
Gaffo2o placet) Est figura artificiosam a cantu desistentiam de-
monstrãs. Uel est tractus per lineas ꝛ spatia, silentium indicans.
Locantur autẽ pause in cantu tripliciter, scilicet essentialiter, indicialiter, et vtroꝗ modo. ¶ Essentialiter quando silentium
demonstrant. ¶ Indicialiter quando non silentiũ, sed modũ pfectũ indi-
cant, et tunc ante temporis signũ locum sibi vendicant. ¶ Utroꝗ modo
quando vtrunꝗ repiesentant,

Regule de Pausis.

¶ Prima, Tot sunt species pausarum, quot notarũ. ¶ Secunda, Pausa omnia tangens spacia, generalis est, vbi omnes voces simul cessant in
calce tantum locanda. ¶ Tertia, Pausa tria occupãs spatia, dicitur modi: quem indicat: in modo perfecto solum ponibilis. ¶ Quarta. Pausa
duo spacia concludens, longa imperfecta nuncupatur. ¶ Quinta, Pausa
vnum occupans spatium, bieuis est, vnum tempus designãs , siue perfectum sit siue imperfectũ. ¶ Serta. Pausa descendens a linea ad medium
spatij, Semibieuis dicitur. ¶ Septima, Pausa a linea ad medium spaciũ
ascendens, minimam siue suspirium demonstrat. ¶ Octaua, Pausa vt
suspirium, vncata dextrorsum, Semiminimam valet. ¶ Nona, Postre-
marum duarum figurarum pause, ob nimiam suam velocitatem in vsu
musico non reperiuntur.

[172

62

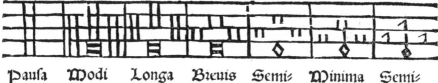

| Pauſa gñalis | Modi | Longa | Breuis | Semi=breuis | Minima | Semi=minima |

Caput decimum de Punctis.

Vnde punctus eſt indiuiſibilis quedã quantitas, notulis ad=
dita, vel diuiſionis, vel augmenti vel certitudis gratia. Vel
eſt minimũ quoddam ſignum notulis accidẽtaliter aut poſt=
poſitum, aut ſupꝛapoſitum, aut interpoſitum.

De puncti diuiſione.

¶ Tria punctoꝛũ ex diffinitione colliguntur genera.
ſcilicet Additionis: et is eſt figurarum augmentatio
Vel eſt imperfectarum notarum perfectio. hic ad me
dium lateris dextri ponitur, in ſignis imperfectis ſo=
lũ reperſ, ac notulas: ꝗbus addiſ : pꝛo medietate ſui
valoꝛ augere dinoſciſ, vt in exẽplo ſubſcripto claret.

TENOR puncti additionis.   BASSUS eiuſdem.

De puncto diuiſionis.

¶ Punctuꝫ diuiſionis eſt duarũ notarũ diſiunctio, nec auferens nec affe=
rens ꝗcꝙ: ſed duaꝫ notaꝫ diſtinguens, primã, ꝑcedẽti, ſecundã aũt ſequẽ=
ti connumerando: pꝛo conſtituenda in notis ternaria perfectione. hic pũ
ctus in gꝛadibus perfectis, nõ perfectis figuris, ſed pꝛopinquis eaꝛũ par=
tꝭbus iungitur. nec ad medium lateris vt additionis, ſed paulo altius vel
pꝛofundius ad medium notarum: quas diuidit: collocatur, hoc modo.
                                          G

TENOR puncti diuifionis.   *BASSUS* eiufdem.

De puncto alterationis.

¶ Alteratiõis punctũ, veteres plus ꝗ recentiores, feruauere.
Ne tamen aliquando repertus, ambiguitatem generet canen=
ti:non nihil de eo placet differere.eſt itaꝗ punctus alterationis
notarum repetitio,notis adueniens non inquantum perfecte :
ſed inquantum perfectarum propinque ſunt partes . Ponitur
autem non ad latus,neꝗ ſurſum aut deorſum , ſed præciſe ſupra
notam quam alterat.vt in ſubſcripto exemplo.

TENOR de pũcto alterationis   *BASSUS* de pũcto alteratõis

¶ Sunt preter hec alia duo punctorũ genera.ſcilicet perfectionis, Et eſt
punctus note perfecte poſtpoſitus,ipſam nec auget nec minuit:ſed ne a ſe
quente imperficiatur preſeruat.Et ponitur vt additiõis,ſed diſcrepat ab
eo,quia circa notas perfectas ſolũ locatur.Tranſportationis autem pun
ctus,notis appoſitus,eas ad diſtantiores figuras transfert cõputandas.
Nec in anteriores ſed poſteriores tantum vim ſuã dirigit:hoc modo.

TENOR   de puncto   pfectionis ac trãſportationis

BASSUS de eiſdem

V Caput vndecimū de impfectiõe

Nde imperfectio est perfectarum notarum degradatio. Est enim imperficere, notam perfectam, imperfectam reddere, Uel est ipsam de suo valore deponere.

De duplici imperfectione.

¶ Imperfectio duplex est. Totalis scilicet, quando precise tertia pars valoris, notulis aufertur: vt dum in tempore perfecto breuis per semibreuem imperficitur. Partialis, qnando nõ tertia pars precise, sed minor ea puta sexta vel huiusmodi ipsis notis abstrahitur, Ut dum longa imperfecti modi, sed imperfecto tempore, vbi duas tantum breues valet: a semibreui imperficitur, respectu breuis in ea contente, Et breuis a minima in prolatione maiore.

Duplex iperfectio

Quibus signis imperfectio cognoscatur.

¶ Imperfectiõis tria sunt signa, scribit Franchinus lib. z. practice. ca. II. scilicet numeralis imperfectio, pūctualis diuisio, et notularum plenitudo.

Imp fectio nis tria signa

Regule de imperfectione.

¶ Prima. Quattuor sunt note impfectibiles, maxia scz. longa, breuis, ac semibreuis. ¶ Secūda, Øis iperfectibilis figura, semper est i nūero sue p fecte quātitatis cõsideranda. ¶ Tertia. Qð semel iperfectū est, ampli⁹ im perfici non potest. ¶ Quarta, Ømnis impfectibilis figura, maior erit im perficiente. ¶ Quinta, Imperfectio non solum fit per partes notarū propinquas, sed et remotas. Ut breuis pfecta, non solū a semibreui ppinqua parte, verū z a duab⁹minimis: que partes remote ipsius existunt: imperfici potest. ¶ Sexta, Due partes propinque alicuius figure pfecte, ipsam non iperficiūt, sed vna tantum. licet due remote idipsum facere possint. Quare si due pause semibreues post breuē perfectā reperte fuerint, pfecta manebit:: nisi diuisio pūctualis interueiat. ¶ Septia, Ø mis figura minor supflua, maiorē impficit pcedētē, nõ sequentē, nisi id ratione pūcti diuisio nis, vel pfectionis, vel etiā transportationis fiat. ¶ Octaua, Similis an similem non impficif: quare omnis imperfectibilis figura. ante maiorem, vel minorē se ponatur. ¶ Nona, Maior nõ imperficit minorē, aut equalis equalem. ¶ Decima, Figura aliam imperficiens, aufert ei tantū quantū ipsa valet. ¶ Undecima, Pausa nõ imperficif sed ipficit. ¶ Duodecia.

G ij

Ligatura non imperficit, fed imperficitur ¶Tredecima, Maxima in im-
perficiendo non agit fed patitur. ¶ Quartadecima, Minima in imperfi
cendo non patitur fed agit.¶ Quintadecima, Longa, breuis, et femibre-
uis imperficiunt, et imperficiunf. ¶ Sedecima, Omnis imperfectio vel
a facie, vel a tergo fit. A facie, quando imperficiens imperfectibilé precedit, A tergo, quando imperfectibili fuccedit, Sunt qui ab vtroqʒ fieri cre
dunt, in partiali imperfectione. ¶ 17. Imperfectio que ante 7 poft fit, nõ
per propinquas partes, fed remotas contingit. ¶18. Omnis imperfectio fit vel per notam, vel per paufam, vel per coloré. Per notam: quan
do fcilicet ante vel poft notam perfectam: figura minoris fpeciei collocatur, eam imperficit, hoc modo.

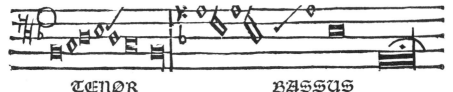

TENOR   BASSUS

Per paufam, quando fcilicet ante vel poft notã perfectam paufa mioris fpeciei reperitur : figura imperfi
citur, paufa autem imperfici non poteft, hoc modo.

TENOR

BARITONANS

¶ Per colorem, quando in figuris color of
fenditur, imperfecte funt : quia tertia pars
eis aufertur, hoc modo.

[17«

TENOR

BASIS huius positionis
De Colore.

¶ Unde color in proposito nihil est aliud:q̃ notularum plenitudo. Uel
est principalium figurarũ denigratio. Cuius tanta vis est vt figuris in sua
perfecta quantitate deductis: tertiam partem valoris adimat: Imperfec
tis vero: modo quartam partem auferat, modo hemiolam proportionẽ
in eis conducat. Quamobrem tabulam tactus resolutoriam, de figuris
perfectis colore notatis, subijcere placuit. hoc notato q̃ spaciola vacua
eam: supra quam ponuntur: figuram incolorabilem eo signo esse demonstrant. Sperica vero figura, quam nihili numerorum periti nominant: et
si figuras colorabiles: integrum tamen tactum non valere, declarat.

⊙3	18	6	Z	0	0
○3	18	6	Z	1	
⊙z	8	4	Z	0	0
○z	4	Z	1		
⊙	8	4	Z	0	0
∅	4	Z	1	0	0
○	8	4	Z	1	
∅	4	Z	1	0	
	▬	▬	◧	◆	◆

Quom i alijs
figur̃ color̃ es-
sentialis exis-
tat: nullã acci-
dentalem no-
tis ĩducit quã-
titatem.

¶ Color etiam interdũ nec aufferre nec afferre quicq̃: apud doctissimos
quosq̃ offenditur: Tũ marie dũ amouẽde alteratiõis gratia, in perfectar
figurarũ propinquis partibus collocatur, hoc modo.

G ij

TENOR   BASIS

henricus ysaac

¶ Pleramᵬ demū color in figuris imperfectis: inquit Franchinus lib.2.ca.11. duplam proportionem efficit. Quod henricus Ysaac,in quodam Alleluia de aplīs : non minus concinne, ᵬ vere disposuit, hoc modo.

TENOR   BASIS.

Caput duodecimum de alteratione.

Joan de murʒ Tinctoꝛ.

Lteratio scōm Joannē de muris ē minoꝛ notule respectu maioris duplicatio. Uel vt Tinctoꝛ ait, est propꝛij valoris geminatio. Uel est vnius et eiusdem note repetitio. Et dicitur alteratio: quasi altera actio:id est secundaria alicuius note decantatio,propter ternarij perfectionem.

De Alteratione regule

¶ Prima, Quattuoꝛ sunt note alterabiles,scribit Franchin⁹.li.2.ca.13. longa,breuis semibreuis,ac minima. ¶ Secunda , Alteratio maximā excludit,et in minima terminatur,quia maxima maioꝛē se:cuius propinqua pars esse possit non habet:diminutioꝛes autē figure numero ternario non sunt computande. ¶ Tertia,Alteratio euenit notulis non perfectis: sed quū fuerint perfectarum propinque partes quoniā perfecta inquantū talis,alterationi non subiacet. ¶ Quarta,Note tantū alteranₜ ₇ nō pause. ¶ 5. In secundā et non in primā cadit alteratio. ¶ 6. Omnis nota alterata continet se ipsam bis. ¶ 7. Similis ante similem nō alteraₜ. ¶ 8. Alteratio solum contingit in gradibus perfectis. ¶ 9. Alteratio fit ob defectum vnius note:cōputata ternarij nūerositate.¶ 10. Quoties inter duas imperfectibiles due alterabiles clauduntur, absᵬ pūcto diuisionis:secunda semper alteratur, vt subscripto exemplo declaratur.

Altera   **TENOR**   Altera

BASIS.

¶ Undecima, Si pauſa cum figura, cui equiualet, inter duas notas perfectas clauditur: Tunc aut pauſa precedit figurā, aut figura pauſam . Si
primum figura alteratur, ſi ſecundū, alteratio nō habet locum, quia note
alterantur tantum, et nō pauſe. Cadit inſuper in ſecundam ſemper, et nō
in primam alteratio, hoc modo.

TENOR

BASIS

¶ Duodecima, Alteratio plenitudine notarū, ac pūcto diuiſionis toll:f.
Et in ligaturis etiam alteratio ſaluatur, vt in ſubſcripta parabola claret.

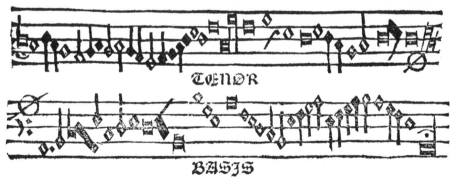

TENOR

BASIS

¶ Decimatertia. Quoties tres alterabiles note inter duas imperfectibiles clauduntur:ambe impfectibiles perfecte manebunt et nulla altera-
bilium alteratur,quia numerus ternarius vbiqȝ est perfectus.

Caput tertiumdecimū
de proportione.

Nde proportio est duoȝū comparatoȝum , in aliquo vniuoco
habitudo. Uniuoco dico, qa in eǧuocis comparatio nulla est.
Stylus eteni et vox acuta non comparantur. Quo fit vt proportio inter equalia ac inequalia,similia ac dissimilia,inueni-
tur proprie dicta.Uel secundū Euclidem,Est duarū quante-
cunqȝ sint,eiusdem generis propinqui quantitatū, alterius ad alterā:cer-
ta habitudo. hinc continua et discreta , quanqȝ sub eodē genere ǧntitatȝ
contineantur non comparantur, quia remota non propinqua existunt,

**Eu-
clideſ**

De proportionum diuisione.

¶ Proportionū alia equalitatis,alia inequalitatis est,Equalitatis est duarum equalium quantitatum relatio.Equale em est quod suo equali nec
plus est nec minus.Jnequalitatis vero est duarū in equalium quantitatū
habitudo.Jnequale siǧdem id dicitur, quod ad aliud relatum, vel plus ,
vel minus eo existit.

Que proportio musicis conueniat.

¶ Quom vocum similitudo consonantiā non pariat, sed dissimilitudo ,
hinc solam inequalitatis proportionem musice disciplina considerat.Et
hec biuariā partitur, in maioȝis scilicet ac minoȝis inequalitatis propor-
tionem.Maioȝis inequalitatis proportio est : numeri maioȝis ad minoȝē
relatio.vt.4.ad.2.6.ad.3.Minoȝis autem inequalitatis econtra est, numeri minoȝis ad maioȝem comparatio, vt duoȝum ad. 4.3.ad 6.

De quinqȝ proportio-
num generibus.

¶ Maioȝis inequalitatis proportionum quinqȝ sunt genera:scilicet multiplex,superparticulare,superpartiens, ꝫ hec simplicia sunt:multiplex superparticulare,et multiplex superpartiens,que sunt composita . his alia

quinq̢ genera minoris inequalitatis opponuntur:inquit Franchin⁹:eiſ
dem etiam nominibus,p̢epoſita tantum p̢epoſitione ſub:vt ſubmulti⸗
plex ꝛc.Uerum cum multiplex p̢oportio p̢ecipuam in muſicis conſonan
tijs vim habeat:Superparticularis deinde,Superpartiens vero cũ duo
bus ſequentibus nullam,quare ſuperpartiẽtium genus cum ceteris ſub⸗
ſequentibus,tanq̢ parum validum,ab harmonico cõcentu relegamus:
duo p̢ioꝛa ſolum amplectendo,

Frã⸗
chin⁹

De genere multiplici.

❡ Multiplex p̢oportionum genus:ceteris et p̢eſtantius et antiquius:
Eſt dum maioꝛ numerus ad minoꝛem relatus, totum minoꝛem pluries:
vt bis vel ter:p̢eciſe comp̢ehẽdit.Cuius ſpecies infinite:ſi ſingulos nu⸗
ros vnitati cõparaueris:apparebũt, vt i ſubſcripto quadrato licet videre

2	3	4	5	6	7	8	9	10
1	1	1	1	1	1	1	1	1
Dupla	Trip	q̃dru	q̃ntu	ſextu.	ſeptu	octup	nonu	decu.

❡ Huic dicto generi, oppoſitum eſt:p̢imum minoꝛis
inequalitatis genus:ſubmultiplex appellatum. hoꝛũ
alterum deſtruit alterum,nec in ſuo eſſe perdurare ſi⸗
nit.hoc genus:eadem relatione vnitatis ad alios nu
meros facta:eaſdem cum multiplici, etiam eiuſdem
nominis ſpecies, adiecta p̢epoſitione ſub, ex ſe p̢o⸗
ducit,hoc modo.

1	1	1	1	1	1	1	1	1
2	3	4	5	6	7	8	9	10
Sub dup	Sub tri	Sub q̃dru	Sub q̃ntu	Sub ſextu	Sub ſeptu	Sub octu.	Sub⸗ nonu	Sub⸗ decu.

De genere Super=
particulari.

❡ Superparticulare ſecundum p̢oportionum genus fit:quando nume⸗
rus maioꝛ minoꝛi comparatus,ipſum ſemel, ꝛ inſuper aliquotã eius par⸗

h

tem, in ſe concludit. Eſt aūt pars aliquota, que aliquoties ſumpta, ipſum totum producit preciſe. Cuius quidem generis ſpecies innumerabiles cõ ducuntur: ſingulos ſi numeros dempta vnitate: ad minorem viciniorem computaueris, modo ſubſcripto.

3	4	5	6	7	8	9	10
2	3	4	5	6	7	8	9
Seſq̃ alfa.	ſeſqui tertia	ſeſqui q̃rta	ſeſqui quita	ſeſqui ſerta.	ſeſqui ſeptia	ſeſqui octa.	ſeſqui nona.

¶ Huius oppoſitum eſt Subſuperparticulare, ſecundũ mino ris inequalitatis genus. Quod et eaſdem ſpecies, eiſdem etiam nominibus ſub prepoſitione mediante cum precedente procre at: ſi ſingulos minores numeros: vnitatem ſemper excipio: ma ioribus vicinioribus compare voluerimus, eo quo ſequiſ mõ.

[181]

2	3	4	5	6	7	8	9
3	4	5	6	7	8	9	10
ſubſeſ q̃alfa	ſubſeſ q̃tertia	ſubſeſ quiq̃r	ſubſeſ quiq̃n	ſubſeſ quiſer	ſubſeſ quiſep	ſubſeſ q̃octa	ſubſeſ q̃nona

Quo pacto ex equalitate proportio. ⁊ ſubinde vna ex alia conducatur.

¶ Cum proportionem ex equalitate, et ex vna aliam creare volueris, id ipſum hac Boetij regula rite efficies. Diſpoſitis trib⁹ equis numeris, pu ta vnitatibus vel quibuſq̃ alijs, Tres alij ſubſtituãtur, ita vt primus pri mo par ſit: ſecundus primo et ſecundo, Tertius primo duobus ſecundis ac tertio, et dupla apparebit, hoc modo.

Boe.

1	1	1	2	2	2	3	3	3
1	2	4	2	4	8	3	6	12
	Duple.			Duple			Duple	

⟨ Oz fi et triplas conducere volueris, conſtitutis ſuperiozi oz
dine duplis iam creatis:ſubſtituantur tres numeri ſecundum re
gule predicte tenozem et habebis effectum, hoc modo.

1	z	4	z	4	8	3	6	1z
1	3	9	z	6	18	3	9	z7
	Triple			Triple			Triple	

⟨ Oz fi has triplas iam creatas ſuperioze ordine po
ſuerimus, quadruplas pzoducemus.per ſubditozum
numerozum conſonam ac regularem appoſitionem,
ez quadruplis quintuplas.et item,ez quintuplis ſez
tuplas.et ſic deinceps vſⱥ in infinitum gradiendo.

1	3	9	1	4	16	1	5	z5
1	4	16	1	5	z5	1	6	36
	Quadruple		Quintuple			Sextuple		

⟨ Oz cum ez duplis ſeſquialteras creare volueris:conuerſis
numeris duplarum ita vt maiozes pzimi ſint,et minozes natu
rali ozdine ſuccedant, Subſtituantur alij tres numeri, pzout
ſepe dicta regula expoſcit,⁊ apparebit effectus, vt in ſubiecto
quadrato licet videre.

4	z	1	8	4	z	1z	6	3
4	6	9	8	1z	18	1z	18	z7
	Seſquialtere	—		Seſquialtere	—		Seſquialtere	

⟨ Et vt ez duplis ſeſquialtere.pari mõ ez triplis ſeſquitertie, et ez qua
dzuplis ſeſquiquarte conducantur, conuerſione nũcrozũ,vt de ſeſquialte
ris dictũ eſt.et ita in infinitũ vſⱥ pzogrediendo, eo quo ſequitur modo.

9	3	1	16	4	1	z5	5	1
9	1z	16	16	z0	z5	z5	30	36
	Seſquitertie		Seſquiquarte			Seſquiquinte		

b ij

Ex quibus proportionibus musice consonantie conducantur.

¶ Proportiones musicas consonantias producentes sex sunt:Boetio ac
Boe. Macrobio testibus:Tres i genere multiplici,scilicet dupla,tripla et qua;
Ma. drupla.Tres insuper insuperparticulari,scilicet sesquialtera,sesquitertia
ac sesquioctaua,Quibus maxime rata musice interualla componuntur:
inquit Plutarchus.Quare dimissis alijs:has tantum, que in notis consi;
stant ac describantur,et preceptis et exemplis breuissimis duximus eno;
dandas.Ac naturali ordine seruato,a dupla : quoniã ceteris ꝗ dignior est
et notior : exordium sumamus.

De proportione dupla.

¶ Dupla proportio prima multiplicis generis species fit, quum maior
numerus ad minorem relatus,ipsum bis in se comprehendit. vt 4.ad 2.
8.ad 4.Sed musicaliter, quũ due note contra vnam sibi et natura,et spe;
cie similem proferũtur.Cuius signũ alij numerũ binariũ esse concludunt,
alij (quoniã proportio non vnius sed duorum relatio existit) numerum
numero supponendum ⌈ 2.4.6. ⌉ idꝗ ꝗ i ceter⸝ seruãdũ eē nõ dubitãt
esse cõtendũt,ħ modo. ⌊ 1 2 3 ⌋

𝕿𝓔𝓝𝓞𝓡 duple

𝓑𝓐𝓢𝓢𝓤𝓢 duple

¶ Non latere vos volo , duplam proportionem, aliasꝗ oēs multiplicis
generis:canonib⁹ designari.dicendo,decrescit in duplo,in triplo,et sic de;
inceps. Qð,quia vel industrie,vel tentatiõis gra sit,nõ improbam⁹.Sũt
qui duplã proportionē in figuris ꝯsiderãt:signis, vn ⌐ cisꝗ si ⌐ nistrorsũ
versus, dicentes hoc.C.huius Ɔ: esse duplũ, hanc ◗ illius ◖ :Jn pau
sis ꝗ3: hui⁹ ꓕillã⌐ , Non alior:vt reor:freti patrocinio : ꝗ ꝗ Franchinus
li,pract. 2.ca.4.dextrũ latus sinistro et auctius et pfectius eē ꝺt: sinistrũ

[183

vero, dextro imbecillius. Cui opinioni nec ipfe refragor multū. Nā apud
Ualerium Probū eruditiſſimū grammaticum, de interpretandis Roma
norum litteris: C.littera: que ſemicirculi formem habet: Caium marem,
eadem inuerſa Caiam femellā inuenio deſignari. Fabius quoq Quinti=
lianus Probi ſententiam corroborans infit. Nam et Caius C littera no=
tatur, que inuerſa mulierem declarat. Et cum maſculi femellis perfectio=
res exiſtant: Semicirculo dextrorſum verſo, perfectio eorum : harū autē
imbecillitas, huius inuerſione, declaratur. hac occaſione moti muſici, la=
tus leuum, dextro dimidium auferre voluerunt: ſic ⊨ ⊨ Ɔ C ⫪

De proportionibus regule.

¶ Prima, Omnis proportio aut per aduentū ſue contrarie proportionis
tollitur, aut per ſigni interpoſitionem infringitur. Ut per aduentum ſub=
duple tollitur dupla, et ſic de alijs. ¶ Secunda, Omnis proportio et pau
ſas et notas reſpicit. ¶ Tertia, Omnis maioris inequalitatis proportio
notas ac pauſas, potētia ſua naturali minuit: minoris vero inequalitatis
adauget. ¶ Quarta, Alteratio ac imperfectio , ijs tantum inſunt
proportionibus , que in gradibus perfectis fiunt. Nec omnibus fi=
guris, ſed ijs dumtaxat: quas illi gradus ſua perfectione reſpiciunt, aut
quibus extra proportionem hec accidentia accidunt. ¶ Quinta Seſqui=
altera proportio figurarum ternariam: niſi eam a ſigno habeant: perfectio
nē excludit. Quare nec alterationē nec ipfectionē, negante ſigno, admittit

De Tripla.

¶ Tripla proportio ſecūda multiplicis gñis ſpecies , fit dū nūerus maior
ad minorem relatus: ipſum in ſe ter cōcludit: vt 6.ad 2.9.ad 3. Sed mu
ſice quum tres notule, contra vnam ſibi ſpecie ſimilem, proferuntur. Cu=
ius ſignum numerus ternarius vnitati ſuprapoſitus: exiſtit. hoc modo

TENOR Triple

BASIS Triple

b iij

De Quadrupla.

❡ Quadrupla, Tertia multiplicis generis species, fit quando nũerus maioz minozem: quater in se cõpzehendit: vt 8. ad z. 1z ad z. Sed musice quando quattuoz note contra vnã pzoferunt. Cuius signa sunt hec.

$$\frac{4}{1} \quad \frac{8}{z} \quad \text{vt sic}$$

TENOR Quadruple

BASIS Quadruple

De Sesquialtera.

❡ Sesquialtera, pzima superparticularis generis species, fit qñ nũerus maioz minozem semel continet: et alterã eius partem: vt 6. ad 4. 9. ad 6 Sed musice, quando tres note, contra duas sibi specie similes pzoferunt. Cuius signa sunt hec. $\frac{3}{z} \quad \frac{6}{4} \quad \frac{9}{6}$ vt in exemplo sequenti.

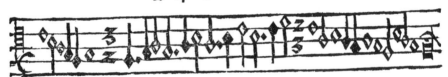

TENOR Sesquialtere

BASIS Sesquialtere.

¶ Sunt qui in figuris numeroꝝ caracteribus ſeſquialteratis, coloꝛẽ ſup
iducunt, ⁊ ediuerſo, ſeſquialteras, ſeſquialterãtes: Et illi tales: teſte Frã
chino: id vitium incidunt, ꝗ ex duabus ſeſquialteris non duplam ſeſqui=
alteram, vt ipſi credunt, ſed duplam ſeſquiquartam pꝛoducunt. Quidam
imperfectionem ac alterationem in ſeſquialteratis imperfecti tempoꝛis
ponunt, pauſam bꝛeuem vno tactu menſurantes, licet in notis tres ſemi=
bꝛeues in vno tactu diſponant. Qua autem id faciant auctoꝛitate, pꝛeter
execrandam atꝗ aſininam ignoꝛantiam, inuenio nullam. neꝗ enim imp=
fectionem ac alterationem ſignoꝝ admittit imperſectio ꞉ neꝗ pauſas ex=
cludit pꝛopoꝛtio.

Frã
chin⁹

De Seſquitertia.

¶ Seſquitertia ꝓpoꝛtio: quã epitritã nominant, eo ꝗ Epitrito cõducaꞇ
ſecundũ Macrobiũ: fit, quando maioꝛ notularum nũerus, minoꝛẽ ſemel
in ſe, et tertiã eius partem concludit: vt 4. ad 3. 8. ad 6. 12. ad 9. Sed mu
ſicaliter quando quattuoꝛ note contra tres ſibi ſpecie ſimiles pꝛoferuntur

Cuius hec ſũt indicia $\frac{4}{3}$ $\frac{8}{6}$ $\frac{12}{9}$. Quidam etiam ſemicirculũ inuerſum

huic pꝛopoꝛtioni aſcribunt: ſed Tinctoꝛ ipꝛobare videꞇ

TENOR Seſquitertie

BASIS ſeſquitertie

Se Seſquioctaua.

¶ Seſquioctaua ꝓpoꝛtio, fit, quũ maioꝛ nũerus minoꝛi cõparatus: ipſum
ſemel includit: et cum hoc octauam eius partem: 9. ad 8. 18. ad 16. Sed
muſice quando nouem note, contra octo ſibi ſpecie ſimiles, decantantur.
Cuius ſignũ eſt numerus nouenarius octenario ſupꝛapoſitus, hoc modo

$\frac{9}{8}$ vel $\frac{C}{8}$

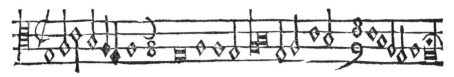

TENOR sesquioctaue

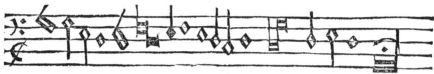

BASIS sesquioctaue

Aul⁹
Gel-
lius.

¶ Sũt insup, qui (qm̃ supueniẽte coloꝛe valoꝛ minuit) sesquialterã nota
rũ plenitudine cõsiderant. Quã et hemiolã noiant . Est em̃ id hemiola,
q̃ sesquialtera:Inquit Aulus Gellius lib.19.ca.14. hec tñ notularũ denigratio ñ nisi sub ipsect̃ quãtitatib⁹,ipis accidere solet,scribit Franchi.

TENOR hemiole

BASSUS hemiole

Hie-
roni-
mus.

¶ Etsi multe sint alie pꝛopoꝛtionum species,quas in harmonico concen
tu musici obseruant, has tamen omnes bꝛeuitatis studio pꝛeterire statui,
ne pueroꝛum:quibus hic liber dicatus est: ingenia impedire magis q̃ iu-
uare videar,Tum pꝛopter illarum difficultatem pꝛopoꝛtionũ, Tũ pꝛopter tenuitatem puerilium ingenioꝛũ.Grandes enũ materias,parua nõ
ferunt ingenia.Dent igitur veniam docti , quoniã ieiunis non delicatis
scriptitatum est:Diuina tamen fauente clementia omnia:que nũc vel bꝛeuitatis,vel alterius rei causa neglecta sunt:olim maioꝛe diligentia,maio-
re cura,maioꝛe deniq̃ rerũ intuitu,in volumie quodã grãdioꝛi elaboꝛata
videbuntur. Sed queso interea ÿs paruis studiosi se exercitent adolescẽ
tes:vt quũ ad maioꝛa gradiendum sit idonei inueniantur.

78

Finit liber Secundus.
Sequitur Tertius.

Perspicacis Ingenij Uiro Philippo Suro Myltenburgensi, bo
narum disciplinarũ Magistro, Musico argutissimo
Sacelli Palatini principis, ac'Bauarie du=
cis moderatori ꝑcipuo:Andreas
Ornitoparchus Mey=
ningẽsis, Sa=
lutem.

Q Uum homo dignissima creaturarũ, animal deiforme, mãsue
tum natura, statura erectũ, prouidum, sagax, memor, acutũ,
secundũ rationẽ legis ac discipline susceptibile, ceteris insen
satis animantibus prelatũ, ac duobus potissimis : sermone
scilicet ac ratiõe, cõditons sui beneficio decoratũ existat, Philippe charis
sime: Ipsius ignorantia tãto est turpior, quanto ipsis hõ bestijs existit di=
gnior. Que cũ alijs turpis sit, Clericis turpissima est . Quorũ vite ad hoc
ordinata est cõditio: vt ceteris bñ viuendo morũ, doctrine, ac probitatis
prebeant exemplũ, fidei feruorẽ in populo augeant, Et quod potissimum
eorũ est officiũ: hymnis et cãticis deum laudando, deuotionẽ in fidelium
cordibus excitẽt. Quéadmodũ eñ militaris disciplina, imperatorũ decus
existit:ita sacerdotũ ac clericorũ oĩm cõcinentia . Cuius tãta est dignitas,
reuerẽtia, atꝗ maiestas, vt oĩa diuina officia, non nisi per eam ordinãtur,
regant̃, cõpleant̃. Sed vtinã bñ:nam hac nostra tempestate:prohpudor,
inter multos vix pauci reperiũt artis huiꝰ periti, qui:ad que ordinati sũt
officia:rite ac rationabiliter ꝑficiũt. Quod an fortune:que sepe promouet
indignos, an prelatorũ incurie, ascribendũ sit, nescio . Nam ij sepius, et si
in alijs parũ sapiant, ab ipsa modulationis disciplina:quã ex patrum de=
creto scire tenentur:penitꝰsunt alieni. Quare retrusis doctis:quos vt cẽ
sores timent:siles sibi ceremonijs preficiũt, prebẽdis onerant, dignitatibꝰ
cumulãt. Quofit : vt alij ere, dolo, fraude, alij mũere, alij fauore, alij alijs
citra canonicã cõstitutionẽ vijs:ad ecclesiasticas dignitates ꝓmoti : nõ se
ecclesie:sed ecclesiam sibi seruire credunt.In choro stãtes , aut vt asini ad
lyram omnino obmutescunt , aut absꝗ lege, modo, ratione, velut boues
vlulando, concinnem cantũ cõfundunt:fideles a deuotione impediũt, in
risum et cachinationẽ male canendo ꝓuocãtes: Et sic ex oratorio speluncã
faciũt Theatralem: dum concinentie disciplinã, aut non ĩ diicerunt, aut:
quia forte magni domini sunt:discere erubescũt. Et hos tales Cõmẽtator
Christiane religionis: licet emulꝰ: his verbis increpat dicens. Ue vobis
hominibꝰ qui de numero bestiarũ cõputati estis: Bonũ quod in vobis est

J

*Im=
pato=
rũ de
cus.*

*Cõ=
mẽta
tor.*

79

non cognofcentes:propter quod ad fuperiora afcenditis, et deo fimiles
eftis.Sed que funt hec bona, que nos deo fimiles faciunt:Nifi ecclefiafti=
ci gradus ac facerdotij dignitas, que omnem terrenā tranfilit dignita=
tem. Sacerdos enim, et regibus eft celfior, et angelis fanctior. Quare pro
pheta Pfalmo 81 ipfis loquitur dices.Ego dixi dij eftis, ꝋ filij excelfi om
nes.Sed id gratia adoptante non natura generante apud diuū Augufti=
num conceditur.Beftijs autem cōnumerātur illi, dum neglecta ratione,
qua cum angelis participamus,fenfualitatem:que nos beftijs fimilimos
efficit:fequuntur.Os fuum, ad dei laudem non apperfentes:Quibus et
iftud propheticum rite cōgruit:Os habent ꝫ non loquentur neꝗ clama=
bunt in gutture fuo.Infuper cum populus beatus dicatur:qui fcit iubila
tionem.Conftat tales a beatitudine longe alienos effe.Quoniā vt de iu=
bilatione a cantu fileam:Uir quidem legere poffunt.Sed vt ipfe verum
fatear,facilius legēdo, ꝗ cantando, errores incurrimus.quia cum alijs ca
nimus,foli autem legimus.Quod cum attēderem:Uir humaniffime, vt
ftudiofos et hac in re iuuarem,Poft concentum:quem fuperioribus duo
bus libris enodauimus:Accentum ecclefiafticum adire libuit.Rem fane
difficilem,Tum ꝗ et grammaticum requirat ꝫ muficum,Tum ꝗ vfu po
tius ꝗ fcripto habeatur.Antea enim aut nulli, aut admodum pauci eccle
fiafticum accentum tractauere.Ob id cum difficultate raritas, opus ali=
quādiu:ne in lucem ederetur:impediuit, Editum autem iam atꝗ perfe=
ctū, tue mando fidei,tue cure,tueꝗ fubijcio cenfure, Ut pro iudicio ftetꝗ
cadetꝗ tuo.Orans quatenus et a medijs eruas, et ab emulorum incurfu
defendas.Quoniam potis es,doct9 es , pius es,Et preter cetera nature
dona habes in dicendo elegantiā, in dictando venam fuauitate fcaturien
tem,in cantu:quo ceteris tuis commilitonibus prestas cū gratia peritā,

in peregrinos vt ipfe:dum coepulo tuus effem:expertuffum, cū hof=
pitalitate liberalitate.Quo fit, vt omnes Budoxini gymnafij:quam hey=
delbergam nominant,magiftri:te vnice diligant,colant, venerentur.Ua
le felix vir prestantiffime,et Andream tuū ab inuidorum liuore, redime,
protege, defende.

Mufice Ornithoparchiane Liber
Tertius ecclefiafticum de =
clarans Accentum.

¶ Argumentum Magiftri Cotberi In librum Tertium.

Tertius accentus:vt erunt ex arte tenendi
Pandit:vt ex ipfo rite legenda legas.

Caput Primum de laude Accentus

Magnam habet cum concentu accentus affinitatem: fraterna nanqʒ cognatione coherent. Sonus nanqʒ ecclesiastice harmonie rex: ambozum pater: Alterum ex Grammatica, alterum ex musica nympha progenuit. Quos cũ vidisset pater, pariter et corporis, et ingenij dotibus pollere, alterumqʒ alteri, in omi genere scibili non inferiozem esse: sibiqʒ (quia grandeuus erat) moztem in dies imminere, cogitare cepit: vtrum eozum regno suo pficeret: nũc hũc, nunc illum intuens: vtriusqʒ mozes contemplabatur. Erat em accentus maioz natu Grauis, facundus, sed seuerus, Ideo populo parum dilectus. Concentus autem hylaris, iucundus, amabilis, omnibus gratiosus, magis amari q̃ timeri studuit, Quare omnium animos: facile sibi cõciliauit. Quod cum notasset pater: plus et plus indies angebatur: quẽ e duobus regem consecraret. Accẽtus enim frugalioz, alter vero populo dilectioz erat. Statuto igitur die, vocatis regni principibus: Quales sunt cãtozes, Poete, ozatozes, philosophi mozales, preterea diuinozum rectozes, qui in ecclesiastico regno: primum post regem locũ tenebant. his cozam Sonus rex, eiusmodi ozationem habuisse dicitur, Proceres mei, varia militie pericula, terra mariqʒ experti: dum me duce victrixia signa, per vniuersum ozbem tulistis, Ecce ozbis paret immensus, hostis nullus, omnia vobis secunda sunt. Soli mihi mozs accedit, vita recedit, cozpus debilitatũ labozibus: animus curis consumptus: Nihil mihi: nisi vt q̃ primum moztem experiar: expectandum. Quare statui vnum e duob², quos genui, filijs: quem cõmuni consilio elegeritis: vobis regẽ constituere, q̃ vos, qui regnum hoc vestro sanguine partum ab inuria, 7 hostium incursione defendat. his dictis, proceres consultare, atqʒ turmatim de communi salute tractare, dissentientes tamen, alij aliũ sibi regẽ postulare. Ozatozes eni et poete accentum: Cantozes vero et mozales, Concentum regem postulabant. Rectozes autem diuinozum: apud quos iura regni erat: altius speculati: neutrũ reijciendũ, sed regnum illis diuidendũ sanxerũt. Quozum sententia, et apud regem preualuit. Diuisum est regnum. Ita vt Concentus omniũ cantabiliũ: vt sunt hymni, Sequentie, Antiphone: Responsozia: Introit²: Tropi et huiusmodi. Accẽtus vero cozum que leguntur: vt sunt Euangelia: Lectiones: Epistole: Ozationes: Prophetie: dux atqʒ moderatoz existeret. Neqʒ em sine Cõcentu: neqʒ sine Accentu: ecclesiastici regni: rite paguf officia. his partes composite cũ regibus suis abierunt. Et non mõ Concentũ: verũ et Accentũ: ab omnibus ecclesiasticis personis reuerendũ concluserunt. Quã rem Sanctissimus in Christo pater: ac dñs: dñs Leo papa decimus: et diuus Maximilianus Romanozũ maxi

189]

Cantozes
Poete
Ozatozes
phi
mozales
Pontificef
Leo.
x.

J ij

milia imperator gloriosissimus, Ambo dij terrent, Ambo Christiãe reipublice
nus. culmina, Ambo bonarũ disciplinarũ ac precipue Musice artis precipua
luminaria: generali patrum ac principum consensu approbarunt, priuile=
gijs dotarunt, atqꝫ omnes contradicentes, tanꝗ lese maiestatis reos, hic
corpore, anima ille damnarũt. hinc ego, attento ꝗ multi sacerdotes (q̀ꝺ
doctorũ pace dixerim) tam scrupulose, tam mõstruose, adeo mendose, le=
genda legant: vt non solum fideles a deuotione impediant, Verũ et in ri=
sum, et cachinationes male legendo inducant. Statui post Concentũ om
nem de accentu: quantum musica est: nodositatẽ, regulis perstringere, vt
vna cum Concentu, Accentus tanꝗ verus heres i hoc ecclesiastico reg=
no habeat. Et laus summi regis: cui honor debet, cui reuerẽtia: rite pficiat

Caput secundum de diffinitione ac diuisione Accentus.

Isi=
dor.

Unde Accent9: vt Isidor9 li.1.ethi.ca.17.scribit: Est certa lex
seu regula, ad eleuandam deprimẽdamue cuiusꝗ dictõis syl
labam. Ul'est regula locutionis. Inepta enim est locutio, que
non exornatur accentu. Et dicitur accentus, quasi sit ad idez
iuxta cantu, secundũ Isidorũ: vt enim aduerbiũ verbum, ita
accentus concentum determinat. Sed quom pscripte descriptiões, gra
matico potius, ꝗ musico accentui conueniant: necessarium erit indagare,
quo nam pacto ecclesiasticus rite describatur accentus. Est igitur accen=
tus, prout ecclesiasticis competit, Melodia quarũlibet dictionũ syllabas,
iuxta accentus sui naturalis erigentiam, regulate pronuntians.

De diuisione.
Accentus.

Pris=
cia.
Isi=
dor9.

Gra=
mati=
ste.

¶ Est autem accentus Tripartitus: Prisciano et Isidoro testibus: Gra=
uis scilicet, acutus ꞇ circumflexus. Grauis est. quo syllaba deprimitur, Sed
musice loquendo. Est finalium dictionũ, secundum ecclesie ritum, regula
ta depressio. Cuius due sunt species: Una que dictiõe finalem vel quã=
libet eius syllabam deprimit per quintam. Et hec proprio vocobulo Gra
uis dicitur. Alia: que dictionem finalem, vel syllabam eius, non per quin
tam sed tertiam tantum grauat. Que a musicis accẽtus vocatur medius
Nec succenseant Grammatiste, si suis legibus contrariũ quid hic offende
rint: Quoniã non grammaticum: quem Priscianus et alij abunde tracta=
uerunt. Sed ecclesiasticum tractare tentabimus accentum, vt in sequenti
exemplo licet videre.

[190

Medius   **Grauis**

Parce mihi dñe   Nihil enim funt dies mei

¶Acutus accentus grammatice, Eſt quo fyllaba eleuatur. Sed muſice:
eſt finalium dictionum, fyllabarum ve ſecundum eccleſie ritum, regulata
eleuatio. Cuius pariter due ſpecies reperiuntur. Una que fyllabam, vel
dictionem finalem reducit ad locum ſui deſcenſus, retinens acuti nomē.
Alia que nõ ad priorem ſui deſcenſus locum: ſed i propriam ſecundam in=
fra: ſyllabam leuat Qui et moderatus appellatur, eo ꝙ moderate fyllabã
ducat in altum: vt in ſubſcripto claret exemplo.

Moderatus   **Acutus**

Illuminare hieruſalem.   quia gloria domini ſuper te orta eſt

¶Circumflexus eſt quo fyllaba eleuata deprimit, Eſt enim teſte Jſidoro,
contrarius acuto circumflexus, ab acuto nanꝗ incipit et in grauem deſi=
nit. Eccleſiaſticis incognitus. Cenobite tamen, et potiſſimum Ciſtercien=
ſis ordinis: Circumflexum habent accentum: Ut apud veterem cellã ci=
uſdem ordinis regale Cenobium expertuſſum. In quo vno:ꝗ vere re=
ligionis ſunt: inuenio ornamenta, diſciplinam, obedientiam, obſeruan=
tiam, vitam regularem, ⁊ ſine qua monaſteria tartara ſunt: charitatem,
bybliothecam preclariſſimam, Cellam pigmentariã precioſam, patrū mſ=
titudinem et piam et deuotam, illuminatiſſimorū virorum turbam copio
ſam, Artiū magiſtros duodecim, Sacre Theologie. Baccalaureos tres,
Domio Martino de Lochen Abbate, Sacre pagine eximio doctore, Ac
domino Michaele Geitano priore eiuſdem pagine baccalaureo: rem ita
adminiſtrantibus, vt et facultatum, et bonarū diſciplinarum copia: apud
eos inueniatur, Nec inter ceteros artium diuerſarum profeſſores deſunt
muſici. Nec preter planum cantum: quem regulatiſſimū habent: menſura
lem aſpernantur. Quippe Dominus prior imprimis: deinde frater Mi=
chael Galliculus vtriuſꝗ muſice ſtudioſiſſimi ſunt. Quorum alter orga=
nice, alter harmonice muſice tantam peritiã aſſecutus eſt: vt ſummis mu=
ſice principibus connumerari non imerito poſſint. Tranſeo alios pleroſꝗ
qui non minus menſuraliter, ꝙ ſi a cunabulis in ſacellis principū vixiſſet,
canūt. Tranſeo deniꝗ precioſiſſimum cãtilenarum theſaurum: quem tan=
tum habent vt nec principi cuiꝗ cedant. Ualeant nunc qui muſicen reli=

                     J iij

(margin notes:) Jſi=
do:o.

Uet⁹
Cel=
la et
laus
cius.

Cantus honestum Cenobitarū solatium.

giosis interdicūt. Qui, preter cantum: solatiū nec vllum habere pñt salubrius: nec honestius, Dum enim solatiose canitur: omnis sollicitudo prauarum cogitationū: preterea oblocutio: detractio, crapula insuper et ebrietas deuitatur. Cantus igitur tum planus tum mensuralis decet religiosissimos quosqꝫ, vt ⁊ laudes deo decantare, ac seipsos, solatij tempore exhylarare valeant. Sed dimissis ijs, ad materiā vnde digressi sumus, reuertamur: atqꝫ de circumflexo accentu sollicitos ad fratrem Michaelē galliculum prenominatum remittimus. Qui rem tanta breuitate expressit: vt alterius elucidatione non egeat.

Caput tertium. generales regulas accentus depromens. [191

QUom a facilioribus, ad difficiliora innat⁹ sit nobis processus, Primum igitur generales accentuationis regulas, et subinde speciales cōgruo ordine placuit enodare. ¶ Prima, Omnis dictio monosyllaba, indeclinabilis vel barbara, acutū exigit accentum: vt Astarot, Senacherib, me, te, sum. ¶ Secunda, Dictiones grece et hebree in latinis terminationibus latinum retinent accentum: vt Parthenopolis, Nazarenus, hierosolyma. ¶ Tertia Dictiones grece et hebree, latinam inflexionem non habentes acuunt, vt Crison, Argyrion, Effraym, hierusalem. ¶ Quarta Grauis accentus in fine complete sententie, acutus pariter, Moderatus autē, ac medius, non nisi in fine incomplete sententie proferuntur. ¶ Quinta. Grauis accent⁹ non debet repeti nullo alio interueniente, nisi oratio adeo breuis existat, vt alius interuenire non possit, vt hic.

Factū est vespere et mane dies secundus Dixit quoqꝫ deus

Caput quartum de regulis specialibus.

Aris.

PRima: Dictio monosyllaba, indeclinabilis, barbara, vl' hebrea: quas acuto accentu proferendas diximus: aut ponitur in fine complete sententie: sic acuitur: aut incomplete et sic moderatur. hinc excipiuntur Encletice coniunctiones que grauantur, vt sic

Dñs locut⁹ eſt Clamate ad me et ego exaudiã vos Deus dñſcʒ

¶ Secunda: Prima diſſyllabe dictionis, ſemper accentum recipit: ſiue breuis: ſiue longa ſit: hoc modo.

Et fugit velut vmbra   Et in amaritudinibus morabif oculos me⁹

¶ Tertia: Dictio poliſyllaba in fine orationis poſita: aut habet penultimam longam:
aut breuem. Si longam: accentus cadit in
eaml. Si breuem: tunc ante penultima accentum recipiet.

Lignum ſi preciſum fuerit rurſum vireſcit.   Et rami eius pullulant

¶ Quarta: Oratio interrogatoria, ſiue habeat in fine dictioné
monoſyllabã ſiue diſſyllabã: ſiue poliſyllabam: accétus ſemper
cadit ſuper vltimam eius: et illa debet acui. Signa autem que-
ſitiue orationis ſunt: quis: que: quod cũ natis: Cur: quare: quã-
do: quamobré: quomodo: qualiter: quorſum: quouſcʒ: quoad.
Quo: qua: vnde: vbi. Cuius cuia cuium: Utrum: an: ne: nonne:
nunquid. Et ſimiles.

Unde tu ⁚   Quid eſt hõ ⁚   Quãtas habeo iniquitates et peccata ⁚

¶ his iunguntur verba queſitiua: vt quero: interrogo: rogo:
poſtulo: inueſtigo: Scruto:: inſuper audio: video: et ſimilia.

Caput quintum de Punctis.

Uoniã eccleſiaſticus aecentus, plerumcʒ punctis cognoſcif:
neceſſariũ videtur: quorundam: noſtro ‚ppoſito ſeruientiũ:
punctorũ naturam regulis aperire. ¶ Prima: Punctus qué
virgulam nominant: ſi inter plures dictiones: eiuſdem partis orationis locaf eas diſtincte legédas deſignat. ¶ Scda Geminus pũ ⁚

ctas, vt punctus preseise ad medium lateris dextri locatus: medium sig-
nat accentum: qui per tertiam descendit. ¶ Tertia, Punctus in fine alicuius orationis vltra medium aliquantulum eleuatus: accentū, aut acu-
tum, aut moderatum secundum sententie tenorem repres[entat. ¶ Quarta, punctus vltra dictionis medium aliquantulum depressus: grauis accentus exstit indicium. ¶ Sexta, Punctus interrogatoriuus qui sic forma
tur? alicubi locorum repertus: vltimam syllabam dictionis: cui iungitur,
acuto accentu proferendam demonstrat. Quorum omnium euidentia, se
quenti elucescit exemplo,

Hesterna luce cum equitassem in campū, virentē, herbosum, floudū,

spaciaturus in eo: occurrit mihi lepusculus cū genitore suo. Insequēs

cum catellis meis ser Apprehendi dūtarat pusillū in valle mōtis Oreb.

Deliberās autē cui amicorū leporias istas carnes essem condo-

naturus? interrogās comitē meū qd esset suasurus? Sano mihi cō

si lio dixit. Hortor cū fidu cia eas donodari consuli de

Brūschuick. Tu aut domine. Misere re nobis

Caput sextum de accen-
tu epistolarum.

❡ Epistolarum accentus totalis, diuersificatur, secundū diocesium ac re-
ligionum diuersitatem. Partialis tamen idem est apud omnes, quoniam
ex syllabarū quantitatibus procedit. vt ex infrascriptis regulis declaraf̄
❡ Prima, Omnis et epistolarum et euangeliorū accentus, ex finalium
dictionum syllabis, ac earundem numero comprehenditur. ❡ Secunda.
Quando in fine orationis dictio monosyllaba collocatur. Accentus vari-
atur secundum precedentium dictionum varietatem. ❡ Tertia, Si monosyllabam finalem precedit alia monosillaba, ɀ ipsam tertia, prima venit
eleuanda. hoc modo.

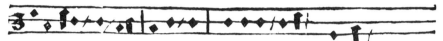

Sic inflati sunt quidā tāꝗ non venturus sit   ad nos

❡ Quo autem Pacto Cenobitarum more accentus
ille distinguatur, frater Michael Muris Galliculus
in Tractatu suo: quem de hac re scripsit: et vere ɀ perite nō sine magna laude sua discussit. ❡ Quarta, Si
monosyllabam finalē precedit dissyllaba, prima eius
est eleuanda, siue sit longa, siue breuis: vt sic.

Mi-
chael
Mu-
ris.

Omnia   em   vestra sunt Si ꝗs diligit deum ex e o est

❡ Quinta, Si monosyllabā finalem, trisyllaba precesserit, Tunc si penultimam longam habuerit eleuetur. Sin autem breuē.
accentus i ante penultimam transferatur.

In pace deus vocauit vos Dispensati o mihi credita est

❡ Sexta, Si in fine orationis dissillaba locaf̄. tunc penultima precedētis
dictiōis debet eleuari, si lōga sit. Sed si breuis, antepenultima, hoc mō.

K

87

Et dixit mihi   Et in plenitudine   sanctorum deten tio   mes

¶ Septima: Si in fine orationis Trissyllaba posita fuerit : et eā
precedat monosyllaba: tunc illa est eleuanda. Sin aūt dissyllaba
eleuetur prima illius: siue longa : siue breuis sit . Q̃ si Trisylla
bā trisyllaba precesserit: ea penultimam eleuat: si sit longa: Q̃ si
breuis: eleuatio in antepenultimam illius transferatur. vt sic .

Tu scis omnia   Nōne dixit dñs   Cantantes de o   gloriam

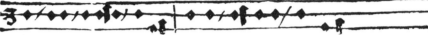

At illi dixerunt domino Nouit   omnia dominus

¶ Octaua: Si in fine orationis ponitur di=
ctio plurium syllabarum q̃ trium: tunc pri=
ma eius debet eleuari: si longa sit. Sin autē
breuis : accentus cadit in precedentem di=
ctionem: hoc quo sequitur modo.

Dixit dñs   omnipotēs   In tēplo solomonis sunt aurei parietes

Caput septimū de accentu Euangelioꝝ.

Euangelioꝝ accentus totalis , ali⁹ est in alia diocesi, ac religio=
ne. Partialis tñ qui vnus est apud omnes infrascriptis regulis
notificatur.   ¶ Prima, Si oratio terminata fuerit in dictio
nem monosyllabā, et illam precedit alia. et ipsam tertia, Accen
tus a prima recipitur hoc modo. ¶ Secunda, si monosyllaba
finalem dissyllaba precesserit, Prima eius accentū recipit, siue longa fue=
rit siue breuis hoc modo .

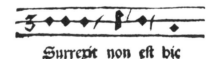

Surrexit non est hic

Omnia verba hec Domin⁹ dedit hoc

¶ Tertia, Si monosyllabā finalē, polisyllaba precedit: accentus cadit in antepenultimam illius, si longa sit. Sin autem breuis antepenultima accentum recipiet.

Dolentes querebamus te Nonne dixit omnia hec

¶ Quarta, Si oratio terminaf in dissillabam: penultima precedentis dictionis eleuetur: si longa sit. Ω si correpta fuerit, antepenultima, hoc modo.

Ut describeret vniuersus orbis Abrahā aūt genuit Jacob

¶ Quinta. Si oratio in trissyllabam desierit, habentem penultimam longam: Tunc accentus cadit super vltimam precedentis dictiōis. Ω si breuis fuerit, penltima illi⁹ accentum recipiet, hoc modo.

Ex e a q̃ fuit Urie Et clausa est ianu a

¶ Sexta, Si finalis dictio oratiōis, pluriū syllabarū q̃ triū extiterit, accentus cadit in primā illius: si lōga sit, sed si breuis, vltima precedētis eleuef.

In transmigratione Babilonis Et filius altissimi voca bitur

De accentu prophetiarum.

¶ Prophetiarū accentuandi duplex est modus. Quedam enim epistolarum more leguntur: Quemadmodum diebus festuitatū diue virginis, Epiphāie, natiuitatis dñi, ⁊ siles. Et ille epistolarū retinēt accentū. Quedam vero more matutinalium lectionum decantātur: vt nocte Christi, et in Jeiunijs quattuor temporum: et hee accentum illarum lectio-

R ij

Sed nec latere vos volo: ꝗ in accentuatione plerumꝗ mos ac ri-
tus patrie seruatur et loci: Sicuti i maiori ecclesia Magdeburgensi: Tu
autem domine, media producta legitur, er consuetudine illi⁹ ecclesie: vbi
alie nationes mediā corripiunt er regula. Dent igitur veniā lectores, Si
aliquando diocesi:i qua sunt: scripta etiam nostra aliquo modo contraire
videbuntur. Quod licet in paucis fiat, in plurimis tn concordiam habe-
bunt. Experientia etenim ductus, non preceptis: vt librum hunc in luce
ederem. Et si citra iactantiam loqui phas sit, eius rei causa, varias mundi regiones: et in ijs varias ecclesias: tam Metropolitanas ꝗ̄ Cathe-
drales: nō sine graui iactura rerum omnium conspeximus, vt posteritati
prodessemus. In qua peregrinatiōe nostra, quicꝗ regna Pannonie, Sar-
matie, Boemie, Datie. ac vtriusꝗ Germanie. Dioceses seragintatres:
Vrbes ter centum quadraginta: populorum ac diuersarum hominum
mores pene infinitos vidim⁹: Maria duo, Balticū scz atꝗ Oceanū mag-
nū, nauigauim⁹, nō vt merces arctoi syderis: sed palladios fruct⁹ cumu-
laremus. Que omnia dirisse volo: Ut experientia potusꝗ preceptis, hūc
de ecclesiastico accentu librū in luce prodijsse, studiosi Lectores cognoscāt

Side notes: gde- / bur- / gen. / eccle- / sie. / Pan- / no. / Sar- / ma. / Boe- / mia. / Da- / cia / Ger- / mia. / Ma- / re / balti- / cum / Ma- / re / mag- / num.

Explicit liber Tertius.
Sequitur Quartus.

Spectabili, nec non Industrio Uiro Mg̃ro Arnoldo Schlick
Musico consumatissimo, ac Palatini Principis Organiste probatissimo, Andreas Ornitoparchus Meyningensis, Salutem.

CUm intellectus noster in ortus sui principio, nudus atꝗ infor-
mis existat: nec preter informandi possibilitatem, in se habeat
quicꝗ: Arnolde charissime: Multi dubitauere, cur summ⁹ ille
rerū opifer de⁹: homini, non vt plerisꝗ insensatis animātib⁹,
a natura scientiā indiderit. Alijs enim nendi, alijs mellificādi,
quibusdam terendi, atꝗ alijs aliam artem fecit connaturalem. hominez
autem nudum. inermē, ignauum, sine arte, sine armis. sine tegumento, ipso natali die abijcit ad vagit⁹ statim et ploratus: risusꝗ ante quadragesi-
mum diem nulli datur, vt Plinius in prologo septimi historie naturalis
scribit. Nunquid igitur homo bestijs inferior erit? Absit. Nam ista homi-
nis nuditas, non ignobilitatem, sed prestantiam eius arguit, Quoniā intus existens prohibet extraneum: hinc videmus ea: quibus artes conna-
te sunt: animalia, preter eam nihil posse, quā habent corriuatam. homo
autem omnibus caret, vt ad omes idoneus sit. Quod naturale sciēdi de-
syderium in eo declarat, Est etenim omnibus nobis, ita naturaliter insitus scientiarū appetitus. vt nullus tam sapiens, nullus tā insipiens. nul

Side notes: Pli- / nus. / Ari- / sto.

lus tam equus, nullus tam iniquus reperiatur:iterrogatus an hanc,vel
illam artem scire vellet:quin vellem respondeat.Ab omnibus etenim ar
tes appetuntur licet non emantur,ab omnibus laudantur,non inuestigā
tur,Ab omnibus diliguntur,non discuntur.Quoniā obsunt pigritia,vo
luptas,inordinatus modus docendi atq egestas.At licet quarūlibet ar
tium,connatus nobis sit appetitus:pre omnibus tamen aliis concinendi
disciplinam,et appetimus et diligimus.Ipsa nanq cunctas res viuentes
allicit iucunditate,trahit vtilitate,vincit necessitate.Cui°partes et si om
nes sacre,ac prope diuine existant:Ea tamen:quam contrapunctū nomi
nant:aliis longe dulcior est,dignior est,prestantior est.Quoniam aliarū do
micilium est omnium.Non q cunctas in se musice difficultates cōtineat:
Sed q in suo effectu,doctum,perfectum atq consumatum musicum re
quirat.Merito igif descisis aliis,ne et in hac vna nostrū claudicet opuscu
lum,loco postremo Contrapunctum (tanq in quo omnia musice secreta
reponuntur Gazophilatiū)studiosis enodare curauimus,Non vt oēs:
nisi q̃s natura fauet:cōdāt,sed vt ab aliis cōdita,bona sint nec ne:diiudica
re valeant.Ualidi enim carminis constitutio:vt ipse optime nosti:non ty
ronum:sed emeritorum militū est opus.7 non omnium:sed eorū dumtax
at (quoniā poete nascimur) quos natura trahit ac allicit.Qui poterint
igif nostris scriptis condant:qui non:quo poterit eāt.Sed ne plus equo
digrediar:Uir prestantissime:Cotrapuncti normas,sparsim pro commu
ni studiosorum fructu,hinc et hinc collectas:in hunc postremo cōportaui
librum.Quem tibi trutinēdum offero,tuo examini subiicio,arbitrio tuo
submitto.Ut te censore crispantes emulorum nasos intrepide queat adi
re.Nam a tua sententia nemo in musica appellabit vnq̃.Quoniā te in hac
re nec quisq̃ doctior existit nec acutor:qui preter visum cetera habes om
nia,prudentiam,eloquentiam,mansuetudinem,ingenii perspicacitatē mi
randam,in omni musico genere,prope diuinam industriam,plurimarum
insuper artium peritiam.Corporea cares lampade,fulget lux aurea men
te.extra nec quicq̃ cernis,intra te omnia conspicis.Deest oculorum cla
ritas,ingenii adest miranda perspicacitas,deficit visus,viget intellectus
Egens es oculo,locuples ingenio,Uisiue virtutis defectum,nobile sup
plet ingenium.Quare non solum a tuis principibus:quos habes gratio
sissimos:amaris,Uerum vt Orpheus et Amphion,ab omnibus predica
ris.Uale Musice decus et delitie,et Andream tuum a Zoilis et Ther
sitis protege ac defende.

Musice Ornitoparchiane.
Liber Quartus Contrapuncti
principia elucidans.

K iij

Pi
gri
tia
Uo
lup.
Inor
di.
docē
dimo
dus.
Ege
stas.

¶ Argumentum Magistri Cotheri In librum Quartum.

Sed contrapuncti postremus continet Artem,
Scita hac compones : que libet ipse tibi.

Caput Primum de diffinitione . diuisione ac nominum contrapuncti differetia.

Nicomachus

REfert Nicomachus Musicus, Canendi disciplinam, adeo simplicem fuisse primitus : vt solo Tetracordo consisteret. Nec plᵘ assa, id est sola voce (assum enim solum dixerunt veteres Unde et assa vox nominatur ore prolata nõ admixtis alijs musicᵍ concentibus : qua maiorũ laudes cantabantur, Scribit Philippus Beros **Philip. Bero al.** aldus Apuleiani Commentarij lib. x) ac eadem simpliciter, et absᵩ vllo modulaminis lepore prolata, perficeretur. Uarijs tamen subide auctoribus : in Tetracorda quattuor : quindecim chordis contexta, excreuit. Qui bus quintum et sextum : atᵩ ijs plura posteritas superduxit, Ita vt non vna voce tantum sed quattuor 5. 6. 8. et interdum pluribus , hac nostra tempestate vocibus : catilena procedat. Nam Joannem Økeken mutetũ. **Joannes. Økeken. Frãchi.** 36. vocum composuisse constat. Que autem id efficit industria. Contrapunctus a musicis appellatur. Est em contrapũctus in genere nihil aliud : ᵩ peritia variarũ catilene partiũ inuentiua, Uel est parens modulationũ Uel vt Franchinus lib. 3. ca. scribit , Est ars flectendi cantabiles sonos, proportionabili dimensione, ac temporis mensura. Ut enim lutũ in manibus figuli : Ita constitutio catilene in manu constituentis est musici. Quare pleriᵩ non contrapunctũ sed compositionem, hanc artẽ nominare con sueuerunt. Talem de nominibus differentiam assignantes , Cõpositionẽ diuersarum harmonie partiũ, per discretas concordantias in vnum collectionẽ dicentes, Est enim componere : diuersas harmonie parteis discre tis concordantijs in vnũ colligere. Contrapũctus vero est plani cantus diuersis melodijs, subita ac improuisa, ex sorte ordinatio. Unde sortisare, est planũ cantum, certis consonãtijs, ex improuiso ordinare. Dicitur autẽ **Bacheus** Contrapunctus : auctore Bacheo : quasi contrapositis vocibus , concors concentus : arte probatus.

De Contrapuncti diuisione.

[198]

¶ Contrapunctus duplex : Simplex scilicet et Coloratus inuenitur. Simplex Est pluriũ catilene partiũ p notas specie sibi similes, cõcors ordinatio. Ut quũ choralis cõtra Choralẽ, breuis cõtra breuem, simpliciter ordinatur. hoc modo.

92

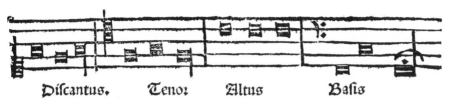

Difcantus.   Tenoz   Altus   Bafis

¶ Coloratus autem contrapunctus, Eft pluriũ can=
tilene partium, difcretis concozdantijs ac diuerfis fi=
guris conftitutio, hoc quo fequitur modo.

Cantus   Tenoz   Altus   Bafis

Caput Secundum de confo= nantijs ac diffonantijs.

Um Concozdantia fecundũ Boetiũ, fit rata dyarũ vel pluriũ
permixtio vocũ, et vox nec abf{ã fono, nec fonus abfq; pulfu,
nec pulfus fine motu fieri poffit, motũ fecare neceffe ẽ. Motuũ
igit alÿ equales alÿ inequales funt. Et rurfus inequalium alÿ
plus. alÿ min⁹ ineꝗles, alÿ mediocriter. Ex motuũ aũt equa=
litate equales fonos fieri, et ex inequalibus:inequales conftat. Et quidẽ
ex mediocri inequalitate fonos confonos. ex omnino aũt a fe diftantibus
diffonos procreari. hinc eft quare Pythagorici vltra Bifdiapafon, vt et
fuperius lib. I. ca. f. claruit: nullã confonantiã:ob nimiã extremozũ diftan
tiam, confiftere poffe concluferunt. Quanto igitur foni propinquiozes, tã
to fuauiozes exiftunt, et quo diftant amplius, eo confonant minus. Quod
(Qm̃ Confonantia duozũ fonoꝛ mixtura fit, vniformiter auribus inci=
dens)ex ineꝗli taliũ fonoꝛũ in aures incidentia euenire potiffimũ argumẽ
toꝛ. Soni em̃ acuti celerius q̃ graues audiuꝛ. Quemadmodu mucro fa
ftigiatus momento penetrat, Quod vero hebetius eft retufus ve non ita,
fed cũ moꝛa et fegniter:Similitꝛ, vibꝛata vox audita, peruellit ac fodicat, Celi=
Gꝛauis obtundit, veluti trudendo, Scribit Celius li. 10. ca. f3. us.

De Vocibus.

¶ Quoniã fimilitudo vocũ cõfonantiã nõ parit, fed diffimilitudo. Uocũ
igitur alie vnifone dicuntur, alie nõ. Unifone funt:quarum vnus eft fo=

93

nus. Non vnisone vero quaruz vna grauioz, altera acutioz est. Non vni-
sonarum.alie equisone,alie consone,alie Emmeles,alie dissone.Equiso-
ne.sunt,que simul pulse,vnum ex duobus sonum efficiunt, vt Diapason
et Bisdiapason.Consone, que compositum seu permixtum sonu reddut.
Diapente et Diapasondiapente.Emmeles sunt:que cum cosone no sunt:
consonis tamen proxime assistunt.Ut ille que tertias, sextas, vel alias im
perfectas concozdantias sonat. Dissone vero sunt:quaru soni impermix-
ti insuauiter sensum feriunt.

Quid sit Concordantia.

¶ Ex pretactis claret cosonantiam, qua alio nomie concozdantiam dici-
mus:esse dissimilium inter se vocum invnum redactam concozdiam.Ut
Tin-
ctoz. est (vt Tinctoz scribit) diuersozum sonozum mixtura:dulciter aurib9 co-
ueniens.Uel secundum Stapulensem lib.3.Est soni acuti grauisq mixtu
ra:suauiter, vniformiterq, auribus incidens.Quaru apud practicos duo
Sta-
pul. decim in vsu seruanf.licet non nulli replicatioe predictaru plures habeat

Scil- Unisonus. 8   15
cet   Tertia.   10   17   Unisonum et eundem causant so-
       Quinta   12   19   num quia fiunt in octaiis
       Sexta.   13   20

De discordantijs.

¶Dissonantia:vt inquit Boetius:Est duozum sonorum sibimet impmixtozum dura atq aspera collisio.
Uel, vt Tinctoz ait, est diuersozum sonozum mixtura,
naturaliter aures offendens. Quarum sunt nouem.

Scilicet Secunda   9   16   Unum et eundem causant so-
          Quarta   11   18   num,quia fiunt in octauis.
          Septima 14   21

Caput tertium de Concor-
dantiarum diuisione.

Oncozdantiarum alie simplices seu primarie, vt Unisonus,tertia,quinta,et sexta, Alie replicate seu secundarie
que et equisone sunt precedentibus, dupla dimensione
concepte. Octaua nanq cum vnisono,decima cum tertia duodecima cum quinta,et tredecima cum sexta,sono
coit. Alie triplicate,scilicet quindecima, que et vnisono

94

et octaue sono equaſ.Decimaſeptima que et tertie et decime. Decimano
na que quinte et duodecime.Uiceſima:que et ſerte et tredecime ſimboli=
zat ſono, ⁊ ſic deinceps. Côcordantiarum item alie perfecte:alie imperfe=
cte. Perfecte ſunt que in certis proportionibus radicate,numeroꝛũ preſi=
dio probabiles eriſtunt. Imperfecte vero cũ probabiles nõ ſint:inter per=
fectas tamen collocate conſonum efficiunt ſonum . Quarum nomina hic
leguntur ſubſcripta.

Perfe= ⎧Uniſonus⎫   ⎧12⎫ Jmper ⎧3 ⎫   ⎧13⎫
cte ſũt. ⎨Quinta ⎬ et ⎨15⎬ ſecte ⎨6 ⎬ et ⎨17⎬
        ⎩Octaua ⎭   ⎩19⎭   ⎩10⎭   ⎩20⎭

❡ Quarum quelibet ſimpliciter ducta,duas tantum
voces recipit:licet ꝑ commixtionem plures recipiat.

Concordantiarum regule.

❡Prima,due concordantie perfecte eiuſdem ſpeciei ſe ſequi,
non permittuntur, ſed bene diuerſarũ. Poteſt tamen octauam
ſequi octaua, dummodo diſſimilibus ac contrarijs procedant
motibus:Inquit Franchinus lib.3.ca.3.ſic.

DISCANTUS   TENOR

❡ Secunda,due concordantie imperfecte,vel etiã plures : ſe ſequi ſimul
aſcendendo vel deſcendendo permittunt. ❡ Tertia , Jmperfectas con=
cordantias ſemper ſequatur proximiꝛ perfecta, puta imperfectã tertiam
vniſonus,perfectam quita,imperfectam ſertam quinta,perfectã.octaua:
vt Gafforus lib.3.ca.3.declarat. ❡ Quarta,Plures eiuſdem ſpeciei pſe Gaſ=
cte concordantie immobiles,ſe ſequi permittuntur:mobiles vero non.   foꝛus
❡ Quinta,Minima nota,vel pauſa illius , inter perfectas eiuſdẽ ſpeciei
concordantias mediare non ſufficit:propter paruum ⁊ quaſi inſenſibilem
eius ſonum. licet a pleriſqʒ contrarũ ſit ſeruatum. ❡ Serta,Contingere
poteſt vt minima,vel ſemuminima:partibus contrarie procedẽtibus:diſ=
cordantia ſit:huiuſmodi enim diſcordantia latet, nullam auribus inferẽs
leſionem. Cauendum tamen eſt:ne due vel plures ſimul iũgantur.
❡ Septima,Breuis vel ſemibreuis diſcordans,a contrapuncto relegaſ.
Sunt tamen qui breuem in quadruplo : et Semibreuem in duplo dimi=
nutam admittunt diſcordantem.

ℒ

Caput quartum.de generalibus contrapuncti preceptis.

Egula prima. Cupiens componere quicpiam : primo formet tenozem vel quacunq̃ aliam vocem : secundũ toni exigentiã : subquo regulatur.¶ Secunda, Modi inusitati omni et parte sunt vitandi:dissonãt nanq̃ omes pzeter decimas. ¶ Tertia, In concozdantijs perfect̃ , nunq̃ ponatur vox mollis contra duram:nec econtra. Sed aut mollis contra mollem, dura contra duram , aut saltem naturalem. Naturales nanq̃ ancipites, et cum bmollibus et cum ♮ duralibus concozdabunt, hoc modo.

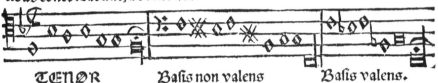

TENOR   Basis non valens   Basis valens.

¶ Quarta, Si tenoz in chozali nimis pzofunde pzocesserit, transponatur ad quintã, vel quartã, si necessitas id efficiat : vt in hymno Quẽ terra,licet videre. ¶ Quita, Omnes cantilene partes:in pzincipio et fine veteres in concozdantijs perfectis posuere : que lex apud nos arbitraria est. ¶ Serta, Una voce sursum, vel deozsum gradiente, non est opus variare reliquas, quia immobili voci plures cõsonantie mobiles possunt coaptari. ¶ Septima, In omni cantilena , consonantie querantur pzopinquiozes.nam que distant nimiũ, dissonantiam sapiunt, Tradunt Pythagozici. ¶ Octaua, Tenoz vna cum alijs dulcem habeat melodiam,in vagis collationibus. ¶ Nona, Si tenoz acutas et excellentes tetigerit, discantus poterit descendere, ad locum tenozis.¶ Decima, Si tenoz cadendo tetigerit graues.bassus scandat in locum tenozis iuxta concozdantiarum exigentiam. ¶ Undecima, Omnis cantilena , formalibus clausulis sepius venit exoznanda. ¶ Duodecima, Si tenoz clausulã discantus habuerit:discantus econtra clausulã tenozis occupabit. clausulando , aut de decima in octauam,aut de tertia in vnisonum, hoc modo.

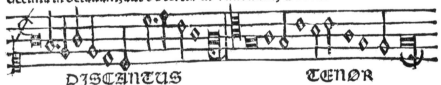

DISCANTUS   TENOR

¶ Tredecima. Si bassus clausulam tenozis assumpserit, tenoz clausulam discantus habebit.Uel si bassus clausulã discantus tenuerit:tenoz suã scr-

Py: tha: gozi: ci.

uabit clauſulando, vt in regula precedente oſtenſum eſt, hoc modo.

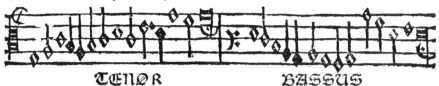

TENOR   BASSUS

¶ Quartadecia, diſcant⁹ raro ſup tenoꝛé quitā teneat, ſed impfectas conꝰ
coꝛdātias ſepius. ¶ 15. Baſſ⁹ infra tenoꝛé raro vl'nnꝗ locet i ſerta: niſ
moꝛ ſequat̃ octaua, ſi i pfectis ſepius. ¶ 16. Si baſſus ſextā ſub tenoꝛe
habuerit, Diſcant⁹ ponat̃ i quita ſupꝛa tenoꝛé clauſulādo i tertiā hoc mõ.

DISCANTUS   TENOR   BASSUS

¶ Decimaſeptima, diſcant⁹ raro faciat ſaltū p quitā ſurſū: ſed per ſertam
et octauā ſepi⁹. Cui et octaua infra ‚phibet̃: reliquis interuallis omnibus
conceſſis. ¶ 18. Baſſus per ſertā ſaltare ‚phibet̃, alios modos oñes
cõmunes habet. ¶ XIX. Jn qnartis mi, contra fa, nõ conſonat, quia cauꝰ
ſat Tritonū. ¶ XX. quarta et ſi ſimpliciter ducta diſſona ſit: cõiuncta tñ **Frā**
concoꝛdi cõmixtioni: concoꝛdé cū extremis efficit medietaté: inquit **Fran** chin⁹
chinus. ¶ XXI. quarta duobus tantū locis in contrapuncto admittitur.
Pꝛimo quando inter duas octauas clauſa quintā infra habuerit: Quia ſi **Ana**ꝰ
ſupꝛa quita ſit, nõ valet conſonātia, Ex ea Ariſtotelis(qui **Anagnoſtes**, gnoꝰ
ideſt lectoꝛ infatigabilis a Platone nūcupat̃) ratione, qua in ‚pblematib⁹ ſtesꝭ
ſonos grauioꝛes diſſonos, acutioꝛib⁹ diſſonis magꝭ ſenſibiles eē declarat ſatꝭ
Scdo qñ tenoꝛ et diſcāt⁹ p vnā, aut plures ſertas ‚pcedunt: tūc voꝛ ꝗ meꝰ gabiꝭ
dia eſt, quartā ſemp ſub cātu, tertiā vero ſupꝛa tenoꝛé ſeruabit. hoc modo, lecꝰ
toꝛ.

VOX ſupꝛema

VOX media.

Z ¶

97

Uox infima,

¶ Uicesima secunda, Celeberrimus qui=
dam Contrapūcti modus efficitur: Inqꝰ it
Frāchinus:Si bassus cum discātu, vel alia
quauis voce per decimā distans simul gra=
diatur:tenoꝛe concoꝛditer ad vtrunꝗ com=
meāte,hoc modo.

TENOR huius.

Discantus exBase
in decimis.

¶ Uicesima tertia, Si nec eandem cosnonantiam
iunxeris, duas partes in decimis concoꝛdabis.

¶ Uicesimaquarta, Necessarium
erit artis huius Tyronibus: scha
lam decemlinealem vt foꝛment,
foꝛmatam, cancellis distinguāt:
Ita vt singula tempoꝛa, singulis
cancellis, clauibus rite signatis:
ne confusa notarum commixtio=
ne impediantur: inscribere vale=
ant. Pꝛestantius tamen est absꝗ
schala condere. quod cum diffici=
le sit, a scala incipiant adulescen
tes,hoc modo.

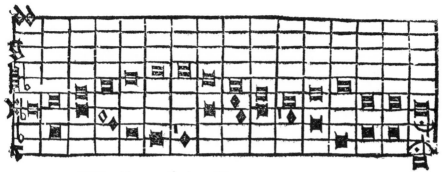

¶ Nec id paruifaciant Tyrones, quo nam pacto
signa ipsa conferantur, et quorum inordinata rela=
tione, tot errores in musica emersere, vt non facile
sit cognitu, quo nam calle quisq tutus incedat.
Quo circa si signo signum conferre quis voluerit,
diminutionis proportionumq naturam caute at=
tendat:ne facta relatiõe hui9 ad hoc:alterius mens
sura vel excrescat vel deficiat.

De cantilene partibus ac clau=
sulis Caput Quintum.

Risce musice simplicitas, varias cãtilene parteis ne=
sciuit:quas nostro euo subtilitas exposcit. Aucto eni
toto augentur et parteis illius. Partes autẽ quibus
nunc musici vtuntur, plures sunt, scilicet Cantus Te
nor, Tenoracutus, Melodia, Cõcordans, Uagans,
Contratenor. Basis, et ijs plures. Sed quoniam in cõmu=
ni vsu omnes non sunt, de frequentioribus nõ nihil dicem9:
de rarioribus autem supersedendum duximus.

De Discantu.

¶ Discantus, vt Tinctor refert. Est cantus diuersis voci=
bus constitutus. Dicitur enim discantus, quasi diuersus can=
tus. Quo nomie oẽz mensuralẽ cantilẽniam veteres nomina=
bant. Nos autẽ quoniã discantus pars est cantilene ab alijs
discreta:ita describem9. Discantus est cuiuslibet cantilene ps
suprema. Uel est harmonia puellari voce modulanda.

Jo̅.
Tin̅
ctor.

L iij

De Tenore.

¶ Tenor est cuiuslibet cantilene vox media. Uel vt Gaffoxus lib .3. ca. 5. scribit · Est cuiuslibet cantilene relationis fundamentum. dictus a tenendo, eo φ omnium in se partium consonantiam respectiue teneat.

De Baritono.

¶ Bassus seu potius Basis, est cuiusuis cãtilene pars infima. Uel est harmonia grauiori voce concinenda. qui z Baritonus dicitur a Uari quod est graue, u in b mutata, eo φ grauiorem cantilene partem possideat.

De Tenore acuto.

¶ Tenor acutus est cantilene pars antesuprema'. Ut est baritonantis decus. plerumφ em bassum decorat, duplam cum eo cõsonantiam faciens · Reliquas partes studiosus quisφ se magistro describet.

De clausulis formalibus.

¶ Quõ omnis cantilena formalibus quibusdam clausulis veniat exornãda: Quid clausula sit dicemus · Est igitur clausula (vt Tinctor scribit) Cãtilene particula, i cuius fine vl'quies vel perfectio reperitur · Uel est vocum diuersimode gradiencium in consonantijs perfectis coniunctio.

Tinctor.

De clausulis regule.

¶ Prima, Ømnis clausula tribus constat notis, vltima, penultima, et antepenultima. ¶ Secunda, Clausula discantus tribus notis conflata, vltimam semper habebit sursum.
¶ Tertia, Clausula tenoris tribus etiam constat notis vltima semper descendente. ¶ Quarta, Baritonantis clausula, vltimam, modo supra, modo infra tenorem requirit. Communiter tamen in octauam infra detrudit. Interdum etiam in quintam supra extollit.
¶ Quinta, Tenoris acuti clausula, vltimam modo eleuat, modo deprimit, modo cum alijs in vnisono disponit: qui cum varijs procedat notibus:eius constitutio carminum conditoribus est arbitraria.

100

¶ Serta, Clanſula diſcantus penultimam ſupra tenorem in ſexta requi
rit: Uel in quinta, ſi baſſus infra ſertam occuparit.

¶ Septima, penultima tenoris ſupra baſſum i quinta rite locatur: Jn ſex
ta quoqᷓ:ſi baſſus tenoris: et ipſe diſcantus clauſulam aſſumpſerit.

¶ Øctaua, Si clauſula tenoris in mi, deſierit, vt i Deutero fit: vel alias:
penultima baſſus, non in quinta, ſed tertia infra tenorem locata, in quin
tam finaliter cadat, abſᷓ diſcantus diſcrimine, vt ſubſcripto concentu de
claratur ⸫

TENØR   **BARITØNANS**

¶ Nona, Si clauſula tenoris terminata fuerit, in re,
vt communiter in protho: baſſus eleganter de quin
ta in tertiam ſupra clauſulabit: diſcantu non variato.
licet et in octauam cadere poſſit.

TENØR   **BASIS**

¶ Decima, omnis cantilena eo eſt ſuauior,
quo clauſulis formalibus abundantior. Tã
ta eñ clauſulis ineſt vis, vt etiam diſſonan
tias faciat conſonas perfectionis gratia. Ui
gilent igitur ſtudioſi, vt in cantilenis ſuis
formales clauſulas q̃ ſepiſſime ponãt. Quo
autem id facilius fiat:clauſularum exerciti
um ſeu promptuarium hic duxim⁹ apponẽ
dum: vt quas ſtudioſi hic decantant: eas
ita i ſuis cantilenis formandas eẽ credant.

Exercitium clauſula-
rum formalium
ſequitur.

DISCANTVS

TENOR

BASSVS

[206

De specialibus contrapũcti. pꝛeceptis. Caput sextum.

¶ Expeditis singulis, que ad cõponendi disciplinã, in generali necessaria visa sut, Nũc essentialit regulisbꝛeuissimis rẽ ipsaꝛ:vt est:apiemus. ¶ Pꝛima, Disposito cantu cũ tenoꝛe in vnisono:bassus tertiã isra, et altus eãdeꝛ supꝛa requirit. Uel bassus quitã infra, et altus quartã supꝛa. ꝗ si bassus ʼoctauã infra occuparit:Altus in tertia supꝛa vel quarta infra concoꝛdabit ꝗ aptissime. Sin autem bassus decimã infra tenuerit, Altus tertiam supꝛa, aut eãdem vel sextam infra requirit. vt in subscripta figura conspicitur.

Exẽ prim̃	Secundi	Tertij	4.ti membri
	Altus ◊		
Altus ◊		Altus ◊	Altus ◊
Discã:Tenor ◊	Discã: Tenor ◊	Cantus Tẽoꝛ ◊	Dis: Tenor ◊
Bassus ◊			Altus ◊
	Bassus ◊	Altus ◊	
			Altus ◊
		Basis ◊	
			Bassus ◊

¶ Secũda, quotiẽs discant⁹ supꝛa tenoꝛe in tertia situaf:Bassus in tertia infra : et altus in sexta supꝛa, vel vnisono locef. Sed si bassus infra octauã habuerit:quitã em̃ habere non põt:Altus quartã infra, tenebit:Basso aũt decimã infra occupante:alt⁹ tertiã vl̕sextã infra requirit.Quod simili vt sup pictasmate studios⁹ quisꝗ pcũctari poterit. ¶ Tertia, Si discãt⁹ quitã supꝛa tenoꝛe:quod raro cõtingit: soꝛtitus fuerit : Bassus occupabit infra sextã,et altus supꝛa tertiã vel infra quartã Qⁱ si bassus octauã infra sonuerit:Alt⁹ tertiã supꝛa, vl̕quartã aut sextã infra postulabit. ¶ Quartã

ꝳ

Diſcantu ſertam ſupꝛa tenoꝛem occupante:Baſſus quintã infra, et altus
tertiam infra, vel quartã ſupꝛa teneat. Uꝶ ſi baſſus octauã infra tenuerit:
Altus in ſola tertia ſupꝛa concoꝛdabit, Baſſo aũt decimã infra occupãte,
Altus tertiam ſupꝛa, vel eandem infra ſonabit. Poſſet et octauam infra
poſſidere, et cũ diſcantu tredecimam ſonare.

⁋ Quinta, Si diſcantus in octaua ſupꝛa tenoꝛem locatur: Baſſus in ter=
tia infra. et altus in tertia, vel ſerta ſupꝛa, aut in quinta infra rite concoꝛ=
dat. Cũ aũt baſſus eandẽ infra tetigerit, altus quartã vel ſertã ſupꝛa, aut
tertiam infra ſonabit. Si vero baſſus octauam infra ſonuerit: Altus ter=
tiam vel quintam ſupꝛa concoꝛditer iubilabit. Baſſo aũt ad decimam in=
fra cadente, Altus tertiam vꝶ ſertã ſupꝛa, et eaſdem infra iure poſſidębit.

⁋ Serta, Quoties diſcantus in decima ſupꝛa tenoꝛem quieuerit: Baſſ⁹
in tertia infra, Et altus in tertia, ſerta vel octaua ſupꝛa locũ ſibi vendica=
bit. Dꝛ ſi baſſus in tertia ſupꝛa reperitur, Altus in tertia infra. aut quinta
vel octaua ſurſum illi conſonabit. Si autem baſſus ſupꝛa tenoꝛem quintã
babuerit: infra enim babere non poteſt: Altus tertiã ſupꝛa, octauã infra,
concoꝛdem ſeruabit. Baſſo vero ad octauã infra cadente. Altus quartã
infra, vel tertiam aut quintã ſupꝛa contingere poteſt.

⁋ Septima, diſcantu ſupꝛa tenoꝛẽ duodecimã occupante: baſſus in octa=
ua infra locetur, Et altus in tertia quinta vel octaua ſupꝛa. Cũ autẽ baſſ⁹
tertiã ſupꝛa ſonuerit: Altus quitã, ꝏctauã, aut decimã, cõcoꝛdif iubilabit.

⁋ Octaua, ſi diſcantus ſupꝛa tenoꝛe in quarta locatus fuerit, baſſus quin
tam infra: et altus tertiã infra, vel ſertam ſupꝛa pꝛo ſua cõcoꝛdia requirit.
Conuerſo modo (ſi baſſum pꝛimo foꝛmare tentaueris) cũ diſcantu face=
re curabis. Si aũt quis plures, ꝙ quattuoꝛ partes conficere voluerit: ſu=
mat concoꝛdantias infra vel ſupꝛa, iuxta aliarum partium exigentiam, ſer
uatis ſeruandis. quod arbitrio committimus conditoꝛis.

Quibus de cauſis pauſe in cõtrapũ=
cto ponantur. Caput ſeptimũ.

**quid
ſit fu=
ga.**

Pauſarũ in contrapuncto, pluribus de cauſis: tolleraf conſtitutio.
Pꝛimo, remouende difficultatis gratia: dum enim due vꝶ plures
cantilene partes ita coaptãtur: vt alias coaptare difficile ſit, pau=
ſas ponimus quoad difficultas illa ceſſauerit. ⁋ Secundo, pꝛop=
ter vitate voces fictas, atꝗ pbibita muſice interualla. ⁋ Tertio,
propter duas concoꝛdãtias perfectas diſtinguere, que ſe mutuo ſequi nõ
poſſunt: niſi vel nota vel pauſa interueniat. ⁋ Quarto, foꝛmandarum fu
garũ gratia. Eſt aũt fuga vnius ꜩ eiuſdem clauſule in exoꝛdio vꝶ quouis
alio loco: per diuerſas cantilene partes ſucceſſiua diſtributio. Uel eſt eiuſ=
dem clauſule in diuerſis cantilene partibus repetitio, boc modo.

DISCANTUS   TENOR   BASSUS

¶ Quinto, pause in cōtrapūcto respiratiōis grā admittunt, Ne ob cantilene celeritatē, vl' spūs cātātis deficiat. Uel ex inordinata respiratiōe cōfusio accidat. ¶ Sexto, vt graduū musicaliū, in sua pfectiōe psiltētū. intriseca signa atꝗ inditia existāt. Modus eīm pfectus trīu temporū pausa, in trisecus designat. Tēpus pfectū, per duas pausas semibreues, cū nota semibreui collocatas. vt supra li. z. ca. ſ. ꝺictū est. ¶ Septimo ob plurali tatē partiū cantilene tollerant pause : Cantilena eīm plurib⁹ ꝗ quattuor partib⁹ incedente : cantantib⁹ quibusdam : ꝗsdā pausare necessum est, Ne vel ex vocū nimia elongatione, vl' consonantiarū inconcinna permixtio ne, suauitas obtundaf : et concentus strepere magis ꝗ cōsonare videat.

De vario canentium ritu ac decē ca= nendi mandatis. Caput. octauū.

Um quisꝗ suo viuat genio: nec eisdem oīes pareant legibus
nationūꝗ diuersitas, diuersos mores habeat atꝗ rit⁹, habitu,
victu, studio, sīmōe, cantu. hic Angli iubilāt, galli cātāt: Inꝗt
Frāchin⁹: hispani plorat⁹ promūt: Italorū ps, qui Januensiū
littora inhabitant Caprisare dicunt, ceteri latrant: Germani
vero: quod pudet dicere: vt lupi vllulant. Et cū sit melius familiaritatē
destruere. ꝗ contra veritatē aliquid temere diffinire: Ueritas dicere co
git: quod amor patrie propalare reprehendit. Germania cātores plures :
musicos paucos nutrit. Nā preter eos: qui in sacellis principū aut sūt, aut
fuerūt: Paucissimi canendi disciplinam: Cleri gloriam: vere cognoscunt.
Magistratus eīm: quib⁹ hec res cōmissa est: Cantores secūdū vocis aspe=
ritate, non artis peritiā, ceremonȳs ac inuētuti preficiūt, deū boatib⁹ mu=
gitibusꝗ placari arbitrātes: qui suauitate magꜩ ꝗ stridore: plus affectu ꝗ
voce in scripturis legit gaudere. Nā vbi in canticis Solomon, vocem ec
clesie in aurib⁹ Christi sonare scribit: mor causam: vt quia dulcis sit: subiū
git. Recte igit Baptista Mantuan⁹ Neotericus ille Uirgilius in oēm tur
gidū insciū, atꝗ boante cantorē inuehif dicens. Cur tantis delubra boū
mugitib⁹ imples. Tu ne deū tali credis placare tumultu ? Quē in cymba=
lis non simpliciter: sed bene sonantibus laudandum propheta precepit.

**An=
gli.
Gal=
li.
his=
pani
Itali
Ger=
mani**

**Bap
tista.
Mā
tua=
nus.
Pro=
phe=
ta.**

De decē mādatis oī canenti necessarȳs.

M ij

¶ Quũ varŷ varŷs in diuina laude abusionibus agitent:mõ indecenter corpus mouendo, mõ indecoros oris hiatus faciendo, mõ vocales mutando, Statui preceptis ꝗ breuissimis,cantores quosꝗ:quo min⁹errẽt:in stituere. ¶ Primũ, Cupiẽs quicpiã decantare, pre omnib⁹tonũ ac repercussionẽ ei⁹ diligenter animaduertat.Nam qui cantũ citra toni cognitionem canit,idem facit quod is:qui syllogismũ extra modũ ac figuram componit. ¶ Secundũ, scalã sub qua cantus decurrit vigilanter attendat:ne

Saxones clari germanie.

ex molli durũ,aut ex duro mollem faciat. ¶ Tertiũ, Uocẽ quisꝗ canẽtũ verbis cõformare studeat:Ita vt in re lamentabili tristẽ, hylari ꝶo ꝗtũ potest iucũdũ cõcentũ promat. Qua in re nõ possum nõ mirari Saxones, preclarissimos germanie populos (quorũ presidio educatus et ipse sum,ꝛ ad scribendã musicã instigatus) ꝗ in mortuorũ exequŷs preacuto, hylari atꝗ iucundo concentu vtant.Non alia vt reor causa ꝗ ꝗ, vel mortẽ (vt

ppli Uale rius.

Macro.

Ualerius de Cleobi ꛉ Bitone fratribus lib.ſ.ſcribit) summũ homini bonũ esse, vľpost corpus animas (vt apud Macrobiũ lib.ꝛ.de Somnio Scipionis est) ad originem dulcedinis musice, id est celũ recidere credant. Quod si ita esset:Ipsos mortis huius terrene strennuos cõtẽptores,ac future glorie zelatores esse iudicaremus.¶ Quartũ, Mensure pre omnib⁹ teneatur equalitas.Nam sine lege ac mensura canere: est deum ipsum offendere, qui omnia numero pondere et mensura bene fecit.Quare resipiscant orientales Franci,gentiles mei,Necꝗt antea in chorali cantu, notu

Orientales fráci. Herbipol Praga.

las iã producãt iã corripiãt,sed ab herbipolensi nobili ecclã:capite suo:in ꝗ optie canit:canẽdi exẽplũ sumãt.Quod et Pragensi ecclẽ nõ min⁹foret vtile ꝗ decorum, qm et ipsa notas iam producit, iam plus equo absumit. Nec hoc inter pretereunda ponam⁹,qd pietas:quã vita funct⁹ debemus: exposcit.Quorũ vigilie:ita ẽ vulgo dicuntur,tanta cõfusione , tanta festinantia,tanta illusione (Nescio quis mentes eorum:quibus hec res cõmissa est:Alasto exagitet) psoluũt, vt nec a voce vox,nec syllaba a sylla ba,nec iterdũ ꝑ itegrũ psalmũ a ꝶsu vers⁹discerni queat. O impietas dirã plectẽda supliciŷs,Talẽ o pastores ŷs:ꝗrũ bñficio et viuitis et hoc habet⁹ qd estis:ꝑ merit⁹ mercedẽ redditis ? Talẽ ꝑ ŷs:quorũ largitõis opẽ indi es postulat⁹,rogitat⁹,extorꝗt⁹:pces fũditis? Tali vlulatu,tali strepitu,ta li murmure:cui nulla deuotio nulla ꝶborũ expressio , nulla syllabarũ articulatio subest,deũ placari creditis? Rixantes canes audiret satius sumus omniũ parens, ꝗ hec vã murmura,nec lege nec modo prolata .Quid de priuatis (bonorũ pace dictũ sit) orationibus dicã:cum publice:quas pro mortuis funditis:tales sint, vt hominibus displiceant,deũ: qui imperfecta dona odit:offendant,quã vereor, illas, ŷs fore peiores.An non credi tis, vos olim de villicatione vestra reddituros rationem? An non illud Ezechielis.33.de manu vestra sanguinẽ eorũ requirã : attenditis? hoc ẽ verbũ cunctis:quibus aliorũ cura cõmissa est:iugiter ruminandũ, hoc est Platonis ipsius speculum, in quo faciẽ suã sepius contẽplari debent pasto

res, vt vita, subditis, sanctitatis prebeāt exemplū, et fidelibus defunctis
oratiōe:prece, cantu pietatis prestent suffragiū Justū cm est, piū est, sanctū
est pro defūctis orare vt a pctis soluant. ¶ Quitū, autentorū tonorū cantica, profunde subiugaliū acute, neutralia vero mediocriter intonēt. hec
enim in pfundū. illa i acutū, verum ista in vtrunq; tendunt. ¶ Sextum,
mutatio vocalium parum docti cantoris est indiciū. At licet varij i hoc
populi varie peccent: multitudo tamen peccatiū non tollit peccatū. Qua
in re attendant. imprimis franci ne u pro o: vt solent:pronuncient, nuster
pro noster dicendo. Religiosi quoq; campestres censuram non euadunt,
dū Aremus pro oremus legunt. Simili abusione Renenses omes a Spy-
ra vsq; Confluentiā vrbem, i vocalem in ei dypthongū vertunt, Marcia
pro Maria dicentes. Uestphali, pro a vocali, a et e coniunctim promunt,
videlicet Aebs te, pro abste. Saxones interiores, ac tota natio Sueuorū
e Uocalem per e et i legunt: deius pro deus dicentes. Germanie quoq;
inferioris incole, omnes coniunctim u et e, pro u vocali exprimunt. Quos
errores licet Germanie lingua persepe requirat: Latina tamen que nihil
commertij cum nostro vulgari habet maximopere abborret. ¶ Septi-
mum, caueat cantor ne asinino clamore cantum plus equo vel incipiat, vł
inceptum vocis instabilitate sursum trahat. Non enim clamor, sed amor
aures demulcet omnipotentis, non strepitus ille labiorum : inquit Erasmus noster:sed ardens animi votum:Uelut vox intēsissima diuinas ferit
aures.Moses nullam edebat vocem et tamen audiuit, quid clamas ad
me. Sed cur Saxones et qui baltica littora accolunt ijs gaudeant clamo-
ribus , causa nulla subest , Nisiq; vel surdum deum habeant.Uel (quia in
austro celos conscendit) ipsum et boreales et australes ob distantiā equa-
liter audire non posse autumant.

¶ Octauū, differentiam festi a festo , quisq; canentium:discernat, Ne sim-
plici feria, velut summa, vel solenniset, vel torpeat omnino.

¶ Nonum, indecens oris hyatus, atq; indecorus corporis motus, canto-
rem declarat insanum.

¶ Decimum, super omnia deo studeat placere cātor, non hominibus. Inter omnes etenim homines:Inquit Guido : fatui sunt cantores : quibus
queren da deuotio contemnitur, vitāda lasciuia queritur,quoniā id quod
canunt:ad homines:non ad deum ordinant, humanam illam glorie lam
querunt, vt eternam amittant,hominibus placere conantur , vt deo dis-
pliceant:Alijs deuotionem:qua ipsi carent,ingerunt . Creature fauorem
laudemq; et venantur et ambiunt:Creatoris autem contemnūt.Cui debet honor Cui reuerentia:cui famłat?.Cui me,meaq; omnia deuoueo, cui
psallam q̃ diu fuero.Jpse enim a terra suscitauit inopē et de stercore erex-
it pauperem.Benedictum igitur sit nomen eius gloriosissimum in secula
seculorum. AMEN.

¶ Finis buius operis.

M ij

Renē
ses.
Spy-
ra.
Con
fluen
tia.
Uest
pha.
Sax-
ones
Sue-
ui.
Infe-
rio.
Ger
mani
Sax-
ones
Bal-
thici.
Colo
ni.
Gui.

Peroratio ac libri Conclusio.

HAs nostra musicaliū Theorematū elucubrationes, aliquot iã
annis:non arrogantie causa, vt quidam Zoili ganniunt, sed
vt dormitantibus alijs, ipse iuuentuti germanice prodessem:
exquisitas, et iam tandem in formam libri redactas, Typogra
phiecʒ oblatas, Studiosi lectores amicis oculis inspicere dig
nentur. Uerū si styli humilitas, et verborū simplicitas quem offenderint.
Ueli materie in qua versamur, et pueris, quibus scribimus, id attribuat.
Non deerunt scio qui laborem hunc nostrum, canino dente lacerabunt, a
tergo ferient, priuscʒ legant despicientes: et antecʒ intelligant annihilan
tes. Qui et videri ǧ esse musici malunt, non autoribus, nõ preceptis, non
rationibus, obtēperantes: Sed quicǭd cerebroso ac fantastico ipsorū capi
ti placuerit, id licitū, id artificiale, id musicū affirmāt. Quib⁹ aurē ne detʒ
Anti oro. Malis enim displicere: laus est. Immo: vt antistenis philosophi vtar
stenes sententia: Superioris persone est detractionem pati, inferioris facere. Et
cum potior sit vnius sapientis laus ǧ decem stultorū, non detrahentium
pluralitatem, sed qualitatem considerate, Attendentes ǧ facile sit garru
las istas picas conuincere, et quasi pulices inter vngues cõprimere. Necʒ
ijs quibus ars odio est ausculate, Quia quod ipsi ob ingenij hebetudi
nem (frustra enim asino lyra canitur) assequi non possunt: hoc alijs et
disuadēt et interdicunt. Sed barbatū me, ǭ manū ferule subduximus
Justi credite magistrū dicere, fides enī pstāda est peritis in arte, inǫt maiestas
anus imperialis. Sint itacʒ Candidissimi lectores, ǫs Ornitoparchiana reficit
diligentia: ijs paucis contenti: ǧ primū enī respirauero maiora videbūt.

Tetrastichon authoris ad Librum.

I liber: et summi laudes diffunde tonantis,
  Nec timeas lingue subdola verba male.
I: tua te pietas: cultus non ipse probabit,
  Ergo age non cultu : sed pietate place.

Libellus ad Lectorem.

Sum pietate liber: tenues modo missus in auras
  Defero Arionios: sub breuitate modos
Pieridum cantus: celi quis numina, manes,
  Placari tellus : pontus: et astra queunt.
Pauperibus pregnans ego sum: medicina: saluscʒ
  Diuitibus splendor : pontificiumcʒ decus.
Icta dionaeis consolor pectora flaminis,
  Me sine nil phebus: nilcʒ Minerua potest.

Martia castricolas: tremulo dum tympana bombo
Instrepitant: plausum concito ad arma viros.
Quicp graues gestant: animorum pondera: curas
Ad me confugiant: mite leuamen ero.
Seria magnanimis: solatia presto iocosis,
Integra: nunc fletus ingero: nunc adimo.
Munus et hoc mihi: cuicp suas ancillor ad artes
Me legat hinc vates: nauita: pastor, eques.
Quo me quiscp vocat cursim sequor: ipse parentis
Sic docuit chari: non sine laude labos.

Henrici Cotberi Brunopolitani Artium magistri, ad Andre
am Ornitoparchum Argutissimum artis modulatorie professorem, Epigramma ·:·

Dij tibi nestorcos vitam dent ducere in annos
Grata iuuentuti, qui modo dona dabas.
Musica enim ingenio nunc diuulgatur in omnes
(Laus superis) homines: Ornitoparche tuo.

Tetrastichon Auctoris in inuidum.

I patriam petito: superum tibi vita negatur.
Inuide tartareis: bestia nata locis.
Tu licet inuideas: mens malesana repugnet,
Phama manet doctos, nil speciosa minus.

¶ Excussum est hoc opus, ab ipso authore denuo castigatum,
recognitumcp: Lipsie in edibus Ualentini Schumanni, calco-
graphi solertissim: Mense Nouebri: Anni virginei partus de-
cimi septimi supra sesquimillesimu. Leone decimo Pont. Max.
ac Maximiliano inuictissimo impatore orbi terrap psidentibus.

Andreas Ornithoparcus
His Micrologus, or Introduction:
Containing the Art
of Singing

BY

JOHN DOWLAND

ANDREAS
ORNITHOPARCVS
HIS *MICROLOGVS,*
OR
INTRODVCTION:
Containing the Art of
Singing.

Digested into Foure Bookes.

NOT ONELY PROFITABLE, BVT
also necessary for all that are studious
of *Musicke.*

ALSO THE DIMENSION AND PER-
fect Vse of the MONOCHORD, *according to*
Guido Aretinus.

BY *IOHN DOVLAND* LVTENIST,
Lute-player, and Bachelor of *Musicke* in both
the Vniuersities.

1609

LONDON:
Printed for *Thomas Adams* , dwelling in *Paules*
Church-yard, at the Signe of the
white Lion.

TO THE RIGHT HONO-
RABLE *ROBERT* EARLE OF
Salisbury, Vifcount *Cranborne*, Baron of *Eßingdon*,
Lord High *Treafurer* of *England*, Principall *Secretarie* to the Kings moft
excellent Maieftie, Maifter of the Courts of Wards and Liueries,
Chancellor of the moft famous Vniuerfitie of Cambridge, *Knight
of the moft Noble Order of the Garter, and one of his* Maiefties
moft honourable Priuie Counfell.

Our high *Place, your princely Honours and Vertues, the hereditary vigilance and wifedome, wherwith* Hercules-*like, you aßift the protection of the
whole State : Though thefe (moft honoured Lord)
are powerfull encitements to draw all forts to the
defire of your moft Noble protection. Yet befides all
thefe (in more particular by your Lordfhips fpeciall Fauors and Gra-
ces) am I emboldened to prefent this Father of Muficke* Ornithoparchus *to your worthyeft Patronage, whofe approoued Workes in my tra-
uailes (for the common good of our Mufitians) I haue reduced into our
Englifh Language. Befeeching your Lordfhip (as a chiefe Author of all
our good) gracioufly to receiue this poore prefentment, whereby your
Lordfhip fhall encourage me to a future tafke, more new in fubiect, and
as memorable in worth. Euery Plant brings forth his like, and of Mufitians,* Muficke *is the fruit. Moreouer fuch is your diuine Difpofition that both you excellently vnderftand, and royally entertaine the
Exercife of Muficke, which mind-tempering Art, the graue* Luther
*was not affraid to place in the next feat to Diuinity. My daily prayers
(which are a poore mans beft wealth) fhall humbly follicite the Author
of all Harmonie for a continuall encreafe of your Honors prefent happi-
neffe with long life, and a fucceßiue bleffing to your generous pofteritie.*

Your Lordfhips humbly deuoted

Iohn Douland.

To the Reader.

 Xcellent men haue at all times in all Arts deliuered to Pofteritie their obferuations, thereby bringing Arts to a certainty and perfection. Among which there is no VVriter
more worthy in the Art of *Muficke*, than this Author *Ornithoparcus*, whofe VVorke, as I haue made it familiar to all
that fpeake our Language, fo I could wifh that the reft in
this kinde were by the like meanes drawne into our knowledge, fince (I am
aflured) that there is nothing can more aduance the apprehenfion of *Muficke*, than the reading of fuch VVriters as haue both skilfully and diligently
fet downe the precepts thereof. My induftry and on-fet herein if you friend-
ly accept (being now returned home to remaine) fhall encourage me fhort-
ly to diuulge a more peculiar worke of mine owne : namely, *My Obferuations and Directions concerning the Art of Lute-playing* : which Inftrument
as of all that are portable, is, and euer hath been moft in requeft, fo is it the
hardeft to mannage with cunning and order, with the true nature of finge-
ring; which skill hath as yet by no VVriter been rightly expreffed : what by
my endeuours may therein be attained, I leaue to your future Iudgement,
when time fhall produce that which is already almoft ready for the Harueft.
Vale, From my houfe in Fetter-lane this tenth of Aprill. 1609.

                        Your Friend,

                        Iohn Douland.

TO THE RIGHT HONO-
RABLE, WORTHY, AND WISE
GOVERNOVRS OF THE STATE OF *LVNENBVRG*,
ANDREAS ORNITHOPARCHVS OF *MEYNING*,
MAISTER OF THE LIBERALL SCIENCES.

E read, that Socrates (*hee that was by* Apollos *Oracle famoused for the wisest man in the world*)*was wont to say, That it had been fit mens hearts, should haue windowes, that so the thoghts might be discerned. This power if we now had, honourable Lords, beleeue it, you should discern my loue towards you and yours. But because speech is the mindes interpretour, and you cannot know men, and their thoughts, but by their words or writing, I am to intreat that you would take in as good part these words, which in my absence I vtter, as if I had in presence deliuered them.*

It is not out of any humor of arrogancy or vain ostentation that I do this: but that vpright, gentle, and religious fashion of yours, wherin you excell more than any Easterlings that border these Baltick coasts, these make me assay the art of Harmony, which the Grecians call Musicke; Musicke the nurse of Christian Religion, and mother of good fashions, of honesty, of Common-wealths, if in any thing we may giue credite to the ancients.

These made me commit my sayles to the furious windes; these made me giue Zoiles *and* Thersites *power to rage ouer me; these made me trauell many Countreys not without endamaging my estate, to search out the Art; these made me many a time to sustaine wearinesse, when I might haue been at rest; greefe, when I might haue solaced my selfe; disgrace, when I might haue liued in good reputation; pouertie, when I might haue liued in plenty. But also these things (right Worthies) seemed to me not worthy the regarding, when I sought how I might whilest others slept, whom your state doth nourish (before all others) profite your youth, and so consequently the youth of all* Germany, *drawing them to good fashions, recalling them by the honest delights of Musicke from vnlawfull attempts, and so by little and little stirre them vp to vertuous actions. For* Socrates, *and* Plato, *and all the* Pythagoreans *did generally enact, that young men and maides should be trayned vp in Musicke, not to the end their mindes might be incited to wantonnesse by those bawbles, which make Art to be so vilely*

B *reputed*

reputed of: but that the *motions of the minde* might be ruled and governed by law and reason. For seeing the nature of young men is vnquiet, and in all things desiring delights, & therfore refuseth seuerer arts, it is by the honest delights of Musick brought to those recreations, which may also solace honest old age.

Among those things wherwith the mind of man is wont to be delighted, I can finde nothing that is more great, more healthfull, more honest, than Musicke: The power whereof is so great, that it refuseth neither any sexe, nor any age, and (as Macrobius *a man of most hidden & profound learning* saith) there is no brest so sauage and cruell, which is not moued with the touch of this delight. For it doth driue away cares, perswade men to gentlenesse, represseth and stirreth anger, nourisheth arts, encreaseth concord, inflameth heroicall minds to gallant attempts, curbeth vice, breedeth vertues, and nurseth them when they are borne, composeth men to good fashion. For among all those things which doe admit sence, that onely worketh vpon the manners of men, which toucheth his eares, as Aristotle in his musicall problemes doth more at large discourse. Hence was it that Agamemnon being to goe Generall for the Troian warres, as Philelphus *reports,* [6] left a Musitian at his house, who by singing the prayses of womens vertues might incite Clytemnestra to a chaste and honest life, wherein he did so farre preuaile, that they say she could not be ouercome by Egistus his vnchaste attempts, till the vngodly wretch had made away the Musitian, who onely hindred him from his wicked purpose. Besides Lycurgus, though otherwise he enacted most seuere lawes for the Lacedæmonians his countrey-men; yet did he very much embrace Musicke, as Quintilian writes. I omit those ancient Philosophers, (for so they rather chose to be called, than to be named wise men) who did repose the summe of their studies in this art as in a certaine Treasure-house. I omit those princes who for the admirable sweetnesse of this art spend many talents. Lastly, I omit the most religious of al men, who though they estrange then selues from al worldly pleasure, yet dwell vpon this delight, as if it were the onely heauenly one. Since therfore this Art is both holy, and sweet, and heauenly, participating of a diuine, faire, and blessed nature, I thought good to dedicate this booke, wherein all the knots of practicke Musicke are vntied, to the gentle youth of your Citie, after it had been first brought forth at Rostoch, that famous Vniuersity of the Baltick coast, and since amended by the censure of the Elders, and publikely read in three famous Vniuersities of Germanie, the Vniuersitie of Tubyng, Heydelberg, and Maguntium. That by their deserts the after ages being helped, might pay the tribute of thanks not to me, but to them, as to the first mouing causes.

Wherefore wise Fathers, I beseech your wisedomes to deigne this booke your gentle fauour and acceptance, not contemning the base stile or little volume of that, which is rather holy than pleasant, and set out not vpon any rash humour, but vpon a true deuotion. For it is written for them that fast, not for them that are filled with delicacies, though euen they may find here that which will fit their stomackes. And since great things fit great men, small things small men, I acknowledge my selfe small; and therefore giue small gifts, yet promise greater whensoeuer I shall grow greater. Farewell most happy, most worthy, most wise.

The

 Eeing it is fitter, as an Emperour faid, to caft out a few fit things, then to be burdened with many vnneceffary fuperfluities, which precept *Horace* put him in minde of, faying :

> *Quicquid precipies efto breuis, vt citò diƈta,*
> *Percipiant animi dolices, teneantą, fideles.*

What ere thou teach, be fhort : the learners braine
Breefe fawes will quicker take, and beft retaine.

Hence it is, that we haue refolued to colleƈt into certaine moft fhort rules, the precepts of Aƈtiue Muficke, if not all, yet the efpeciall, out of diuers Authours. For to know all things and faile in nothing, is a mark rather of diuine then of humane nature. Now thofe, whom I herein followed as my leaders, and acknowledge as my fpeciall Patrons, are thefe :

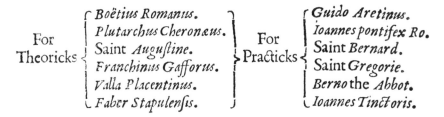

For Theoricks	For Practicks
Boëtius Romanus.	*Guido Aretinus.*
Plutarchus Cheronæus.	*Ioannes pontifex Ro.*
Saint *Auguftine.*	Saint *Bernard.*
Franchinus Gafforus.	Saint *Gregorie.*
Valla Placentinus.	*Berno* the *Abbot.*
Faber Stapulenfis.	*Ioannes Tinƈtoris.*

[7]   Wherefore omitting all needleffe circumlocutions, and affeƈting fhortneffe, the mother of truth, wee purpofe to open all Praƈtick *Muſick* in foure Bookes, for of fo many parts it doth confift. The firft whereof, fhall fhew the principles of plaine Song: The next Meafurall Song: The third the Accent: The fourth and laft the Counterpoint, as it were the gouernour and mother of the reft. The head of each Booke, fhall in their places be mentioned, as occafion fhall ferue.

B 2   **THE**

THE FIRST BOOKE OF
ORNITHOPARCHVS HIS
Muſicke, declaring the Principals of
plaine Song.

Eing to deliuer the Art of ſinging, than which in the world there is nothing ſweeter, leſt out of a ſmall errour a great may ariſe, let vs begin with the definition, by which the nature of all things is knowne: that is with the eaſieſt things firſt, that ſo the Art may be more fitly deliuered. And then, hauing vnfolded the nature thereof in generall, wee will proceede to the perticulars, firſt making the generall diuiſion, and afterward handling each part ſeuerally.

The generall Deſcription of Muſicke.

Mᵛſicke (as *Franchinus Gafforus* in the third Chapter of the firſt booke of *Theorie* writeth) is a knowledge of *Tuning*, which conſiſts in *ſound* and *Song*. In *ſound* (I ſay) becauſe of the muſicke which the motion of the cœleſtiall Orbes doth make. In *Song*, leaſt that melody which our ſelues practiſe, ſhould be ſecluded out of our definition.

The Diuiſion of Muſicke.

Bᵒ*ētius* (to whom among the Latine writers of Muſicke, the praiſe is to be giuen) doth ſhew in the ſecond Chapter of his firſt booke of Muſicke, that Muſicke is three-fold. The *Worlds Muſicke: Humane Muſicke:* and *Inſtrumentall Muſicke.*

Of the Muſicke of the World.

[8]

VVHen God (whom *Plutarch* prooues to haue made all things to a certaine harmonie) had deuiſed to make this world moueable, it
was

was neeeſſary, that he ſhould gouerne it by ſome actiue and moouing power; for no bodies but thoſe which haue a ſoule, can moue themſelues, as *Franchinus* in the firſt Chapter of his firſt booke of *Theoric* ſaith. Now that motion (becauſe it is the ſwifteſt of all other, and moſt regular) is not without ſound: for it muſt needs be that a ſound be made of the very wheeling of the Orbes, as *Macrobius in Somnium Scip. lib.2.* writeth. The like ſayd *Boêtius,* how can this quick-mouing frame of the world whirle about with a dumb and ſilent motion? From this turning of the heauen, there cannot be remoued a certaine order of Harmonie. And nature will (ſaith that prince of Romane eloquence *Cicero,* in his ſixt booke *de Re pub.*) that extremities muſt needs ſound deepe on the one ſide, & ſharp on the other. So then, the worlds Muſicke is an Harmonie, cauſed by the motion of the ſtarres, and violence of the Spheares. *Lodouicus Cælius Rodiginus, lectionum antiquarum lib.5. cap.25.* writeth, That this Harmony hath been obſerued out of the conſent of the heauens, the knitting together of the elements, and the varietie of times. Wherefore well ſayd *Dorilaus* the Philoſopher, That the World is Gods Organe. Now the cauſe wee cannot heare this ſound according to *Pliny* is, becauſe the greatneſſe of the ſound doth exceede the ſence of our eares. But whether wee admit this Harmonicall ſound of the Heauens, or no, it skils not much; ſith certaine it is, that the grand Work-maiſter of this *Mundane Fabricke,* made all things in number, weight, and meaſure, wherein principally, *Mundane Muſicke* doth conſiſt.

Of Humane Muſicke.

HVmane Muſick, is the Concordance of diuers elements in one compound, by which the ſpirituall nature is ioyned with the body, and the reaſonable part is coupled in concord with the vnreaſonable, which proceedes from the vniting of the body and the ſoule. For that amitie, by which the body is ioyned vnto the ſoule, is not tyed with bodily bands, but vertuall, cauſed by the proportion of humors. For what (ſaith *Cælius*) makes the powers of the ſoule ſo ſundry and diſagreeing to conſpire oftentimes each with other? who reconciles the Elements of the body? what other power doth ſoder and glue that ſpirituall ſtrength, which is indued with an intellect to a mortall and earthly frame, than that Muſicke which euery man that deſcends into himſelfe finds in himſelfe? For euery like is preſerued by his like, and by his diſlike is diſturbed. Hence is it, that we loath and abhorre diſcords, and are delighted when we heare harmonicall concords, becauſe we know there is in our ſelues the like concord.

Of Inſtrumentall Muſicke.

INſtrumentall Muſicke, is an Harmony which is made by helpe of *Inſtruments.* And becauſe Inſtruments are either artificiall, or naturall, there is one fort of Muficke, which is made with artificiall Inftruments; another, which is made with naturall inftruments. The Philofophers call the one *Harmonicall*; the other *Organicall.*

Of Organicall Muficke.

ORganicall *Muficke* (as *Cælius* writeth) is that which belongeth to artifici- [9] all Inftruments : or it is a fkill of making an *Harmony* with beating, with fingring, with blowing : with beating, as Drums, Tabors, and the like : with blowing, as Organs, Trumpets, Fluits, Cornets : with fingring, as thofe Inftruments which are commanded, either with the touching of the fingers, or articulating of the Keyes. Yet fuch Inftruments as are too voluptuous, are by *Cælius Rodiginus* reiected.

Of Harmonicall Muficke.

HArmonicall *Muficke*, is a faculty weighing the differences of high and low founds by fence and reafon, *Boetius* : Or, it is a cunning, bringing forth the founds with Humane voyce, by the helpe of naturall Inftruments, and iudging all the Sounds which are fo brought forth. This as *Placentinus* writeth in the third Chapter of the fecond booke of his Muficke: is twofold, *Infpectiue* and *Actiue.*

Of Infpectiue Muficke.

INfpectiue *Muficke*, is a knowledge cenfuring and pondering the Sounds formed with naturall inftruments, not by the eares, whofe iudgement is dull, but by wit and reafon.

Of Actiue Muficke.

ACtiue *Muficke*, which alfo they call *Practick*, is (as Saint *Auftine* in the firft booke of his Muficke writeth) the knowledge of finging well : or according to *Guido* in the beginning of his *Doctrinall*, it is a liberall Science, difpenfing the principles of finging truely. *Franchinus* (in the third Chapter of his firft Booke of his *Theorick*) doth fo define it : It is a knowledge of perfect finging, confifting of *founds, words,* and *numbers* ; which is in like fort two-fold, *Menfurall,* and *Plaine.*

Of Menfurall Muficke.

MEnfurall *Muficke*, is the diuers quantitie of Notes, and the inequalitie of figures. Becaufe they are augmented or diminifhed according
as

as the *moode*, *time*, and *prolation* doth require : of this wee will speake at large in the second Booke.

Of Plaine Musicke.

P *Laine Musicke*, (as Saint *Bernard* an excellent searcher into regular and true Concinence) doth write in the beginning of his Musicke, saying : It is a rule determining the nature and forme of regular Songs. Their nature consists in the disposition, their forme in the progression and composition. Or plaine Musicke is a simple and vniforme prolation of Notes,which can neither be augmented nor diminished.

Of the Profitablenesse of this Art.

[10] T He *Profit* of this Art is so great, (as writeth Pope *Iohn* the 22. of that name,in the second Chapter of his Musick) that whosoeuer giues him-selfe to it, shall iudge of the qualitie of any Song, whether it be *triuiall*,or *curious*, or *false* : He knowes both how to correct that which is faulty,and how to compose a new one. It is therefore (saith he) no small praise,no lit-tle profit, no such labour as to be esteemed of slightly, which makes the Artist both a *Iudge* of those *Songs* which be composed, and a *Corrector* of those which be false, and an *Inuentor* of new.

Of the difference betwixt a Musitian,and a Singer.

O F them that professe the Art of *Harmony*,there be three kindes ; (saith *Franchinus* in the first Book the 4.chap.of his *Theoric*) one is that which dealeth with Instruments ; the other maketh Verses ; the third doth iudge the workes both of the instruments, and of the verses. Now the first,which dealeth with Instruments, doth herein spend all his worke ; as *Harpers*, and *Organists*,& all others which approue their skil by Instruments.For they are remoued from the intellectuall part of Musicke, being but as seruants, and vsing no reason : voide of all speculation, and following their sence one-ly. Now though they seeme to doe many things learnedly and skilfully, yet is it plaine that they haue not knowledge, because they comprehend not the thing they professe, in the purenesse of their vnderstanding ; and therefore doe we deny them to haue Musicke, which is the Science of ma-king melodie. For there is knowledge without practise, and most an end greater, than in them that are excellent Practitioners. For we attribute the nimblenesse of fingring not to Science, which is only residing in the soule, but to practise, for if it were otherwise,euery man the more skilfull he were in the Art,the more swift he would be in his fingring. Yet doe we not de-ny the knowledge of Musicke to all that play on Instruments ; for the Or-ganist, and he that sings to the Harpe,may haue the knowledge of Musick, which if it be, we account such the best Artists.

The second kind is of *Poets*, who are led to the making of a verse, rather by a naturall instinct, than by speculation. These *Boêtius* secludes from the speculation of Musicke, but *Austin* doth not.

The third kind of Musitians, be they which doe assume vnto them the cunning to iudge and discerne good *Ayres* from bad : which kind, (sith it is wholy placed in speculation and reason) it doth properly belong to the Art of *Musicke.*

Who is truely to be called a Musitian.

THerefore he is truely to be called a *Musitian*, who hath the faculty of speculation and reason, not he that hath only a practick fashion of singing : for so saith *Boêtius lib.*1.*cap.*35. He is called a Musitian, which taketh vpon him the knowledge of Singing by weighing it with reason, not with the seruile exercise of practise, but the commanding power of speculation, and wanteth neither speculation nor practise. Wherefore that practise is fit for a learned man: *Plutarch* in his Musicke sets downe (being forced vnto it by *Homers* authoritie) and proues it thus : *Speculation breedeth onely knowledge, but practise bringeth the same to worke .*

Who be called Singers.

[11]

THe *Practitioner* of this facultie is called a *Cantor*, who doth pronounce and sing those things, which the Musitian by a rule of reason doth set downe. So that the *Harmony* is nothing worth, if the *Cantor* seeke to vtter it without the Rules of reason, and vnlesse he comprehend that which he pronounceth in the puritie of his vnderstanding. Therefore well saith *Ioan. Papa* 22. *cap.* 2. To whom shall I compare a *Cantor* better than to a *Drunkard*(which indeed goeth home,)but by which path he cannot tell. A *Musitian* to a *Cantor*, is as a *Prætor* to a *Cryer* : which is proued by this sentence of *Guido* :

Musicorum, ac Cantorum, magna est distantia,
Isti sciunt, illi dicunt, quæ componit Musica,
Nam qui facit, quod non sapit, diffinitur bestia
Verum si tonantis vocis laudent acumina,
Superabit Philomela, *vel vocalis Asina.*

Twixt *Musitians*, and *Practitians*, oddes is great :
They doe know, these but show, what Art doth treat.
Who doeth ought, yet knoweth nought, is brute by kind :
If voices shrill, voide of skill, may honour finde?
   Then *Philomel*, must beare the bell,
   And *Balaams* Asse, Musitian was.

Therefore

Therefore a *Speculatiue Mufitian,* excels the *Practick*: for it is much bet-ter to know what a man doth, than to doe that which another man doth. Hence is it, that buildings and triumphs are attributed to them, who had the command and rule; not to them by whofe worke and labour they were performed. Therefore there is great difference in calling one a Mufitian, or a Cantor. For *Quintilian* faith, That Mufitians were fo honoured a-mongft men famous for wifedome, that the fame men were accounted *Mufitians* and *Prophets,* and *wife men.* But *Guido* compareth thofe *Cantors,* (which haue made curtefie a farre off to Muficke) to brute Beafts.

Of the Inuentors of Muficke.

THe beft writers witneffe, That Muficke is moft ancient : For *Orpheus* and *Linus* (both borne of Gods) were famous in it. The inuention of it is attributed to diuers men, both becaufe the great antiquitie of it, makes the Author incertaine; and alfo becaufe the dignitie of the thing is fuch, and maketh fo many great men in loue with it, that euery one (if it were poffible) would be accounted the Authors of it. Wherefore fome thinke *Linus* the Thebane; fome, that *Orpheus* the Thracian; fome, that *Amphion* the Dircean; fome, that *Pythagoras* the Samian found out this Art. *Eufe-bius* attributes it to *Dionyfius, Diodorus,* to *Mercury, Polybius,* to the Elders of *Arcadia,* with whom there was fuch eftimation of Muficke, that it was the greateft difgrace that could be in that place to confeffe the ignorance of Muficke. Neither did they this, faith *Cœlius lib.* 5. *antiquarum lection.* for wantonneffe or delicateneffe, but that they might mollifie and temper their dayly labours, and befides their aufteritie and feuere fafhions, which befell them by a certaine fad temperature of the clyme with this fweetneffe and gentleneffe. Yet if we giue any credit to *Iofephus,* and the holy Writ, *Tubal* the Sonne of *Lamech* was the chiefe and moft ancient Inuentor of it, and left it written in two tables, one of Slate; another of Marble before the flood for the pofteritie. The Marble one (fome fay) is yet in *Syria.* But leaft fome errour arife out of the multitude of thefe Inuentors, it is cleere that *Tubal* before the flood, that *Mofes* among the Hebrewes, that *Orpheus, Amphion,* and fuch like among the Gentiles, that *Pythagoras* among the Græcians, that *Boëtius* among the Latines, was firft famous for Muficke.

---

[12]

THE SECOND CHAPTER.

Of Voyces.

 Oncord, (which rules all the Harmony of Muficke) cannot be without a *Voyce,* nor a *Voyce* without a *Sound,* faith *Boëtius, lib.* 1. *cap.* 3. Wherefore in feeking out the defcription of a *Voyce,* we thought fit to fearch out this point, what *Sounds* are properly called *Voyces.* Note therefore, that the found

D   of

of a fenfible creature is properly called a *Voyce*, for things without fence haue no *Voyce*, as *Cælius* writes, *antiquar. lect. lib.10. cap.53.* When we call pipes *Vocal*, it is a tranflated word, and a *Catachrefis*. Neither haue alfenfible cretures a *Voice*: for thofe which want blood, vtter no *Voice*. Neither do fifhes vtter any *Voyce*, becaufe a *Voyce* is the motion of the ayre, but they receiue no ayre. Wherefore onely a fenfible creature doth vtter a *Voyce*, yet not all fenfible creatures, nor with euery part of their bodies (for the hands being ftroken together make a clapping, not a *Voyce*.) A *Voyce* therefore is a found vttered from the mouth of a perfect creature, either by aduife, or fignification. By aduife, (I fay) becaufe of the coffe, which is no *Voyce* : By fignification, becaufe of the grinding of the teeth. But becaufe this defcription of a *Voyce*, doth agree onely to a liuely *Voyce*, and not to a deafe muficall *Voyce*, which efpecially, being a fole fyllable is deafe, vnleffe it be actually expreffed, we muft find out another defcription more agreeable to it. Therefore a muficall *Voyce*, is a certaine fyllable expreffing a tenor of the Notes. Now Notes is that by which the highnes, or lownes of a Song is expreffed.

Who firft found out the Muficall Voyces.

BEing that al Harmony is perfected by *Voyces*, and *Voyces* cannot be written, but remembred: (as *Gafforus lib.5. Theor. cap.6.* and 1. *Pract. cap.*?. faith; that they might therefore be kept the better in memory, *Guido Aretinus* a Monke, led by a diuine infpiration, deuoutly examining the Hymne of Saint *Iohn Baptift*, marked, that the fixe capitall fyllables of the Verfes, *viz, Vt, Re, Mi, Fa, Sol, La,* did agree with muficall Concords. Wherefore he applyed them in the chords of his introductory : which deuife *Ioannes* the 22. Bifhop of Rome allowed.

Of the Diuifion of Voyces.

IN the Fourth part of this Worke, I will handle that Diuifion, by which *Voyces* are diuided into *Vnifones, æquifones, Confones, Eumeles, &c.* Here I will only touch that which will ferue our turne ; Therefore of *Voyces*,

Some are called
$$\begin{cases} \text{b } Mols \\ Naturals \\ ♮ \ Sharps \end{cases} Viz. \begin{cases} Vt \ Fa \\ Re \ Sol \\ Mi \ La \end{cases} \text{becaufe they make a} \begin{cases} Flat \\ Meane \\ Sharpe \end{cases} \text{found.}$$

Befides of *Voyces* fome be Superiours : *viz. Fa, Sol, La.* Others be Inferiours : as *Vt, Re, Mi.*

Rules for the Voyces.

[13]

FIrft, *Vt,* (in *Harmonicall Songs*) is the head and beginning of the other Voyces.

The

The second, The Superiour Voyces are fitly pronounced in *Defcending*, and the Inferiour in *Afcending*. Yet to this Rule there be Foure places contrary.

The firft is this. In *F faut* you neuer fing *vt*, vnleffe you muft fing *fa*, in *b fa ♮ mi*.

The fecond, In *b fa ♮ mi*, you muft always fing that Voice which the Scale requires.

The third, The fame Voyce may not be repeated in *feconds*, though in *fourths*, *fifths*, and *eights* it may very fitly.

The fourth, Neither muft the fuperiour Notes be fung in the *defcending*, nor the inferiour Notes in the *afcending*, becaufe they make a needleffe change.

A Progreffion of the Six Muficall Voyces, according to the Rule *of* **Arfim** *and* **Thefim.**

THE THIRD CHAPTER.

Of the Keyes.

THe Wifedome of the Latine Mufitians, imitating the diligence of the Græcians (whereas before the Singers did mark their Chords with moft hard fignes) did firft note a muficall Introduction with Letters. To this *Guido Aretinus* ioyned thofe Voices he found out, and did firft order the Muficall *Keyes* by lines and fpaces, as appeareth in his Introductory. Therefore a *Key* is a thing compacted of a Letter and a Voyce. For the beginning of euery *Key* is a Letter, and the end a Syllable: Of a Voice (I fay) not of Voyces, both becaufe all the Keyes haue not many Voyces, and alfo becaufe the names of *Generalities*, of *Specialties*, and of *Differences*, of which a definition doth confift, cannot be expreffed in the plurall number. For *Animal* is the *genus*, not *Animalia*; a *Man* is the *fpecies*, not men: *rationale* is the *difference*, not *rationabilia*: Or more formally, A *Key* is the opening of a Song, becaufe like as a *Key* opens a dore, fo doth it the Song.

Of the Number and Difference of Keyes.

KEyes, (as *Franchinus lib.1. pract. cap.* 1. doth write) are 22. in number. Though Pope *Iohn*, and *Guido* (whom hee in his Fift Chapter faith to haue been the moft excellent Mufitians after *Boëtius*) only make 20. Thefe

D 2   Two

Two and Twentie *Keyes* are comprehended in a three-fold order. The firſt [14] is of Capitall Letters; the Second of ſmall; the Third of double Letters. And all theſe *Keyes* differ one from the other in *ſight*, *writing*, and *naming* : becauſe one is otherwiſe placed, written, or named than the other. Of the Capitall there be eight, *viz.* г. A. B. C. D. E. F. G. Of the ſmall alſo Eight, *a. b. c. d. e. f. g.* for *b fa* ♮ *mi*. is not one *Key* onely, but two : which is prooued by *mutations*, *voyces*, and *inſtruments*. The ſame you muſt account of the vpper *bb fa* ♭ ♮ *mi* his Eight: of the double ones there be Six, *viz. aa. bb.* ♭ ♮ *cc. dd.* and *ee.* The order of all theſe is expreſſed in Ten lines and ſpaces in the Table following.

Here followes the Introductorie of *Guido Aretinus* a Benedictine Monke, a moſt wittie Muſitian, who onely (after *Boëtius* did giue light to Muſicke) found out the *voyces*, ordered the *keyes*, and by a certaine diuine induſtry, inuented a moſt eaſie way of practiſe, as here followeth to be ſeene.

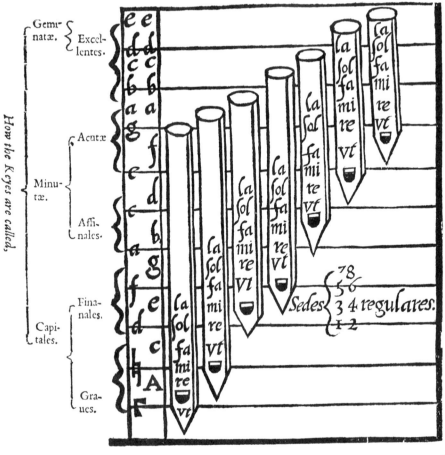

[15]

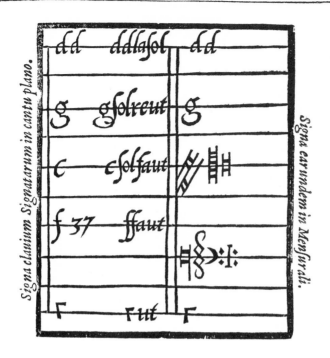

Of the Keyes which are to be marked.

OF *Keyes* some are to be marked, or (as others call them) *marked Keyes,* others are called *vnmarked Keyes.* Of the marked, there are fiue principall, *viz.* г *vt, F faut, C sol faut, G sol reut,* and *Dd la sol:* which the Ambrosians (as *Franch. lib. 1. pract. cap. 3.* reports) did mark with colours. *F faut,* with red, *C sol faut* with blew, double *bb* with skie-colour. But the Gregorians (whom the Church of Rome doth imitate) marking all the lines with one colour, to describe each of the marked *Keyes* by his first Letter, or some other signe, as in the Scale was mentioned.

Those *Keyes* which are lesse principall, are two, *b* round, and ♮ square: The first shews that the Voyce is to be sung *fa,* the second that it is to be sung *mi* in the place wherein it is found. And vnlesse one doe heedily discerne *b* from ♮, he doth confound the Song (as *Berno* sayth) euen as wine and water being mingled together, one can discerne neither.

To the Readers.

SEeing it is a fault to deliuer that in many words, which may be deliuered in few (gentle Readers) leauing the hand, by which the wits of yong beginners are hindered, dulled, and distracted, learne you this fore-written Scale by numbring it : for this being knowne, you shall most easily, and at first sight know the *voyces, Keyes,* and all the *Mutations.*

E *Rules*

Rules for the Keyes.

F Irſt, Of the marked *Keyes* one differs from the other a Fift, except г *vt*, which is remoued from *F faut* a Seuenth.

2. The *Keyes* of an odde number are contained in line, the *Keyes* of an euen number in ſpace.

3. All the ſigned keyes, from which the Iudgement of other *Keyes* is fetched, are ſet in line.   [16

4. The Greeke Letter is placed in the baſer part of the *Introductory*, in honour of the Greekes, from whom *Muſicke* came to vs : For *Berno* the Abbot (in his firſt Booke of Muſicke) ſaith, The Latines choſe rather to put the Greeke letters than the Latine, that the Greekes may be noted hereby to be the Authors of this Art.

5. All *Keyes* beginning with one Letter, doe differ an Eight, ſaith *Guido cap* .5. of his *Microl.*

6. Of Eights there is the ſame iudgement.

7. It is not lawfull for plaine-Song to goe vnder, г *vt*, nor aboue *Eela.* Hereupon it is, that the Three higheſt *Keyes* haue no inferiour *Voyces*, becauſe beyond them there is no riſing : Neither haue the three lowermoſt ſuperiour *voyces*, becauſe there is no deſcending vnder them.

8. As oft as in a broken Song, you goe beyond the extreame *Keyes* (as you doe often) take your *voyces* from Eights.

T H E F O V R T H C H A P T E R.

Of Tones in Generall.

 *Tone* (as *Guido* ſaith) is a rule iudging the Song in the end, or it is a knowledge of the beginning, middle, and end of euery Song, ſhewing the riſing and falling of it.

Of the number of Tones.

B Y the authoritie of the Grӕcians, we ſhould only obſerue 4.*Tones*, (ſaith *Guido Microl.*11. 1.*Proton.*2.*Deuteron*, 3.*Triton*, 4.*Tetarton.* But the Latines conſidering the riſing & falling, and diuiding each of the Greeke *Tones* into authenticke & plagall: to conclude euery thing that is ſung within Eight *Tones*, agreeable to the eight parts of Speech. For it is not amiſſe, (ſaith *Ioan Pont. cap.* 10.) that euery thing which is ſung, may be comprehended within Eight *Tones*, as euery thing which is ſpoken, is confined within Eight parts of Speech.

Now theſe Eight *Tones* (as *Franch. lib.* 5. *Theor.* and laſt Chapter, and
lib.

*lib.*1.*pract.*7. *cap.* faith) are by the Authors thus named, The firſt *Dorian;* the ſecond, *Hypodorion* ; the third, *Phrygian;* (which *Porphyrio* cals barba- rous ; the fourth, *Hypophrygian* ; the fift, *Lydian* ; the ſixt, *Hypolydian ;* the ſeuenth, *Myxolydian* ; the eight, ſome call *Hypermyxolydian ;* others ſay it hath no proper name.

Of the Finals belonging to the Tones.

Finals, (as Saint *Bernard* in his Muſicke ſaith, both truely and briefely) are the Letters which end the Songs. For in theſe muſt be ended euery Song which is regular, and not tranſpoſed, and are in number Foure, as *Guido* writeth in the Dialogue of his *Doctrinall:*

$$
\text{To wit,}
\begin{cases}
D\ \text{ſol re}\\
E\ la\ mi\\
F\ faut\\
G\ \text{ſol re vt}
\end{cases}
\begin{array}{c}\text{In which}\\ \text{euery}\\ \text{Song}\\ \text{ends}\end{array}
\begin{cases}
First\\
Third\\
Fift\\
Seuenth
\end{cases}
\text{and}
\begin{cases}
Second\\
Fourth\\
Sixth\\
Eight
\end{cases}
\text{regular}\ Tones
$$

Of the Compaſſes of the Tones.

The Compaſſe is nothing elſe, but a circuite or ſpace allowed by the authoritie of the Muſitians to the *Tones* for their riſing and falling.

Now to euery *Tone* there are granted but Ten Notes or Voices, wherein he may haue his courſe, (as Saint *Bernard* ſaith in the Prologue of his Mu- ſicke. Hereof hee aſſignes Three reaſons: to wit, The authoritie of the *De- cachorde* of the Pſalter : the worthineſſe of equalitie : and the neceſſity of ſetting the Notes downe. Although at this time the licentious ranging of our modern Muſitians, doth adde an Eleuenth to each, as in the figure fol- lowing appeares.

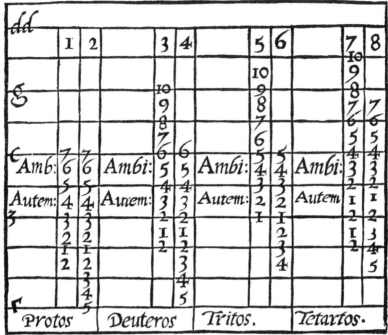

Ambitus Plagales.

The First. The Second. The Third. The Fourth.

Of the Repercußions of Tones.

WHerupon the *Repercußion*, which by *Guido* is alſo called a *Trope*, and the proper and fit melodie of each *Tone*. Or it is the proper interuall of each *Tone*, as in the Examples following appeareth.

Re la giues the firſt, *Re fa* giues the ſecond,

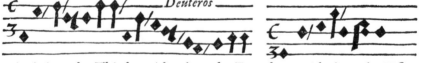

[18]

Mi mi giues the Third, *Mi la* giues the Fourth, *Vt ſol* giues the Fift,

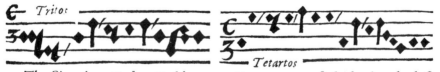

The Sixt giues *Fa la*, *Vt ſol* vneuen *Tetartos*, *vt fa* doth giue the laſt.

               Rules

Rules for the Tones.

Irst, All the odde *Tones* are *Authenticall,* all the euen *Plagall* : thefe are fo called becaufe they defcend more vnder the final *Key* : thefe, becaufe they doe more afcend aboue the finall *Key.*

Thefecond, Euery Song in the beginning, rifing ftraight beyond the finall Note to a Fift, is *Authenticall:* but that which fals ftraight way to a Third, or a Fourth, vnder the finall *Key,* is *Plagall.*

The third, A Song not rifing in the middle beyond the finall Note to an Eight, although it haue a Fift in the beginning, is *Plagall:* vnleffe the *Repercufsion* of an *Authenticall* being there found, preferue it: as an *Antiphone* is newly found, which is iudged to be of the Eight *Tone,* becaufe it hath not the rifing of an *Authent* in the middle. But the *Repercufsion* of a feuenth, appearing ftraight in the beginning, doth preferue it, and make it remaine *Authenticall.* See *Pontifex cap.* 12.

By how many wayes we may know the Tones.

E may know the *Tones* by three meanes: by the beginning: the middle: and the end. By the beginning; for a Song rifing in the beginning ftraight wayes aboue the finall *Key* to a Fift, is *Authenticall,* as before was fayd in the fecond Rule. By the middle, and firft, by the rifing ; For the Song which toucheth an Eight in the middle, is *Authenticall:* that Song which doth not, is *Plagall:* fecondly by the *Repercufsion,* which is proper to euery *Tone,* as before was fayd ; by which at firft hearing you may iudge of what kinde a Song is. By the end, as before we fpake of the finall Notes.

[19]   Befides there be certain Songs, which do afcend as an *Authentical,* & defcend as a *Plagall,* and thofe are called *Neutrall,* or mixt Songs, though indeede Saint *Bernard* doeth not allow of them: for he faith, what execrable licentioufneffe is this, to ioyne together thofe things, which are contrary one to the other, tranfgreffing the bonds of Nature ? furely as it doth make a difcontinuance in conioyning, fo doth it open wrong to Nature. Therfore they are ftarke mad, which prefume fo farre as to rife a *Plagall,* and defcend an *Authenticall.*

Yet are thefe Songs (in my iudgement) to be very diligently marked in the end, to which *Tone* they encline moft. For whileft they difcend from a Fift to the finall Note, they are *Authentickes;* but whileft they rife from a Third or a Fourth to a finall, they are *Plagals* : See *Pontifex* in his 12. and 16. *chap.*

F   THE

The Fift Chapter.

Of Solfaing.

 Herevpon, *Solfaing* is the orderly finging of euery Song by Muficall *Voyces*, according as *Mi* and *Fa* fhall require. For to *Sol fa* (as *Gafforus* witneffeth) is to expreffe the Syllables, and the names of the *Voyces*.

Of three manners of Singing.

E Very Song may be fung three manner of wayes: that is, by *Solfaing*, which is for *Nouices*, that learne to fing: By founding the foundsonly, which belongs to Inftrumentifts, that they may affect the mindes of them that heare or conceiue them with care or folace: Thirdly, by applying, which is the worke of the *Cantor*, that fo he may expreffe Gods praife.

Of Scales.

B Ecaufe the diuerfitie of *Tones* caufeth a diuerfitie in the *Solfaing*, efpecially about *mi* and *fa*, in *b fa* ♮ *mi*, which before wee concluded was not one onely *Key*, but two: therefore the induftrious Mufitians haue deuifed Two Scales, in which euery Song doth runne, and is gouerned: and hath ordayned, that the firft fhould be called ♮ durall of the ♮; the fecond, *b moll* of *b Flat.*

The generall defcription of the Scale.

T Herefore generally a Scale is nothing elfe, but the knowledge of *mi* and *fa*, in *b fa* ♮ *mi*, and in his Eights.

What the Scale ♮ *Durall is.*

T He Scale ♮ *Durall* is a Progreffion of Muficall Voyces, rifing from *A* to ♮ fharpely, that is, by the *Voyce Mi.*

What the Scale b Moll is. [20]

B Vt the Scale *b Moll* is a Progreffion of Muficall *Voyces*, rifing from *A* to *b flatly*, that is by the Voyce *fa*: therefore a *b Moll* Scale doth alwayes require *fa* in *b fa* ♮ *mi*, and a ♮ *fharpe* Scale, *mi*: as in the draft following you may fee.

Rules

The Scale of ♮ dure, *and where the* Mutations *are made.*   *The Scale of* b Moll, *and where the* Mutations *are made.*

Rules of Solfaing.

THe Firſt, He that will *Solfa* any Song, muſt aboue all things haue an eye to the *Tone.* For the knowledge of the *Tone* is the inuention of the Scale, vnder which it runnes.

The Second, All the *Tones* runne vnder the Scale of ♮ Dure, excepting the fift and the ſixt.

[21]   The Third, To haue a Song runne vnder ♮ Dure, is nothing elſe, but to ſing *Mi* in *b fa* ♮ *mi,* and *fa* in a *flat* Scale.

The Fourth, When a Song runnes vnder a Scale ♮ *Dure,* the lowermoſt Notes of that kinde are to be ſung; but vnder a Scale *b Moll,* the vppermoſt Notes.

The Fift, Euery *Solfaer* muſt needs looke, whether the Song be regular, or no; for the tranſpoſition of a Song is oft times an occaſion of changing the Scale.

The Sixt, Euery Song ending in the *Finals,* is regular, and not tranſpoſed, ſaith Saint *Bernard* in his Dialogue.

The Seuenth, Whenſoeuer a Song aſcends from *D ſol re* to *A la mi re* by a ſift, mediately or immediately, and further onely to a ſecond, you muſt ſing *fa* in *b fa* ♮ *mi* in euery *Tone,* till the ſong do againe touch *D ſol re,* whether it be marked or no. But this Rule failes, when a ſong doth not ſtraightwayes fall to *F faut,* as in the Hymne, *Aue maris ſtella,* you may ſee.

The Eight, In *b fa* ♮ *mi,* and his eights, you may not ſing *mi* for *fa,* nor

F 2   contrariwiſe,

contrariwife;becaufe they are difcording and repugnant voyces,faith *Fran-chinus lib.*1.*praĉt.cap.*4.

The Ninth,*b* in places,where he is marked contrary to his nature,doth note Mutation.

The Tenth, The Scale being varied,the *Mutations* are alfo with it varied, both in the whole and in part. In the whole,as in tranfpofed Songs; in part, as in conioyned Songs.

The eleuenth, As often as *fa* or *mi* is marked contrary to their nature, the *Solfaer* muft follow the marke fo long as it lafts.

The twelfe, Seeing there is one and the felfefame iudgement of eights, the fame *Solfaing* of *Voyces* muft be.

The Sixt Chapter.
Of Mutations.

Hereupon *Mutation* (as *Georg. Valla lib.*3.*cap.* 4. of his Muficke proueth) is the putting of one *Voyce* for another. But this defi-nition, becaufe it is generall, doth not properly agree to a Mu-fitian: therfore *Mutation* is(to apply it to our purpofe)the putting of one concord for another in the fame *Key.* And becaufe all *Voyces* are not concords,al do not receiue *Mutation.* Therfore it is neceffary to confider, to which *Voyces* Mutation doth agree, and to which not; for ♮ *dures* are not changed into *b mols,*nor cõtrarily: as you may fee in the example following.

[22]

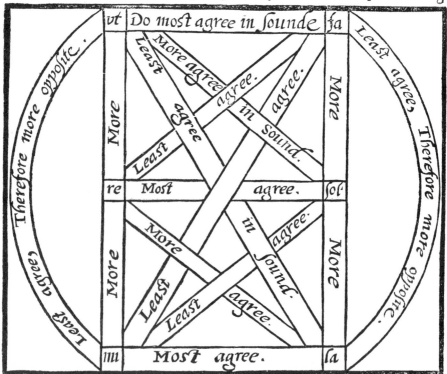

Rules

Rules for Mutations.

Irſt, As often as the Progreſſion of ſixe Muſicall *Voyces* wants, there muſt neceſſarily be *Mutation.*

2   No *Mutation* can be in a *Key* which hath but one *Voyce*, becauſe there one *Voyce* is not changed into it ſelfe, although it may well be repeated.

3   In *Keyes* which haue two *Voyces*, there be two *Mutations*, the firſt is from the lower to the vpper; the ſecond contrarily. From this Rule are excepted *Keyes* which haue *Voyces* of one kinde, as *cc ſolfa*, and *dd la ſol.*

4   A *Key* hauing three *Voyces*, admitteth ſixe *Mutations*, although therein you muſt needs varie the Scale.

5   Let there be no *Mutation*, vnleſſe neceſſitie force you to it.

6   The *b moll Voyces* cannot be changed into ♮ ſquare, nor contrarily: becauſe they are diſcords.

7   Naturall *Voyces* are changed both into ♮ *Dures*, and into *b mols*, becauſe they are doubtfull. excepting *mi* and *ſol*, *re* and *fa*, which are not changed one into another; becauſe they are neuer found dwelling in one *Key.*

8   In the falling of a Song, let the lower be changed into the higher, in the riſing contrarily.

9   In a *Key* which hath one *Voyce*, there may be ſo many *Mutations*, as there may be in his eight, becauſe of them there is the ſame iudgement.

[23]   10   You muſt make a mentall, not a vocall *Mutation*, vnleſſe two or three Notes be put in the ſame place that receiues *Mutation.*

The Seventh Chapter.

Of Moodes, or Interuals.

N *Interuall* (as *Boëtius*, whoſe conceit for Muſicke, no man euer attained *lib. 1. cap.8.* writeth) is the diſtance of a baſe and high ſound. Or (as *Placentinus lib.2.cap.8.* ſaith) it is the way from lowneſſe to height, and contrarily. Or it is the diſtance of one *Voyce* from another, conſidered by riſing and falling. Whence it is manifeſt, that an *Vniſon* is not a *Moode*, although it be the beginning of *Moodes*, as vnitie is of numbers. For *Boëtius* ſaith, As vnitie is the beginning of pluralitie, and number, ſo is æqualitie of proportions. Now an *Vniſon* is, (according to *George Valla lib.2.cap. 2.*) a *Voyce* ſo qualified, that it neither tendeth to depth nor to height. Or it is a conioyning of two or three Notes in the ſame place, as appeareth in exerciſe.

Of the number of the Moodes.

N Ow the vſuall *Interuals* are in number 9, *viz.* a *Semitone*, and that is a riſing from one *Voyce* to another, (by an imperfect ſecond) ſounding flatly: and it is onely betwixt the *Voyces Mi, fa.* It is called a *Semitone,* not becauſe it is halfe a *Tone,* (for a *Tone* cannot be diuided into two equall parts) but becauſe it is an imperfect *Tone,* for *Semum* is called that which is imperfect, as ſaith *Boëtius lib.*1. *cap.*16. Of how many ſorts a *Semitone* is, I ſhall hereafter in my *Theoricks* diſcuſſe.

A *Tone* (as *Faber Stapulenſis* writeth) is the beginning of *Conſonances*: or it is a *Conſonance* cauſed by the number of eight. For *Macrobius* ſaith, that the eight, is an number, by which *Symphonie* is bred ; which *Sympho-nie* the Græcians call a *Tone.* Or it is the diſtance of one *Voyce* from ano-ther by a perfect ſecond, ſounding ſtrongly, ſo called a *Tonando,* that is, *Thundring.* For *Tonare,* (as *Ioannes Pontifex* 12.*cap.* 8. ſaith) ſignifieth *to thunder powerfully.* Now a *Tone* is made betwixt all *Voyces* excepting *mi* and *fa,* conſiſting of two ſmaller *Semitones,* and one *Comma.*

A Semiditone.

WHich *Faber Stapulenſis* calleth *Seſquitonium,* is an *Interuall* of one *Voyce* from another by an imperfect third: conſiſting of a *Tone,* and a *ſemitone* according to *Placentinus.* It hath two kindes, as *Pontifex* in the eight Chapter ſaith ; the firſt is from *re* to *fa*; the ſecond from *mi* to *ſol,* as in exerciſe will appeare.

A Ditone.

[24]

IS a perfect third : ſo called, becauſe it containes in it two *Tones,* as *Placen-tine* and *Pontifex* witneſſe. It hath likewiſe two kindes, the firſt is from *vt* to *mi* ; the ſecond from *fa* to *la.*

Diateſſaron.

IN *Boëtius lib.*1.*cap.*17. It is a *Conſonance* of 4. *Voyces,* and 3. *Interuals.* Or it is the leaping from one *Voyce* to another by a Fourth, conſiſting of two *Tones,* and a leſſer *ſemitone.* It hath three kinds in *Boëtius lib.*4.*cap.*13. and in *Pontifex cap.*8. the firſt is from *vt* to *fa,* the ſecond from *re* to *ſol,* the third from *mi* to *fa.*

Diapente.

IS a Conſonance of fiue *Voyces,* and 4. *Interuals,* as ſaith *Boëtius lib.*1.*cap.* 18. Or it is the leaping of one *Voyce* to another by a fift, conſiſting of three *Tones,* and a *ſemitone.* It hath foure kinds in *Boëtius lib.* 4. *cap.*13. Therefore *Pontifex* cals it the *Quadri-moode Interuall.* The firſt, is from *vt* to *ſol* ; the ſecond, from *re* to *la* ; the third, from *mi* to *mi* ; the fourth, from *fa* to *fa.*

Semitone

Semitone Diapente.

IS an *Interuall* of one *Voyce* from another by an imperfect sixt, according to *Georgius Valla lib. 3. cap. 21.* consisting of three *Tones,* and two *Semitones.*

Tonus Diapente.

IS the distance of one Voyce from another by a perfect sixt. Which *Stapulensis* affirmes to consist of foure *Tones,* and a lesser *semitone.*

Diapason.

WHich onely is called a perfect *Consonance* by *Guido* in the 9.Chapter of his *Microl.* according to the same Author in the 5. Chapter is an *Interuall:* wherein a *Diatessaron* and *Diapente* are conioyned. Or (as *Franchinus lib.1.pract.c.7.*writeth) is a *Consonance* of eight *sounds,* and seuen *Interuals.* Or (as *Plutarch* saith, it is a *Consonance* weighed by a duple reason. Now for example sake 6. and 12. will make a duple reason. But they to whom these descriptions, shall seeme obscure, let them take this. It is a distance of one Voyce from another by an eight, consisting of fiue *Tones,* and two lesser *semitones.* It hath seuen kindes, according to *Boëtius* and *Guido* the most famous *Musitians.* For from euery Letter to his like is a *Diapason.* Besides euery *Moode* hath so many kindes excepting one, as it hath Voyces.

[25]

Here followeth a Direction for the Moodes.

Ter tri ni sunt mo di qui bus omnis cantile na contexitur, scilicet, Unisonus, Se mi-

tonium, To nus, Semiditonus, Di to nus, Di a tes se ron, Di a pen-

te, Semitoniū cū diapente, To nus cum diapente, adhuc modus di a pa son, Si quē delectat

G 2

[26]

lectat eius hûc modũ eê cognoscat cũq̃, tã paucus mo du lis to ta harmonia formetur,

vtilissimum est eam altæ memoriæ cõmendare, nec ab homini studio re quiesce re, Do-

nec vocũ interuallum cog ni tũ Harmõtæ totius facilime queat cõprehẽdere noticiam.

Of the forbidden Interuals.

THere be some other *Interuals*, very rare, and forbidden to yong beginners. For as the learned licence of Orators & Poets, doth grant certaine
things to thofe which are as it were paffed the age of warfare, but doth de-
ny the fame to frefh-water fouldiers ; fo is it amongft Mufitians. The names
of thofe are thefe.

Tritonus.

ANd it is a leaping from one Voyce to another by a fharp Fourth, comprehending three whole *Tones* without the *femitone*. Wherefore it is
greater than *Diateffaron* ; *Stapulenfis* faith thus, A *Tritone* doth exceed the
Confonance of a *Diateffaron*. And this *Moode* is vfed in the anfwere, *Ifti funt
dies*, *Dominica Iudica*: and in the anfwere, *Vox Tonitrui*, in the saying, *Euan-
gelifta*, as thus :

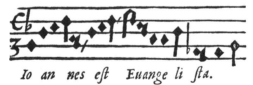

Io an nes eft Euange li fta.

Semidiapente.

[27]

IS an *Interuall* by an imperfect fift, comprehending two *Tones*, with two
femitones, which though it be not found in plaine-fong, yet doth the
knowledge thereof much profit compofers, who are held to auoide it.

Semiditones

Semiditonus Diapente.

IS an *Interuall* by an imperfect seuenth. This according to *Placentinus lib.3.cap.* 24. comprehends foure *Tones*, and two *semitones*. The example of this is in an *Antiphone* called, *Dum inducerent puerum Ihesum*, in the speech, *Accepit*

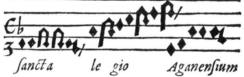

Parentes   e   ius   ac ce pit.

Ditonus Diapente.

IS the distance of one Voyce from another by a perfect seuenth : consisting of fiue *Tones*, and one *semitone*, according to *Georg.Valla lib.3.cap.* 26. It is found in the *Responsorie, sancta legio de sancto Mauritio*, in the word, *Aganensium*.

sancta   le gio   Aganensium

Semidiapason.

IS an imperfect eight, consisting of foure *Tones*, and three **Semitones**, not to be vsed in any plaine Song, yet worthy to be knowne by componists.

Semitonium Diapason.

IS a leaping by an imperfect Ninth, consisting of fiue *Tones*, and three *semitones.* Now a *Tone* with a *Diapason* is a perfect Ninth, consisting of sixe *Tones*, and two *semitones*.

Semiditonus Diapason.

IS an *Interuall* by an imperfect Tenth, as witnesseth *Valla* the 31.Chapter, consisting of sixe *Tones*, and three *semitones*. A *Ditone* with a true *Diapason* is a perfect Tenth, consisting of seuen *Tones*, and two *semitones*.

[28]

Diapason Diapente.

IS a consonance of twelue *sounds*, and eleuen *Interuals*, consisting of eight *Tones*, and three *semitones*. The examples of these *Moodes* are verie rarely seene in plaine Song; in mensurall often.

Disdiapason.

IS an *Interuall* by a Fifteenth, occasioned (as saith *Macrobius*) by a quadruple proportion. Wherein antiquitie sayd we should rest, and goe no

H   further,

further,as *Ambroſius Nolanus* doth proue in the prouerb *Diſdiapaſon*, which is in *Eraſmus* that other light of *Germany*. Both becauſe this is the naturall compaſſe of mans voice, which going aboue this,is rather a ſqueaking;and going vnder,is rather a humming than a *Voyce* : And alſo becauſe *Ariſtotle* doth deny Muſick to be meerely Mathematicall.For Muſick muſt be ſo tempered, that neither ſence be againſt reaſon, nor reaſon againſt ſence.

The Eight Chapter.

Of the Dimenſion of the Monochord.

Monochord, that is,an Inſtrument of one ſtring, is thus truely made.Take a peece of wood of a yard long, or what length you pleaſe, of two fingers bredth,and ſo thicke, make it hollow in the middle, leauing the ends of it vnhollowed. Let it be couered with a belly peece well ſmoothed, that hath holes in it,like the belly of a Lute:through the middle of this,let there be ſecretly drawne one line,and in the beginning of it, let one pricke be marked with the letter *F.* for that ſhalbe the firſt *Magade* of the Inſtrument : then diuide the whole line from the pricke *F.* into nine equall parts, and in the firſt pricke of the diuiſions place *vt*, in the ſecond nothing, in the third *Cfaut*, in the fourth nothing,in the fift *Gſolreut*,in the ſixt *Cſolfaut*, in the ſeuenth *G ſolreut* ſmall, in the eight nothing, in the laſt o *Cifer*, which ſhall poſſeſſe the place of the ſecond   *agade.* This done, againe diuide the ſpace,which is from *vt* to the ſecond *Magade*,into nine parts.

In the firſt part ſet *A* Baſe; in the third *Dſolre;* in the fift *Alamire;* in the ſixt *D laſolre;* in the ſeuenth *aalamire.* Then from *A re* to the ſecond *Magade* againe make nine parts;in the firſt ſet ♮ *mi* Baſe; in the third *Elami;*in the fift ♮ *mi* in the ſmall letters ; in the ſixt *Elami* ; in the ſeuenth ♮ ♮ *mi* double.

This done, diuide all this ſpace from the firſt to the ſecond *Magade* into foure parts: in the firſt put *B fa* Baſe ; in the ſecond *Ffaut* finall ; in the third *Ffaut* ſharpe. Then begin in *B fa* Baſe, and diuide the whole line towards the *Cone* into 4.parts ; in the firſt,*b* the *Semitone* betwixt *D & E* capitals ; in the ſecond,*b fa;* in the third, *bb fa* This done,begin in the *ſemitone*,which is betwixt *D & E*, and diuide the whole line into 4. equall parts. In the firſt, place *b* the *Semitone*, betwixt *G* capitall and ſmall ; in the ſecond,*b Semitone*, betwixt *D* and *E* ; in the third,*b fa*, betwixt *dd* and *ee*: and if you further diuide the third into two equall parts,you ſhall haue a *ſemitone* betwixt *g* and *aa.* Then place the foot of your compaſſe in *C ſolfaut*,and diuide the ſpace towards the ſecond *Magade* into two parts ; in the middle whereof place *cc ſolfa.* In like manner diuide the ſpace from *dlaſolre* towards the *Cone* into two equall parts ; and in the middle place *ddlaſol.* Laſtly,diuide the ſpace from *e* towards the ſecond *Magade* ; and in the middle you ſhall haue *ee la*, with the true *Dimenſion* of the *Monochord.* This done,in the extreame points

[29]

points of the *Magades*, fet little props to hold the ftring, leaft the found of the ftring be dulled with touching the wood. This readied, fet to one ftring of wyre, ftrong, big & ftretched inough, that it may giue a found which may be eafily heard, and you fhall haue your *Monochord* perfect. The forme of it is this.

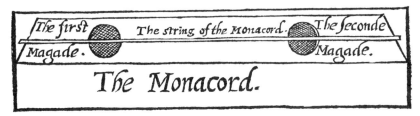

points of the Magades

The first | The string of the Monacord. | The feconde
Magade. | | Magade.

The Monacord.

THE NINTH CHAPTER.

Of the Definition, Profit, and vfe of the Monochord.

A *Monochord* (as *Guido* proues in the beginning of his *Doctrinall*) is a long fquare peece of wood hollow within, with a ftring drawne ouer it; by the found whereof, we apprehend the varieties of founds. Or it is a rude and vnskilfull Maifter, which makes learned Schollers. For it fhewes to others that which it felfe conceiues not, it tels truth, it cannot tell how to lye, it inftructeth diligently, and reprehendeth no mans flow conceit. Now it is called a *Monochord*, becaufe it hath but one ftring, as a *Tetrachord* is called that which hath foure. And a *Decachord* which hath tenne, faith *Ioan. Pont. 22. cap.7.* of his Muficke.

---

[30]

Of the profit of the Monochord.

THe *Monochord* was chiefly inuented for this purpofe, to be iudge of Mufical voices and interuals: as alfo to try whether the fong be true or falfe furthermore, to fhew haire-braind falfe Mufitians their errors, and the way of attaining the truth. Laftly, that children which defire to learne Muficke, may haue an eafie meanes to it, that it may intice beginners, direct thofe that be forward, and fo make of vnlearned learned.

Of the vfe of the Monochord.

THe vfe of the *Monochord* (faith *Berno Cluniacenfis lib. 2.* of his Muficke) is, that we may know how much each voyce is higher or lower than other. When therefore thou wilt learne a Song, euen the deepeft, of thy felfe by the helpe of thy *Monochord*, fet thy *Monochord* before thee on the table, and marke in what *Key* the firft Note of that Song is, which thou defireft to know. This being found, touch the fame in the *Monochord* with a quill, and the found it giues, is that thou defireft. Thus runne ouer each Note of the

Song, and so mayest thou by thy selfe learne any Song though neuer so weighty.

The Tenth Chapter.

Of Musica Ficta.

Ained Musicke is that, which the Greekes call *Synemenon*, a Song made beyond the regular compasse of the Scales. Or it is a Song, which is full of Coniunctions.

Of Coniunctions.

THe Coniunct sounds were called by the ancients *Diiuncts* because it is added to songs besides their nature, either to make them more sweet, or to make the *Moodes* more perfect: for thus saith Saint *Bernard*: In euery kinde, where it is meet a flatter sound should be, let there be put a flat in stead of a sharpe; yet couertly, least the Song seeme to take vpon it the likenesse of another *Tone*. Now a *Coniunct* is this, to sing a Voyce in a *Key* which is not in it. Or it is the sodaine changing of a *Tone* into a *Semitone*, or a *semitone* into a *Tone*.

Of the Diuision and number of Coniuncts.

COniuncts are two-fold: that is, Tolerable ones, when a Voyce is sung in a *Key*, wherein it is not, yet is found in his eight: as to sing *Mi* in *A re, La* in *Dsolre*. Intolerable ones, when a Voyce is sung in a *Key* which is not in it, nor in his eight, as to sing *Fa* in *Elami, Mi* in *Ffaut*. Of these *Coniuncts* there be two signes, *viz. b* round and ♮. The first sheweth that the Coniunct is in ♮ *dure* places; the second, that it is in *b flat* places. [31]

There be 8. *Coniuncts* most vsuall: although there may be more. The first in a Base, is marked with round *b*. The second in *E* finall, is marked with the same signe. The third is in *Ffaut*, and is marked with ♮. The fourth in a *fmall*, is knowne by *b flat*. The fift, in *c* affinall by ♮ *dure*. The sixt, in *e* by *b* round. The seuenth, in *f* by ♮. The eight in *aa* by *b*. There be examples enough to to be found of these both in plaine and mensurall Songs.

Here followes the fayned Scale.

THe fained Scale exceedes the others both in height and depth. For it addeth a *Ditone* vnder *Vt* base, because it sings *fa* in *A*, and it riseth aboue *eela* by two degrees, for in it it sounds *fa*. Wherfore for the expressing of it, there are necessarily required twelue lines, as appeareth in the figure following.

Rules

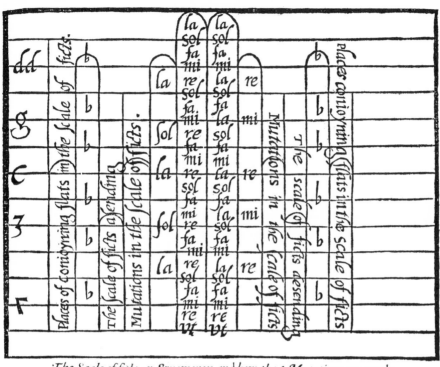

The Scale of ficts or Synemenon, and how the Mutations are made.

Rules for Ficta Musicke.

Frst, It is better, and sweeter to sing by tolerable *Coniuncts*, than by the proper Voyces of *Keyes.*

2 The tolerable *Coniuncts* doe not spoyle the Song, but the intolerable ones.

3 Musicke may Fict in any Voyce and *Key*, for Consonance sake.

4 Marking *fa* in *b fa* ♮ *mi*, or in any other place, if the Song from that shall make an immediate rising to a Fourth, a Fift, or an Eight, euen there *fa* must necessarily be marked, to eschew a *Tritone*, a *Semidiapente*, or a *Semidiapason*, and inusuall, and forbidden *Moodes* : as appeareth in the example vnder-written.

An Exercise of Ficta Musicke.

I

THE ELEVENTH CHAPTER.

Of Song and Transposition.

Herfore a Song is a melody formed of a *Sound, Mood, & Tone,* by a liuely Voice. I fay by a *found,* becaufe of the writing of the Notes, which improperly we call a Song: By the *moode,* I vnderftand rifing and falling, becaufe of the prayers which are read in an Vnifon. By the *Tone,* becaufe of the chirping of birds, which is comprehended within no *Tone.* For within a *Syllogifme* is *moode* and *figure,* that in a Song is the *Tone* and Scale. I fay a liuely Voyce, becaufe of Muficall Inftruments. Or otherwife : A Song is the fitting of a liuely Voyce according to rifing, and falling, Or (as *Gafforus* writeth in his *Theoricks lib.5.cap.6.*) it is the deduction of many Voyces from the fame beginning. And this defcription doth properly agree to this progreffion of fyllables, becaufe it is not a Song.

[33]

Of the number of Deductions.

THere are therefore three Deductions of this kinde: the firft is called ♮ *durall,* to be fung fharpely, becaufe it requires *mi* in *b fa* ♮ *mi,* and in his Eights.

The fecond is *b* flat, which runneth with a fweet and flattering Harmonie, and requires *fa* in *b fa* ♮ *mi.*

The third is *neutrall,* and is called *naturall.* For it receiueth in *b fa* ♮ *mi,* neither *mi,* nor *fa* : becaufe it comes not to fuch places.

Rules for Deductions.

FIrft, Wherefoeuer *Vt* is put in the Scale, there is the beginning of fome Deduction : where *fa* is put, there the middle : where *la,* there the end : as appeareth in the figure following.

$$\text{In} \begin{Bmatrix} C \\ F \\ d \end{Bmatrix} \textit{Naturall,} \begin{Bmatrix} F \\ b \\ d \end{Bmatrix} b \textit{ Moll} \begin{Bmatrix} b \\ c \\ e \end{Bmatrix} \text{and} ♮ \textit{ dure} \begin{Bmatrix} \text{the beginning,} \\ \text{middle,} \\ \text{end.} \end{Bmatrix}$$

The fecond Rule. Of which *Deductions* this or that rule is, you fhall thus eafily know. Confider the voice that is there to be fung, with which it defcends to his foundation, I fay to *Vt* : and where you find any fuch, fee what *Deduction* begins fo: for it will be of that Note which you feeke.

Of Transposition.

WHereupon *Transposition* is the remouing of a Song, or a *Key* from his proper place. For to tranfpofe is to remoue a fong, or a *Key* from the proper place. And *Transposition* is two-fold, *viz.* Of the Song and of the *Key.*

of

Of Transposition of a Song.

IT is the auoiding of *Coniuncts*, for whilst we striue to auoide *Coniuncts*, (because they marre the Song) we doe eleuate the Song from the proper place of his end, aboue to a Fift, as directly appeareth in the Responsorie, *Ite in Orbem.*

I　　te in Orbem　　I　　te in or bem

[34]

Of the Affinall Keyes of Tones.

THe *Keyes* (which we call *Affinall*) be the Letters, which end irregular Songs : whereof according to *Guido, Berno,* and Saint *Gregory,* there be three : Although the *Ambrosians* make more.

Viz. $\begin{cases} alamire \\ b fa \natural mi \\ c solfaut \end{cases}$ wherein ends euery Song of the $\begin{cases} First \\ Third \\ Fift \end{cases}$ and $\begin{cases} Second \\ Fourth \\ Sixt \end{cases}$ transposed *Tone*.

Now this irregularnesse of Songs (as writeth *Pontifex* 14. chapter of his Musicke) comes sometime by licence, sometime by the negligence of the *Cantors*, sometimes by reason of ancientnesse, which cannot be gainesaid, sometimes because of the *Counterpoint*, that the Base may haue place to descend.

Of the Transposition of a Rule.

FIrst, A Song of the seuenth and eight *Tones* is not transposed. Not vpward to *Dlasolre*, as the *Ambrosians* are of opinion, because an *Authentick Tone* hath no place of rising to the tenth, neither down to *Cfaut*, because a *Plagall* hath no place of falling to a fift: neither must you clime aboue *eela*, nor descend vnder *г vt*, as before hath been declared. Wherfore (saith *Ioan. Pontif.*) It is fit, that he which cannot haue a Vicar, doe administer his businesse himselfe.

2　A Song ending in *Dlasolre*, or in *Cfaut*, is either an *Ambrosian* Song, or corrupted with the ignorance of *Cantors*, as *Pontifex* saith; Whensoeuer in a Song of the fourth *Tone*, there fals any missing, let vs say, that it proceeds from the vnskilfulnesse of the *Cantors*, and is to be corrected with the cunning of the Musitians. But the authoritie of the *Gregorians* admits no such Song.

3　The placing of one strange Voice in any *Key*, is a cause, why the whole Song is transposed.

4 . *Transposition* is an helpe and excuse of the *Coniuncts*.

5　Let euery transposition be from a *Finall*, to a fift the proper *Affinall*:

I 2　　　　　　　　　　　　　　　　　　　vnlesse

vnleſſe neceſſitie compell, that it be to be made to a fourth. For then are we forced to transpoſe it to a fourth, when after the Transpoſition to a fift more *Coniunĉts* riſe than were before : as in the anſwere, *Quæ eſt iſta,* vnder the third *Tone* may appeare.

Quæ eſt iſta regu-   *Transpoſitio quin-*   *Transpoſitio quar-*
lariter.   *taria non valens.*   *taria bene valens.*

6 The ſame Voices after Transpoſition are to be ſung, which were [35 ſung before.

7 In irregular Songs transpoſed to a fift, you muſt ſing *Mi* in *b fa♮ mi* in euery *Tone,* vnleſſe it be ſpecially marked with *fa.*

8 In Songs transpoſed to a fourth, *fa* is alwaies founded in *b fa♮ mi* : vnleſſe *Mi* be ſpecially noted.

9 Transpoſition to a fourth is knowne, when a Song is ended by a voice which agrees not to his Scale. Or when in the beginning of a transpoſed Song, *fa* is found. To which transpoſition Saint *Bernard* ſeemes to be oppo
Note. ſite, in ſaying this: It is fit that they which propound to themſelues an orderly courſe of life, haue alſo the Art of Singing ; and reſtraine from the liberty of thoſe men, which regarding rather likeneſſe than nature in Songs, diſioyne thoſe things which are ioyned together, and ioyne together thoſe things which are diſioyned, begin and end, make low and high, order and compoſe a Song, not as they ſhould, but as they liſt : for by the fooliſh transpoſition that ſuch men vſe, there is growne ſuch confuſion in Songs, that moſt are thought to be of a contrary faſhion.

10 A Song ending in *Gſolreut,* marking *fa* in *b fa♮ mi* is of the firſt or ſecond *Tone* transpoſed to the fourth. And that which is in *alamire,* is of the third or fourth, as *Quæ eſt iſta,* and ſo of others.

Of the Transpoſition of Keyes.

THe *Transpoſition* of a *Key* is the raiſing or low carying of a marked *Key* for want of lines, of which there are theſe Rules giuen.

1 The transpoſition of *Keyes* doth not make the Song irregular, becauſe it varies not the regular end.

2 By how much a transpoſed *Key* doth deſcend from the former going before ; ſo much doth the following Note aſcend aboue that transpoſed *Key* : and contrarily, as in the examples following is manifeſt.

Hæc ſunt cōniuia quã tibi placēt ô patris ſa pi en tia

                                                        THE

THE TVVELFTH CHAPTER.

Of the Tones in speciall.

[36] **B**Eing that to proceed from generaltie to specialty is more naturall to vs, as *Aristotle* the Prince of all Philosophers, and light of naturall knowledge, in the first Booke of his Phisickes sheweth. Therefore in a fit order after the generall deliuery of the *Tones*, let vs goe to the speciall, discussing more largely and plainely of the nature of each. And first,of the first.

Of the first Tone.

THe first *Tone* (as S. *Bernard* saith) is a Rule determining the *authentick* of the first kinde. Or it is the *authenticall* progression of the first. Now an *authenticall* progression, is the ascending beyond the *Finall Key* to an eight, & a tenth. And the progression of the first is formed by that kind of *Diapente*, which is from *d* to *a*: and of that kind of *Diatessaron*, which is from *a* to *d*, saith *Franchinus lib.*1.*pract.cap.*8.It hath his *Finall* regular place in *Dsolre*, or his vnregular in *alamire*. The beginnings of it according to *Guido* are *C. D.E.F.G.* and *a*, whose capitall forme is this :

Capita. primi toni. Sacerdos in æternum.   Gaudeamus omnes in do.

Of the differences of Tones.

DIfferences of the Essences of *Tones* there be none, but for the vnlearned there are some framed, that they may the easilier begin in the diuers beginnings of *Tones* : saith *Pontif.*23.chapter of his Musicke. Therefore I find no cause of this, but onely vse : neither haue I found it written by any Musitian. Neither doth Saint *Bernard* much like it. For the differences giue occasion of many confusions and errours. Wherefore seeing our obsequiousnesse,which we performe to God,must be reasonable, leauing the differences,which are by no reason approued, let the Readers onely be carefull of the Capitall tenours of *Tones*,least they wind themselues in vnprofitable and superfluous precepts, put on the darkenesse of the night, and make an easie thing most hard and difficult. For God delights not in vnreasonable turnings,but in Songs well fashioned and regular, being he himselfe hath made all things in a most regular and orderly fashion. Wherefore the Psalmist saith, *Praise the Lord in well-sounding Cymbals*:for he would not haue said well sounding, if he would haue had God praised with euery bellowing, screaming,or noyse.

K

Of

Of the Diuiſions of the Pſalmes.

I Find there are two ſorts of Pſalmes, which we vſe in praiſing God, the greater and the leſſer : all Pſalmes are called leſſer, except thoſe two, *viz.* Of the bleſſed Virgin, and of *Zacharias.* Alſo the Song of *Symeon,* in ſome Dioceſſe is accounted for a greater Pſalme, in ſome for a leſſer; as I in going ouer the world haue found.   [37]

Of the true manner of Singing Pſalmes.

THe authoritie both of *Cælius Rhodiginus,* and of al the Diuines doth teſtifie, That the Prophet had a great myſterie in the Harmony of the Pſalmes : wherefore I thought good to interlace ſome within this booke of the true manner of ſinging. Whence to ſing pſalmes, is to ſing the praiſes of almighty God with a certaine ioy. In which matter there is ſuch diuerſitie, (the more is the griefe) that euery one ſeems to haue a ſeuerall faſhion of Singing. Neither doe they obſerue the Statutes, and precepts of their forefathers, but euery one ſings Pſalmes, and other things euen as they liſt. Wherevpon there is ſuch diſcention growne in the Church, ſuch diſcord, ſuch confuſion, that ſcarce two ſing after one manner. This doth *Pontifex* in the 22. chapter of his Muſicke, very much reprehend, and ſurely with good reaſon, ſaying : Seeing that one God is delighted with one baptiſme, one faith, and the vnity of manners, who may think but that he is grieuouſly offended with this multiplicity of Songs? Wherfore I had deliuered certaine Rules of the true order of ſinging, vnleſſe I had found them both copiouſly and learnedly written by maiſter *Michael Galliculo de Muris,* a moſt learned man. Wherefore I ſend all that are deſirous to be inſtructed in this point to him, onely medling with thoſe things which belong to the tuning of pſalmes.

Rules for the tuning of Pſalmes.

FIrſt, All the greater Pſalmes are to be tuned with a riſing, the leſſer without a riſing.

2   The indeclinable words, the Hebrew, and Barbarous, are to be pronounced in the middle accent high.

3   The tuning of the leſſer Pſalmes of the firſt *Tone* is thus out of *alamire,* and out of *Ffaut,* the tuning of the greater thus:

Laudate pueri do laudate nomen domini . memento do. Dꝰ. Magnificat anima mea dominum.

The melodie of verſes in Reſponſories, is framed by later Muſitians at their pleaſure : but of entrances the manner is as yet inuiolably kept, according to the decrees of the Ancients, in this manner.   [38]

The

The Melodie of the Verses in the answeres of the first Tone.

The Melody in the beginnings of the Verses of the first Tone.

Of the second Tone.

THe second *Tone,*(as Saint *Bernard* saith)is a Rule determining the *Pla-gall* of the first fashion. Or it is a plagall Progression of the first. Now a *plagall* Progression is a descending beyond the *Finall* to a Fift, or at least a fourth. His beginnings (according to *Guido*) are *A.C.D.F.*& *G.*& doth right-ly possesse the extreames of the eight *Authenticke,* because the souldier by law of Armes, doth dwell in the Tents of his captaine. The manner of the se-cond *Tone,* is thus:

Cap. secúdi toni.   Miserator   do   mi nus.   Hunc mundú spernes.

The tuning of the smaller Psalmes is thus out of *Ffaut;* the tuning of the greater out of *Cfaut,* thus:

Laudate pueri do. laudate nomé do-   Memento do da. Magnificat anima mea dominum.

The Melodie of the Verses in the answeres of the second Tone.

The Melodie in the beginnings of the Verses of the second Tone.

Of the third Tone.

THe third *tone,* is a Rule determining the *Authenticall* of the second ma-ner. Or it is the *authentical* progressió of the secód, hauing the final place

K 2   regular

regular in *Elami*: His beginnings(according to *Guido*) are *E.F.G.*&c. The chiefe forme whereof, is this :

Capitale tertij. O   gloriosum.   Fauus distillans.

The tuning of the lesser Psalmes out of Csolfaut, *and of the greater out of* Gsolreut, *is this* :

[40]

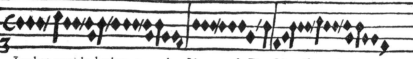

Laudate pueri do laudate nomen do.   Memento do Da.   Magnificat anima mea.

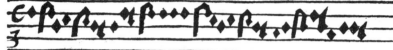

The Melodie of the Verses in the answeres of the third Tone.

The Melodie in the beginnings of the Verses of the third Tone.

Of the Fourth Tone.

THe Fourth *Tone* (as witnesseth *Bernard*) is a Rule determining the *plagall* of the second manner. Or it is a Progression of the second *plagall*, holding the same end that his *Authenticke* doth. It hath sixe beginnings, *C. D.E.F.G.* and *a*, whose principall tenour is this, as it followeth :

Capitale quarti   Tota pulchra es   Hæc   est dies.

The tuning of the smaller Psalmes out of *alamire*, and the greater out of *Elami*, is thus :

[41]

Laudate pueri dominú, laudate nomé domini. Memento do. Da. Magnificat anima mea dominú.

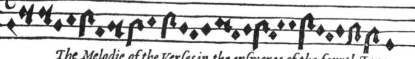

The Melodie of the Verses in the answeres of the fourth Tone.

The

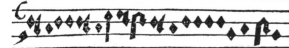

The Melodie in the Diuine Offices of the Verses of the Fourth Tone.

Of the fift Tone.

THe fift *Tone* is a Rule, determining the *Authenticke* of the third manner, or it is an *Authenticall* Progreſſion of the third. Whoſe regular end is in *Ffaut;* and irregular end in *Cſolfaut.* The beginnings of it (as *Franchinus* witneſſeth) are Foure, *F.G.a,* and *c.* whoſe chiefe forme is this :

Capitale quinti.   Gaude Dei genitrix.   Gau di a.

The tuning of the ſmaller Pſalmes out of *Cſolfaut,* and of the greater out of *Ffaut,* is in this ſort.

[42]

Laudate pueri dominum.   Memento do. Da. Mag. anima mea dominum.

The Melody of the Verſes in the anſweres of the Fift Tone.

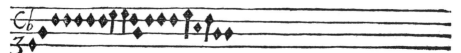

The manner in the beginnings of the Verſes of the Fift Tone.

Of the Sixt Tone.

THe Sixt *Tone* is a Rule, determining a *plagall* of the third ſort. Or it is the *plagall* Progreſſion of the third, participating iuſtly with his *Authenticall* in the finall Notes. To whom there befall foure beginnings, *viz. C.D.F.* and *a,* ſaith *Franchinus* in the 13. chapter of his *Practick;* and *Guido* in his doctrinall Dialogue. The chiefe forme of it is this :

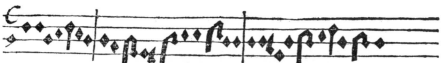

Capitale Sexti   Veni electa   mea.   Diligebat   eam.

The tuning of the leſſer Pſalmes out of *alamire,* and greater out of *Ffaut,* is this :

[43]

Laudate pueri dom. laudate nomen do. Me. dom. Da. Magnificat anima mea dom.

The Melodie of the Verses in the answeres of the Sixt Tone.

The Melody in the beginnings of the Verses of the Sixt Tone.

Of the Seuenth Tone.

THE Seuenth *Tone* is a Rule determining the *Authenticke* of the fourth sort. Or it is the *authenticall* Progression of the Fourth. It hath his end in *Gsolreut* regular only. To this belongs fiue beginnings, *viz. G. a. ♮. c. & d.* The chiefe forme of it, is this:

Capitale septimi.   Exortum   est.   Clamauerunt.

The tuning of the lesser Psalmes out of *Dlasolre*, and of the greater out of *b fa ♮ mi*, is thus:

[44]

Laudate pueri dom. laudate nomen dom. Memento do. Da. Magnificat anima mea dom.

The Melodie of the Verses in the answeres of the Seuenth Tone.

The Melodie in the beginnings of the Verses of the Seuenth Tone.

of

Of the Eight Tone.

THE Eight *Tone* is a Rule determining the *plagall* of the fourth ſort. Or it is the *plagall* Progreſſion of the fourth, poſſeſſing the ſame end that his *Authenticke* doth. The beginnings of it are *D. F. G. a.* and *c*. The chiefe forme of it, is this following :

Capitale octaui.   Dum ortus.   Iuſti confitebuntur.

The tuning of the leſſer Pſalmes out of *Cſolfaut*, and of the greater out of *Gſolreut*, is thus :

Laudate pueri dominū,   laudate nomé do. Memento do. Da. Magnificat anima mea dom.

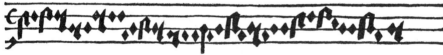

The Melodie of the verſes in the anſweres of the Eight Tone.

The Melodie in the beginnings of the verſes of the Eight Tone.

Of the ſtrange Tone.

THere is another *Tone*, which many call the *Peregrine*, or ſtrange *Tone*, not that it is of ſtrange Notes, but that it is very ſeldome vſed in our Harmony. For his Tenor is not ſung to any but to one *Antiphone, Nos qui viuimus, &c* and to two Pſalmes, *In exitu &c.* and *Benedicite.* His end is in the finall Note of the Seuenth *Tone*, as *Franchinus* demonſtrates it. The Tenour of it followeth :

Peregrinus tonus. In exitu Iſrael   de Ægy domus Iacob de pop. barbaro.

That diuers men are delighted with diuers Moodes.

Very mans palate is not delighted with the same meate (as *Pon.* writes in the 16.ch. of his Musick.)but some delight in sharp, some in sweet meates: neither are all mens eares delighted with the same sounds : for some are delighted with the crabbed & courtly wandring of the first *Tone*. Others do affect the hoarse grauitie of the second: others take pleasure in the seuere, & as it were disdainful stalking of the third: others are drawn with the flatring sound of the fourth: others are moued with the modest wantonnes of the fift: others are led with the lamenting voyce of the sixt: others do willingly heare the warlike leapings of the seuenth: others do loue the decent, & as it were, matronall carriage of the eight. Neither is it maruell(saith *Guido* in the 13.cha. of his *Mic*.)if the hearing be delighted with the variety of sounds, seeing that the sight, is pleased with the variety of colours, the smelling power, with the variety of odours, & the taste, with diuersity of meats. Wherfore let a Musitian diligently obserue that he dispose his song in that *Tone*, wherein he knows his auditors are most delighted. As if he will compose a song at the request of yong men, let it be youthfull and frolicke; If at the request of old men, let it be testy, and full of seuerenes. For as a writer of Comedies, if he giue the part of a yong man vnto an old man, or the part of of a wanton fellow to a couetous person, is laughed to scorne: so is a singer if he bring in a dauncing merry moode, when occasion requires sadnes, or a sad one, when it requires mirth. Now by what means that may be performed, the property of the *Moodes* declareth. Because(as *Cassiodorus* writes in an Epistle to *Boëtius*, & *Cælius* repeats it in *antiq.lect.lib.5.cap.*22.)The Darian *Moode* is the bestower of wisedome, and causer of chastity. The *Phrygian* causeth wars, and enflameth fury. The *Eolian* doth appease the tempests of the minde, and when it hath appeased them, luls them asleepe. The *Lydian* doth sharpen the wit of the dull, & doth make them that are burdened with earthly desires, to desire heauëly things, an excellët worker of good things. Yet doth *Plato lib.3. de Rep.*much reprehend the *Lydian*, both because it is mournful, and also because it is womanish. But he alloweth of the *Dorian*, both because it is manly, & also doth delight valiant men, & is a discouerer of warlike matters. But our men of a more refined time do vse somtime the *Dorian*; somtime the *Phrygian*; sometime the *Lydian*; sometime other *Moodes*. because they iudge, that according to diuers occasions they are to choose diuers *Moodes*. And that not without cause: for euery habit of the mind is gouerned by songs, (as *Macrob.* writeth)for songs make men sleepy, and wakefull, carefull, & merrie, angry, & mercifull, songs do heale diseases, & produce diuers wonderful effects (as saith *Fran. Petrac.*) mouing some to vain mirth, some to a deuout & holy ioy, yea ofttimes to godly teares. Of al which I had rather be silent, than to determine any thing rashly: least I do burthen the wits of children with vnprofitable & vnnecessary precepts. Because who so in expounding any thing doth poure on more than is needful, increaseth the darknesse, and maketh not the mist thinner, as *Macrobius* saith in the second booke vpon the dreame of *Scipio*. Therfore let learners study those few precepts, because they are necessary for the vnderstanding of that which followes.

Here endeth the first Booke.

47]

TO THE VVORTHY HIS

kinde friend *George Brachius*, a moſt ſkilfull Muſitian, and chiefe Doctor of the Duke of *Wittenberg* his Chappell: *Andræas Ornithoparchus* of *Meyning*, wiſheth health.

Hen I had throughly ruminated of that ſaying of Plato, *That we were not made for our ſelues, but to doe good to our Countrey, and friends, I was euen out of heart) my moſt reſpected friend) euen as if my powers had fayled me, and as one ſtroken with amazement. And as that firſt Monarch of the Romane Empire, when he firſt ſaw* Alexanders *ſtatue at* Gades, *lamented for that he himſelfe had done nothing worthy the remembrance: euen ſo I, becauſe I haue done no ſuch thing, did euen lament; conſidering that beauty, pleaſures, age, health, and delicacies doe fade away,* Sed famam extendere factis, hoc virtutis opus. *Wherefore after many harty ſighes, taking heart againe (though I were toſſed with many flouds of Cares, many guſts of aduerſities, and many ſtormes of diuers perturbations) yet began I to thinke what I ſhould leaue to poſteritie for witneſſe that I had liued. Now my mind being turned hether and thither, in the end I choſe the learning of Harmony; both becauſe it is fit for morall education, and alſo becauſe it is the ſeruant of Gods praiſe. For amongſt all Scholler-like Arts, (which they commonly call Liberall) none is more morall, more pleaſant, more diuine, than Muſicke. Whereof although there be many Profeſſors, yet be there very few writers (I know not whether it grow out of hatred to the Art, or their owne ſlothfulneſſe) that haue deliuered the Art in a good forme. Hence is it, that excepting thoſe which are, or haue been in the Chappels of Princes, there are none, or very very few true Muſitians. Wherupon the Art it ſelf doth grow into contempt, being hidden like a Candle vnder a buſhel, the praiſing of the almighty Creator of all things decreaſeth, and the number of thoſe which ſeeke the ouerthrow of this Art, doth dayly increaſe throughout all Germany. By this occaſion ſtirred vp, & further relying vpon your kindnes, moſt worthy Sir, (a great teſtimony wherof you gaue me, when I came fro the Vniuerſity of* Tubyng, & *turned in at your pleaſāt (indeed moſt pleaſant houſe) which you haue of your Princes gift) I turned my pen to the writing of Menſural Muſick, hauing before writtē of Plain-Song. And what flowers ſoeuer other mens volumes had in them, like a Bee I ſucked them out, and made this ſecond Book the hiue to lay them vp in. Now as I haue dedicated it in your name, ſo doe I ſubiect it to your cenſure, that you may both mend thoſe faults you find in it, and detect it from the barking of thoſe who doe commonly defame all good men. For hauing a fit iudge of theſe things which I write, I doe fitly ſubmit my ſelfe to his Cenſure; euen his whom alreadie both my owne experience hath found, and all Sueuia doth acknowledge, and all high Germanie doth honour, for a godly, vpright, and learned man. Farewell, (moſt learned friend) and defend thy* Andræas *from the tooth of Enuie.*

M   THE

THE SECOND BOOKE [48]
of *Ornithoparchus* his Muficke: wherein are
contained the Rudiments of Menfurall Song.

THE FIRST CHAPTER.

Of the Profit and Praife of this Art.

Oêtius that Romane, (whofe wit in Muficke no man euer mended; nay, neuer attained to, in the firft Chapter of his Muficke) writes, That there is fuch efficacie in Harmonicall Confents, as a man though he would, cannot want them. For Muficke driueth away thofe cares which driue away fleepe, ftilleth crying children, mitigateth the paine of thofe which labour, refrefheth wearied bodies, reformeth appaffionate minds. And euery liuing foule is fo ouercome with Muficall founds; that not onely they which are of the gallanter fort (as faith *Macrobius*) but euen all barbarous Nations doe vfe Songs, either fuch as ftirre them vp to an ardent embracing of vertue; or doe melt them in vnworthy pleafures: and fo are they poffeffed with the fweetneffe of Harmony, that by Muficke the *Alarum* to warre is giuen, by Muficke the Retraite is founded, as if the Note did both ftirre vp, and after allay that vertue of fortitude. Now of the two, that Muficke which we call Menfurall, doth fpecially performe thefe effects. For this (as *Ifidorus* faith) ftirreth vp not onely men, but alfo beafts, ferpents, birds, and Dolphins with the fweetneffe of the harmony. By this did *Arion* preferue himfelfe in the middle of the fea; by this did *Amphion* the *Dircæan* gather together ftones for building the *Theban* walles. By this did *Timotheus* the *Phrygian* fo enflame *Alexander Magnus*, the Conquerour of the whole world, that he rife from the table where he fat, and called for his armes; and afterwards changing his *Moode* on the Inftrument, did caufe him to put off his armour, and fit downe againe to banquet. By this did *Dauid* the princely Singer, helpe *Saul* the King of Ifrael, when he was vexed with an vncleane Spirit; by this, not onely the great God, the maker of all things, but alfo the furies of the *Stygian* God are delighted, appeafed, and mitigated. For this is the Lady and Miftreffe of all other Arts; which can delight both thofe that be in *Plutoes* iurifdiction, and thofe that abode in *Neptunes* fields; and thofe that liue in *Iupiters* eternally-lightfome Manfions. This Art onely, leauing the earth, flyeth vp before the

the tribunall feat of the higheſt Iudge; where together with the Inſtruments of the Saints it foundeth, where the Angels and Archangels doe inceſſantly ſing Hymnes to God, where the Cherubins, and Seraphins, cry with a continuall voyce,*Holy,holy,holy*.Beſides,no Art without Muſicke can be perfect : wherefore *Pythagoras* appointed his Schollers they ſhould both when they went to reſt, and when they awaked vſe Melodies. Beſides, Muſicke doth gouerne and ſharpen the manners and faſhions of men.For euen *Nero* whilſt he gaue himſelfe to Muſicke, was moſt gentle, as *Seneca* witneſſeth : but when hee leauing of Muſicke, and ſet his minde on the Diabolicall Art of Nicromancie, then firſt began that fierce crueltie of his;then was he changed from a Lambe to a Wolfe,and out of a moſt milde prince transformed into a moſt ſauage beaſt.But leaſt I digreſſe too farre, and leaſt we proceede from vnknowne beginnings, Iwill briefly ſet downe what this Muſicke is.Therefore *Menſurall Muſicke* is a knowledge of making Songs by figures,which are in forme differing,and hauing the quantity of *Moode,time,* and *Prolation*:Or it is an Art,whoſe Harmony is effected by the variety of figures and voyces.

[49]

THE SECOND CHAPTER.

Of the Figures.

 Herefore a *Figure* is a certaine ſigne which repreſents a voyce, and ſilence. A Voyce, (I ſay) becauſe of the kindes of Notes which are vſed:Silence,becauſe of the Reſts which are of equall value with the Notes,and are meaſured with Artificiall Silence.

Of the number of the Figures.

THe Ancients obſerued onely fiue *Figures*, as principall Figures, and ſuch as receiue the quantitie of the three Degrees of Muſicke: Out of which after ages haue drawne out others for quickneſſe ſake, according to that ſaying of *Ouid* :

         Ex alijs alias reparat natura figuras.

The bodies of the *Figures* are of the forme following.

A *Large* is a figure,whoſe length is thriſe as much as his breadth, hauing on the part toward your right hand a ſmall tayle, bending vpward,or downeward.

A *Long* is a Figure,whoſe length is twiſe as much as his breadth,hauing ſuch a tayle as the *Large* hath.

A *Breefe* is a Figure,which hath a body foure-ſquare,and wants a tayle.

A *Sembreefe* is a Figure,which is round in forme of an egge,or(as *Franchinus* ſayeth) Triangular.

A *Minime* is a Figure like a *Sembreefe*,hauing a tayle, aſcending or deſcending.

A *Crochet*, is a Figure like a *Minime* in colour varying.

A *Quauer* is a figure like a *Crochet*, hauing a daſh to the right hand-ward.

A *Semiquauer* is a figure like a *Quauer* which hath two daſhes, and therby is diſtinguiſhed from it, as thus:

The Eight Figu-
-rall bodies.
{
Large.
Long.
Breefe.
Semibreefe.
}

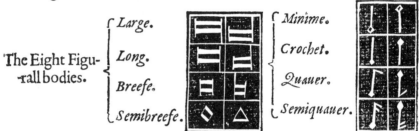

{
Minime.
Crochet.
Quauer.
Semiquauer.
}

There is a certaine Figure, in ſhape like a *Minime*, but ioyned with the number of Three, which is called *Seſquialterata*, becauſe three are ſung for two.   [50]

Beſides, a Figure which hath two tayles, is as if it had none, becauſe one doth hinder another.

THE THIRD CHAPTER.

Of Ligatures.

Herefore a *Ligature* (as *Gaff*. writes in the fift chap. of his ſecond Booke) is the conioyning of ſimple Figures by fit ſtrokes. Or (according to the ſtrokes vpward or downward) it is the dependence of the principall figures in ſtraightneſſe, or crookedneſſe.

Generall Rules for the Ligatures.

First, There are foure ligable Notes, that is a *Large*, a *Long*, a *Breefe*, and a *Semibreefe*.

2 Euery ligable Note, except a *Large*, may be figured with a two-fold body, a ſquare body, and a crooked.

3 Euery ligable Note is to be iudged according to the aſcenſion and deſcenſion, either of it ſelfe, or of the Note following.

4 Euery ligable Note is either beginning, middle, or finall.

5 The Accidents of ſimple Notes, ſay for example, *alteration*, *imperfection*, and the like (as *Franchinus* witneſſeth) are alſo the Accidents of the bounden Notes.

Rules for the beginning Notes.

First, Euery Beginning (whether ſtraight, or crooked) wanting a tayle, when the ſecond Note deſcends, is a *Long*.

2 Euery Beginning Note without a tayle, if the ſecond Note aſcend, is a *Breefe*.

3 Euery Beginning Note hauing a taile downe-ward on the left ſide of it, is a *Breefe*.

4 Euery

4 Euery Initiall, howfoeuer fashioned, hauing a taile on the left fide vp-ward, is a *Semibreefe*, together with the Note next following; fo that you need not care whether it afcend, or difcend.

Rules for the middle Ligatures.

Irft, Euery Note betwixt the firft and the laft, is called middle.

2 Euery middle Note howfoeuer fhaped, or placed, is a *Breefe.*

3 A *Long* may begin and end a *Ligature*, but can neuer be in the middle of it.

4 A *Breefe* may be in the beginning, middle, and end of a *Ligature* very fitly.

5 A *Semibreefe* may be in the beginning, middle, and end of a *Ligature*: fo that it haue a taile in the left part vpward.

Rules for the finall Ligatures.

Irft, Euery laft Note that is ftraight, and defcends, is a *Long.*

2 Euery Finall Note that is ftraight, and afcending, is a *Breefe.*

3 Euery crooked Finall whether it afcend or defcend, is a *Breefe.*

4 A *Large* wherefoeuer it is fet, is alwaies a *Large.*

The Examples of thefe Rules are in the following *Tenor* fet out.

Tenor Exercife of Ligatures.

Bafe Exercife.

Of Ligatures.

THE FOVRTH CHAPTER.

Of Moode, Time, and Prolation.

He degrees of Mufick, by which we know the value of the principal figures, are three: to wit, *Mood, Time,* and *Prolation.* Neither doth any of them deale vpon all Notes, but each only with certaine

N   Notes,

Notes that belong to each. As *Moode* dealeth with *Largs*, and *Longs*; *Time*, with *Breefes*; *Prolation*, with *Semibreefes*.

A *Moode* (as *Franchinus* faith in the fecond Booke, *cap.* 7. of his *Pract:*) is the meafure of *Longs* in *Largs*, or of *Breefes* in *Longs*. Or it is the beginning of the quantitie of *Largs* and *Longs*, meafuring them either by the number of two or the number of three. For euery Figure is meafured by a double value.

[52]

To wit, by the number of { Two, Three, } *and fo is called* { Perfect, Imperfect; } *becaufe we make 3. perfect, and limit the imperfect by 2.*

Of the Diuifion of Moode.

Moode (as it is here taken) is two-fold; to wit, The greater, which is in the *Largs* and *Longs*, and the leffer, which is in the *Longs* and *Breefes*. And each of thefe is diuided into the perfect and imperfect.

Of the greater Moode.

The greater perfect *Moode* is, when a *Larg* contains in it three *Longs*: or it is the meafuring of three *Longs* in one *Larg*. The figne hereof is a perfect circle accompanied with the number of three, thus; O3. The greater imperfect is a *Larg*, comprehending in it two *Longs*: which is knowne by an imperfect circle, ioyned to the number of three, thus; C3.

Of the leffer Moode.

The leffer perfect *Mood* is a *Long* hauing in it three *Breefes*. Or it is the meafuring of three *Breefes* in one *Long*, whofe figne is a perfect Circle, accompanied with the number of 2, thus; O2. But the leffer imperfect, is a *Long* which is to be meafured onely with two *Breefes*. The figne of this is the abfence of the number of 2. Or a *Semicircle* ioyned to a number of 2. thus; C2. O. C. as followeth:

Of Time.

Time is a *Breefe* which contains in it two or three *Semibreefes*. Or it is the meafuring of two or three *Semibreefes* in one *Breefe*. And it is two-fold, to wit, perfect: and this is a *Breefe* meafured with three *Semibreefes*. Whofe figne is the number of three ioyned with a Circle or a Semicircle, or a perfect Circle fet without a number, thus; O3. C3. O. The imperfect is, wherein a *Breefe* is meafured onely by two *Semibreefes*. Which is knowne by the number of two ioyned with a perfect Circle, or a Semicircle, or a Semicircle without a number, thus; O2. C2.

[53]

O

Of Prolation.

WHerefore *Prolation* is the effentiall quantitie of *Semibreefes* : or it is the fetting of two or three *Minims* againft one *Semibreefe*. And it is twofold, to wit the greater, (which is a *Semibreefe* meafured by three *Minims*, or the comprehending of three *Minims* in one *Semibreefe*, whofe figne is a point inclofed in a figne thus, ⊙.℃) The leffer *Prolation* is a *Semibreefe* meafured with two *Minims* onely, whofe figne is the abfence of a pricke. For *Franchinus* faith, They carry with them the imperfecting of the figure, when the fignes are wanting, thus :

Time perfect.   Imperf. time.   Greater Prol.   Leffe Prolation.

There was one well feen in this Art, that made this vnderwritten Example of thefe three degrees, reafonable learnedly and compendioufly for the help of yong beginners : which (by his fauour) wee will not thinke vnworthy to fet downe here.

The Tenor, in the leffer   The Defcant, in the greater Prolation.
   Moode perfect.

The Bafe, in time perfect.

THE FIFT CHAPTER.

Of the Signes.

THough there be fuch diffention betwixt Mufitians about the Signes, fuch confufion of rules and examples, that euen to a perfect Mufitian they feeme to breed doubts : fo that *Plutarch* (a man furnifhed with all learning) faith in that Booke, which hee wrote of Muficke: In our time, the forme of difference hath fo much increafed, and fo farre varied from the Cuftome of our Auunceftors, that there is no mention, no precept, no certaintie of Art left. And alfo though wee be not to make a definitiue fentence in doubtfull matters, but rather to hold queftion: yet that yong beginners, which are defirous to learne this Art, may not be either difcouraged from proceeding, or miffed, leauing thofe things

N 2   which

which more vnuſuall, wee will briefly ſhew thoſe things which are in vſe a-
mongſt thoſe Muſitians, who now are in credite : by ſeeking out that doubt
of the circle and number, which was among the *Theoricks*. Therefore a ſigne
is, a certaine figure ſet before a Song, which ſheweth the *Moode*, *Time*, and
Prolation.

Of the Diuiſions of Signes.

OF Signes ſome be principall, and ſome leſſe principall : The principall
are thoſe, which are fit for the vnderſtanding of *Moode*, *Time*, and *Prolation*. And they are two-fold, to wit, *Extrinſecall*, and *Intrinſecall* : *Extrinſecall*
are thoſe called, which doe outwardly preſent themſelues, and ſhew the degrees of Muſicke, as *Number*, a *Circle*, and a *Point*.

Rules for the Extrinſecall Signes.

FIrſt, A Circle ſet alone by it ſelfe ſheweth time : if it be perfeƈt it ſhewes
perfeƈt time, if imperfeƈt, imperfeƈt time. VVhen it is ioyned to a number, it ſignifies the *Moode*.

2 A *Circle* accompanied with the number of 3. doth repreſent the greater *Moode*, but ioyned with a number of 2. the leſſer.

3 Whereſoeuer is the greater *Mood*, there is the leſſe, but not contrarily.

4 The number of three ioyned to a Circle, is a ſigne of the perfeƈt time:
but the number of two, of the imperfeƈt.

5 A point incloſed in a ſigne of time noteth the greater *Prolation*, thus:

Of Signes,
ſome be

$$O_3, C_3$$ of the greater *Moode* $\begin{cases}Perfeƈt\\Imperfeƈt\end{cases}$ of the perfeƈt time.

$$O_2, C_2$$ of the leſſer *Moode* $\begin{cases}Perfeƈt\\Imperfeƈt\end{cases}$ the time imperfeƈt.

$$O, C$$ the greater *Prolation* $\begin{cases}Perfeƈt\\Imperfeƈt\end{cases}$ Time.

$$O, C$$ Time $\begin{cases}Perfeƈt\\Imperfeƈt\end{cases}$ in the leſſer *Prolation*.

But when out of the mingling of three principall Signes, to wit; of the
number, *circle*, and *point*, there be diuers ſignes made, that you may the eaſi-
lier haue the knowledge of them, and euery figure may haue his value, I
thought good in this forme following to ſet downe a Table, by which you
might at firſt ſight iudg of the value of any figure, thogh placed in any ſigne.

[55

A

A Resolutorie Table, shewing the value of the Signes, by the beholding of euery figure.

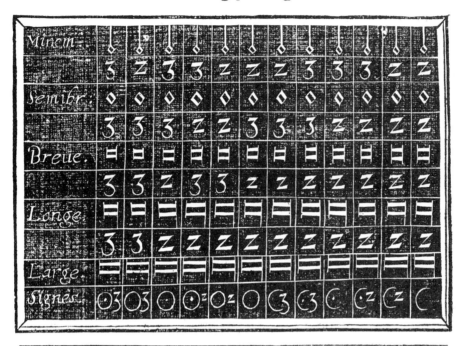

Of the Intrinsecall Signes.

THe *Intrinsecall* signes are those, by which the perfection of Musicall degrees in the figures is shewed, without the adioyning of any of the *Extrinsecall* Signes. Of these there are three, to wit;

1 The inuention of a rest of three times. For when in a Song, there is found a Rest which toucheth three spaces, it signifies the lesse perfect *Moode*. If it touch two, it sheweth the greater perfect. For saith *Franchinus*, It is not vnfit, that two Rests of three Times be adioyned to the greater *Moode*, if one be adioyned to the lesser.

[56]

2 The blacking of the Notes. For as oft as you find three *Longs* coloured, the lesser perfect *Mood* is signified. When three *Breefes*, the perfect time. When three coloured *Semibreefes*, the greater Prolation.

3 The doubling of certaine Rests. For as oft as two *Semibreefe* Rests are placed with a *Semibreefe*, the perfect Time is signified. So by two *Minims* with a *Minime* Note, the greater Prolation, thus;

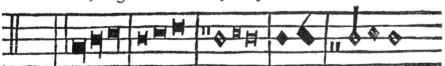

The greater   The lesser   *Time perfect.*   The greater   Prolation.
Moode.   Moode.

O

Of

Of the leſſe principall Signes.

THe Signes leſſe principall are thoſe, which are not neceſſary for the knowledge of *Moode,Time,*and *Prolation.*And theſe are diuers, as you may plainely ſee in the quadrate following.

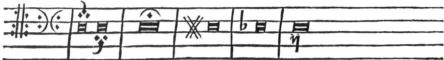

Repetition.   Conueni-   Concordance Aſpiration.b Moll.Dealbation.
          ence.   Cardinalis.

THE SIXT CHAPTER.
Of Tact.

Herefore *Tact* is a ſucceſſiue motion in ſinging, directing the e-qualitie of the meaſure:Or it is a certaine motion, made by the hand of the chiefe ſinger,according to the nature of the marks, which directs a Song according to Meaſure.

Of the Diuiſion of Tact.

TAct is three-fold, the greater, the leſſer, and the proportionate. The greater is a Meaſure made by a ſlow,and as it were reciprocall motion. The writers call this *Tact* the whole,or totall *Tact*.And,becauſe it is the true *Tact* of all Songs, it comprehends in his motion a *Semibreefe* not dimini-ſhed : or a *Breefe* diminiſhed in a duple.

The leſſer *Tact*,is the halfe of the greater,which they call a *Semitact*. Be-cauſe it meaſures by it motion a *Semibreefe*, diminiſhed in a duple : this is allowed of onely by the vnlearned.

The Proportionate is that, whereby three *Semibreefes* are vttered againſt one,(as in a Triple)or againſt two,as in a *Sefquialtera*.Of this we ſhall ſpeake more at large in the Chapter of proportions.

A Rule for Tact.

A *Semibreefe* in all Signes(excepting the Signes of Diminution, augmen-tation,and proportions)is meaſured by a whole *Tact*,as in the example following appeareth: [57

⊙3	Z1	9	3	1					
O3	Z1	9	3	1	𝄽				
C3	1Z	6	3	1	𝄽				
⊙z	1Z	6	z	1					
⊙	1Z	6	3	1		4.or to one Stroake.	8.to one Stroake.	16.to one Stroake.	The Table of Tact reſolued.
ℂ	8	4	z	1					
O	1Z	6	3	1	𝄽				
C	8	4	z	1	𝄽				
				◇	↓	↓	↓	↓	

THE SEVENTH CHAPTER.

Of Augmentation.

BEcause in the Chapter before going, we haue made mention of *Augmentation* and *Diminution*, therefore leaſt we proceed from vnknowne things, we will ſhew what each is.

Therefore *Augmentation* is the making of more Notes in a Song: or it is the excrement of ſome Note. For in it is put a *Minime* for a *Semibreeſe*; a *Semibreeſe* for a *Breeſe*; a *Breeſe* for a *Long*.

By what ſignes you ſhall know Augmentation.

OF *Augmentation* there be 3.Signes. The firſt is, the fewnes of the Notes in one part of the Song.

The ſecond is, the adioyning of the *Canon*, by ſaying, Let a *Breeſe* be a *Large*, let a *Semibreeſe* be a *Long*, let a *Minime* be a *Breeſe*. Or let it increaſe in *Duplo, Triplo, vel hexagio, &c.*

[58]

The third is, a point in the Signe of time, found onely about one part of the Song : One I ſay, for if it be found about all; it is not a ſigne of *Augmentation*, but of the greater *Prolation*,

Rules of the Augmention.

FIrſt, *Augmentation* is the contradiction of *Diminution*.

2 In *Augmentation* the *Minime* figure is meaſured with an whole *Tact*.

3 Betwixt *Prolation* and *Augmentation*, there is this difference, *Augmention* ſounds one *Minime* to a *Tact* ; *Prolation* ſounds three, that is a perfect *ſemibreeſe* : which then is meaſured with a proportionate *Tact*.

4 The Reſts are diminiſhed and augmented, as well as the Notes.

5 *Augmentation* muſt ſeldome be, but in the Tenor.

6 A *Large* is not augmented, becauſe it hath none greater than it ſelfe, whoſe value it may aſſume. Therefore they are in an errour, which ſay there are 81.*Tacts* in a *Large* which is ſet vnder ſuch a ſigne ⊙3 : becauſe a *Large* neither growes to aboue 27.*Tacts*, nor admitteth any thing greater than it ſelfe, becauſe it is the greateſt, than which there is nothing greater. Beſides as in nature, ſo in Art it is in vaine to place a nothing : therefore ſhould a *Large* be in vaine augmented, becauſe no Song was euer found of ſo long time, that 81.*Tacts* might be Song in an Vniſon.

7 *Augmentation* comprehends vnder it ſelfe all the kinds of Notes excepting a *Large*, for which point marke the example following :

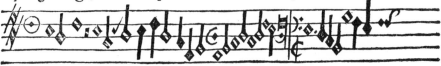

Augmentation.   The greater   The *Bariton or Baſe,*
                     Prolation.

O 2   *vnder*

vnder the signe of Semiditie.   *The greater Prolation.*

What a Canon is.

BEing we haue made mention of a *Canon*, least I hold the learner in a mammering, I will shew what a *Canon* is.

A *Canon* therefore is an imaginarie rule, drawing that part of the Song which is not set downe out of that part, which is set downe. Or it is a Rule, which doth wittily discouer the secrets of a Song. Now we vse *Canons*, either to shew Art, or to make shorter worke, or to try others cunning, thus;

[59]

THE EIGHT CHAPTER.

Of Diminution.

Iminution, which is more truely called *syncopation*, is the varying of Notes of the first quantity, as writeth *Fran. li. 2. Pr. 14*. Or it is a certain cutting off of the measure. For as in Grammer we say *sæcla* for *sæcula*, so in Musicke we do curtall the naturall and essentiall measure of the Notes by this *syncopation*. Therefore generally it shall be called *syncopation*, not *Diminution*, because it is a kind of *syncopation*.

Of the kindes of Syncopations.

OF this there be two kindes; *Semiditie*, and *Diminution*. *Semiditie* is the middle of the chiefe measure of Notes, which can be placed onely in an imperfect time, which hath these Signes, O2. C2. ₵. Є. ₵.

For in all these, the halfe of the measure is put off by the dash properly, and by the number, for so much as it hath of Duple proportion. Therefore *Erasmus Lapicida* doth well in placing one number vnder another in all these signes, thus; O$\frac{2}{1}$ C$\frac{2}{1}$.

For proportion is the relation of two quantities, not of one, as elsewhere we will more largely shew.

Of Diminution.

Iminution (as the Ancients thought) is the taking away of the third part from the measure. But the opinion of the Modernes, is more true and laudable, which make no difference betwixt *Diminution* and *Semiditie*, as *Ioan: Tincteris*, of all that euer excelled in Musicke the most excellent writer,

writer, and *Franchinus Gafferus lib.2.cap.14.* haue pofitiuely fet downe.

Therefore *Diminution* is the cutting off of the halfe part in the meafure, nothing differing from *femiditie*, but that it is found in perfect Signes, and in figures which are to be meafured by the number of 3. Wherefore I cannot but fcorne certaine Componifts (for fo they will be called) though indeed they be the Monfters of Muficke) who though they know not fo much as the firft Elements of the Art, yet proclaime themfelues, The *Mufitians* of *Mufitians*, being ignorant in all things, yet bragging of all things, and doe (by their foolifh toyes which contrarie to the maieftie of the Art, they haue gotten an habite of, rather by vfe, than wit) difgrace, corrupt, and debafe this Art, which was in many ages before honoured, and vfed by many moft learned, (and to vfe *Quintitians* words) moft wife men: vfing any Signes at their pleafure, neither reckoning of value, nor meafure, feeking rather to pleafe the eares of the foolifh with the fweetneffe of the Ditty, than to fatisfie the iudgement of the learned with the maieftie of the Art. Such a one know I, that is now hired to be Organift in the Caftle at *Prage*, who though he know not (that I may conceale his greater faults) how to diftinguifh a perfect time from an imperfect, yet giues out publikely, that he is writing the very depth of Mufick: and is not afhamed to fay, that *Franchinus* (a moft famous writer, one whom he neuer fo much as tafted of) is not worth the reading, but fit to be fcoffed at, & fcorned by him. Foolifh bragging, ridiculous rafhnes, groffe madnes, which therfore only doth fnarle at the learned, becaufe it knows not the means how to emulate it. I pray God, the Wolfe may fal into the Toiles, and hereafter commit no more fuch outrage; nor like the Crow brag of borrowed feathers. For he muft needs be counted a Dotard, that prefcribes that to others, the Elements whereof himfelfe neuer yet faw. As *Phormio* the Greeke Orator (in *Tullies* fecond Booke *de Orat.*) who hauing before *Antiochus* the King of *Afia*, (in the prefence of *Haniball*) made a long Oration of the dutie of a Generall, when as hee himfelfe had neuer feene Campe, nor armes, and had made all the reft to admire him, in the end *Haniball* being afked, what his iudgement was of this Philofopher, his anfwere was, That hee had feene many doting old men, but neuer any man that doted more, than *Phormio*. Now come I to the matter, and leaue thefe vnlearned ridiculous *Phormio's*, many whereof (the more is the fhame) haue violently inuaded the art of *Mufick*, as thofe which are not compounders of Harmonies, but rather corruptors, children of the furies, rather than of the Mufes, not worthy of the leaft grace I may doe them. For their Songs are ridiculous, not grounded on the Principles of the Art, though perhaps true inough. For the Artift doth not grace the Art, but the Art graceth the Artift. Therefore a Componift doth not grace Muficke, but contrarily: for there be that can make true Songs not by Art, but by Cuftome, as hauing happily liued amongft fingers all their life-time: yet do they not vnderftand what they haue made, knowing that fuch a thing is, but not what it is. To whom the word our Sauiour vfed on the Croffe, may be well vfed; *Father pardon them, they know **not** what*

P

they

[60]

*they doe.*Wherfore allow of no Componists,but thofe,who are by Art worthy to be allowed of:now fuch are *Ioan.Okeken,Ioan: Tinctoris,Loyfet,Verbonet,Alex: Agricola,Iacobus Obrecht,Iofquin,Petrus de Larue,Hen:Ifaack,Hen: Finck, Ant: Brummel, Mat: Pipilare, Geor: Brack, Erafmus Lapicida, Cafpar Czeys,Conradus Reyn,* and the like : whofe Compofitions one may fee doe flow from the very fountaine of Art.But leaft by laughing at thefe fellowes we grow angry,and by being angry grow to hate them, let vs euen let them alone,and returne to *Diminution.*

   Whereof we will refolue with *Franchinus* and *Tinctor*,that it taketh not away a third part,as the Ancients thought,(for it is hard finding out that) but one part: for as this figne ₵. is the Duple of this figne C,fo is this ₵ of this O. Wherfore euen approued Componifts doe erre,becaufe they mark not that there is a double Progreffion of meafure in a perfect Circle diuided with a dafh,befides the *Ternarie* number of the figures, becaufe they are of a perfect time : finging one *Semibreefe* to a *Tact*, when they fhould fing 2. For in that figne the Song is fo to be placed,that keeping the perfection of the *Ternarie*, it may receiue the Clofes, and end in a Binarie meafure. For in this Signe ₵. the Notes keepe the fame value, which they haue in this O, but the meafure onely, is to be meafured by the Binarie number,thus :   [61

     A Table for the Tact of Diminution.

Sign					to one ftroake.	4 or. 8. to one ftroake.	16. to one ftroake.	3 2. to one ftroake.
Ø	6	3	Z	X				
Ø	6	3	Z	X				
O:	6	3	1	X				
₵	4	Z	1	X				
C	4	Z	1	X				
₵	4	Z	1	X				

    By what fignes Diminution is marked.

Now *Diminution* is marked by three wayes, to wit : By a *Canon*, by a *Number*,and by a *Dafh*.By a *Canon*,faying; It decreafeth in *Duplo,Triplo*, and *Quadruple*,and fuch like.

   By a *Number*,for euery number adioyned to a Circle,or a Semicircle,befides that which effentially it betokens, doth alfo diminifh according to the naming of his figure.As the number of 2,being placed with a whole Circle befides the time, which it betokens to be imperfect, doth alfo fignifie a duple *Diminution*, the number of three a Triple, the number of foure a Quadruple,and fo forth.

                     By

By a *Dash*, to wit, when by a *Dash*, the signe of Time is diuided, thus; $\oplus$. ¢.$\oplus$.¢.

Rules of Syncopation.

Irst, *Syncopation* belongeth to the measure of Time, not to the figures themselues.

2 *Syncopation* doth respect both the Notes, and the Rests.

3 *Syncopation* doth not take away the value, but the measure of the Notes.

4 The number doth not diminish *Prolation*, because it cannot work vppon the pricke, whilst a Circle doth keepe it.

5 Betwixt *Diminution* and *Semiditie*, there is no difference of *Tact*, or *Measure*, but onely of nature.

6 *Diminution* is the contradiction of *Augmentation*.

7 It is not inconuenient, that to the same Signe there may belong a double *Diminution*, to wit; *virgular* and *numerall*, thus; ¢2.

8 *Virgular Syncopation* is much vsed, *Numerall* seldome, *Canonicall* most seldome: the Example therefore following is of the first, and the second.

[62]

The Rule of Semiditie in Diminution.

Syncopation by number.

THE NINTH CHAPTER.

Of Rests.

Rest (as *Tinctoris* writeth) is the Signe of Silence. Or (as *Gafforus* saith) it is a figure which sheweth the Artificiall leauing off from singing: Or it is a stroke drawne in line and space, which betokens silence. Now *Rests* are placed in songs after three manners, to wit; Essentially, Iudicially, and both wayes. Essentially, when they betoken silence. Iudicially, when they betoken not silence but the perfect *Moode*: and then their place is before the signe of Time. Both wayes, when they represent both.

Rules for the Rests.

Irst, There be as many kinds of *Rests*, as of Notes.

2 The *Rest*, which toucheth all the spaces, is generall, where all the voyces cease together, and is onely to be placed in the end.

P 2   3 The

3 The reft which takes vp three fpaces, is called of the *Moode*, which it betokens, and is to be placed onely in a perfect *Moode*.

4 A *Reft*, which doth conclude two fpaces, is called an imperfect *Long*.

5 A *Reft*, which takes vp but one fpace, is a *Breefe* betokening one Time · whether perfect or imperfect.

6 A *Reft*, defcending from the line to the middle of the fpace, is called a *Semibreefe*.

7 A *Reft*, afcending from the line to the middle of the fpace, betokens a *Minime*, or a figh.

8 A *Reft*, like a figh, being forked to the right hand-ward, betokens a *Crochet*.

9 The *Refts* of the two laft figures, becaufe of their too much fwiftneffe, are not in vfe among Mufitians.

[63]

Refts *Larg.* *Long.* *Breefe.* *Semi-* *Minim.* *Crochet.*
generall. *breefe.*

THE TENTH CHAPTER.

Of Prickes.

Herefore a *Pricke* is a certaine indiuifible quantity, added to the Notes, either for *Diuifion*, or for *Augmentation*, or for *Certainty* fake. Or it is a certaine Signe leffer than any other accidentally fet either before, or after, or betweene Notes.

Of the Diuifion of a Pricke.

Vt of this Definition, there are collected three kindes of *Prickes*, to wit: That of *Addition*, and that is the *Augmentation* of the figures. Or it is the perfection of imperfect Notes. This is fet in the middle on the right fide, and is found onely in imperfect Signes, and doth augment the Notes to which it is added, the halfe of his owne value, as in the Example following appeareth.

Tenor point of Addition. *The Bafe is the fame.*

Of the Pricke of Diuision.

THe *Pricke* of Diuision is the disioyning of two Notes, neither taking
away nor adding any thing, but distinguishing two Notes by reckoning
the first with the former, & the second with the following Notes, to the end
that the *Ternarie* perfection in Notes may be had. Here the *Pricke* in perfect
degrees, is ioyned not to perfect figures, but to their neere parts, neither is
adioyned to the middle of the side, as that of Addition, but a little higher,
or lower about the middle of the Notes, which it diuides, thus:

[64]

The *Pricke* of *Diuision* in the *Tenor*.   *Also in the Base*.

Of the Pricke of Alteration.

THe *Pricke* of *Alteration*, was obserued more by the Ancients, than the
later Musitians. Yet least it may breed some doubt to the Singer, that
shall light on it by chance, it is not amisse to speake somewhat of it. Therfore
the *Pricke* of *alteration* is the repeating of Notes, which doth accidentally
befall them, not as they are perfect, but as their parts neighboring the perfect. Now is it set neither on the one side, nor vpward, nor downe-ward, but
directly ouer the Note, which it alters, as in this Example appeareth.

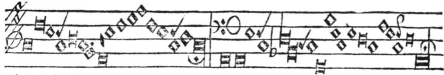

The *Pricke* of *Alteration* in the *Tenor*.   *Also in the Base*.

There are besides these, two other kindes of *Prickes*; to wit, of perfection.
And this is a *Pricke* set after a perfect Note ; neither increasing nor dimini-
shing it, but onely preseruing it from being imperfected by the following
Note. It is set as the *Pricke* of Addition, but differs from it, because it is alwayes, and onely placed about perfect Notes.

There is another *Pricke* of *Transportation*, adioyned to Notes, which it
doth translate to be reckoned with figures remooued further off: and this
doth direct his force not vpon the precedent Notes, but onely vpon the
following ones, thus;

The *Pricke* of perfection or *Transportation* in the *Tenor*.

Q   *Also*

Also in the Base.

THE ELEVENTH CHAPTER. [65]

Of Imperfection.

Herefore *Imperfection* is the degrading of perfect Notes. For to imperfect is to make a perfect Note imperfect. Or it is this, to bring it from his value.

Of two-fold Imperfection.

IMperfection is two-fold : to wit, *Totall*, when precisely the third part of the value is taken from the Notes : as when in perfect time a *Breefe* is imperfected by a *Semibreefe.* Or partiall, when not precisely the third part, but a lesse than that, say a sixt part, or so, is taken from the Notes : as when a long of the imperfect *Moode*, but in the perfect time, where it is valued at two *Breefes*, is imperfected by a *Semibreefe*, in regard of the *Breefe* in it contained : and as a *Breefe* by a *Minime* in the greater *Prolation*.

By what Signes Imperfection is knowne.

OF *Imperfection* there be three Signes, (as writeth *Franchinus li*.2.*Pract. cap*.11.) to wit, numerall *Imperfection*, punctuall *Diuision*, and *fulnesse* of the Notes.

Rules of Imperfection.

FIrst, There is foure Notes which may be imperfected, to wit, a *Larg*, a *Long*, a *Breefe*, a *Semibreefe.*

2 Euery figure, which may be imperfected, is alway to be considered in the number of his perfect quantitie.

3 That which is once imperfect, cannot be more imperfected.

4 Euery figure that may be imperfected, is greater than the imperfecting figure.

5 *Imperfection* is made not onely by the neere parts of the Notes, but also by the remoued parts. As a perfect *Breefe* can be imperfected, not onely by a *Semibreefe*, which is the neere part, but also of two *Minims*, which are remote parts of it.

6 Two neighbouring parts of one perfect figure doe not imperfect it, but onely one : although two remoued ones may doe the same. Wherefore if you finde two *Semibreefe* Rests after a perfect *Breefe*, it shall remaine perfect, vnlesse punctuall Diuision come betweene.

7 Euery

7 Euery leſſe figure being ſuperfluous doth imperfeƈt the greater going before, not the following one : vnleſſe it happen by reaſon of the *Pricke* of *Diuiſion, Perfeƈtion,* or *Tranſportation.*

8 A Note of one ſort comming before his like is not imperfeƈted, wherby euery figure that is to be imperfeƈted, muſt be put before a figure that is greater, or leſſe th an it ſelfe.

9 The greater Note doth not imperfeƈt the leſſe, nor an equall Note an other equall Note.

10 The figure which doth imperfeƈt another figure, takes ſo much from it, as it ſelfe is valued at.

11 A *Reſt* is not imperfeƈted, but doth imperfeƈt.

[66] 12 A *Ligature* doth neuer imperfeƈt, but is imperfeƈted.

13 A *Larg* doth nothing, but ſuffereth onely in *Imperfeƈtion.*

14 A *Minime* doth, and neuer ſuffereth in *Imperfeƈtion.*

15 A *Long, Breeſe,* and *Semibreeſe* doe imperfeƈt, and are imperfeƈted.

16 Euery *Imperfeƈtion* is either before or behinde: Before, as when the imperfeƈting Note doth goe before the Note that is imperfeƈted: Behind, as when it followeth. There be that thinke it is cauſed both wayes in partiall *Imperfeƈtion.*

17 That *Imperfeƈtion,* which is cauſed before and behind, is cauſed not by the neighbouring, but by the remote parts.

18 All *Imperfeƈtion* is cauſed either by the Note, the Reſt, or the colour. By the Note, to wit, when a figure of a leſſer kind is placed before or after a perfeƈt Note, and ſo imperfeƈts it, thus :

Tenor.   Baſe.

By a *Reſt,* to wit, when a *Reſt* of a leſſe kind is found before or after a perfeƈt Note: but the *Reſt* cannot be imperfeƈted, as thus :

Tenor.

Baſe.

Q 2   *Colour.*

By Colour: when in the perfect figures you finde Colour, the Notes are Imperfect ; becaufe their third part is taken away, thus :

Tenor.

Baſſus and his Poſition.

Of Colour.

WHerfore *Colour* in this place is nothing, but the fulnes of the Notes : Or, it is the blacking of the principall figures : the force whereof is fuch, that it takes away the third part of the value from figures placed in their perfect quantitie: and from imperfects fometime it takes away the fourth part, fometimes it makes them of the *Hemiola* proportion. Where-fore I thought good to place here a Table of the perfect figures coloured. VVherein note this, that the voide fpaces doe fhew that that figure, ouer which they are placed is not to be coloured in that figne. But the Sphærical figure (which the learned call the figure of nothing) declares that the figures may be coloured, yet that they haue not the value of one *Tact*.

Colour being in other figures effentiall, induce no accidentall quantity into Notes.

⊙3	18	6	z	o	o
O3	18	6	z	1	
⊙z	8	4	z	o	o
Oz	4	z	1		
⊙	8	4	z	o	o
∅	4	z	1	o	o
O	8	4	z	1	
∅	4	z	1	o	
	▬	▬	◫	◆	▐

Colour is oftentimes found among most of the learnedst, neither to take away nor to adde any thing: but specially, when to remoue *Alteration*, it is placed in the neighbouring parts of perfect figures, thus:

[68]

       Tenor.   *Base.*

Most commonly the *Colour* doth cause a Duple proportion in the imperfect figures, (as *Franchinus* saith. *lib.2. cap.11.*) which *Henry Isaack* in a certaine *Alleluia* of the Apostles, did thus both wittily, and truely dispose.

       Tenor.   *Base.*

THE TVVELFTH CHAPTER.

Of Alteration.

Lteration according to *Ioannes de Muris*, is the doubling of a lesser Note in respect of a greater, or (as *Tinctor* saith) it is the doubling of the proper value. Or it is the repetition of one, and the selfe same Note. And it is called *Alteration, Quasi altera actio,* it is another action, to wit: A secundary singing of a Note, for the perfecting of the number of three.

Rules of Alteration.

Irst, There be foure Notes, which may be altered, (saith *Franchinus lib. 2.cap.13.*) a *Long,* a *Breefe,* a *Semibreefe,* and a *Minime.*

2   *Alteration* doth exclude the *Larg,* and is limitted by a *Minime,* because a *Larg* hath not a greater than it selfe, whose neighbouring part it may be: and the lesse figures are not to be reckoned after the number of three.

3   *Alteration* happens in numbers which be not perfect, but are parts neighbouring to perfect Notes, because a perfect Note in as much as it is a perfect Note is not lyable to *Alteration.*

4   Onely the Notes are altered, not the *Rests.*

5   *Alteration* falleth vpon the second Note, not vpon the first.

6   Euery altered Note containeth it selfe twise.

7   A like Note is not altered before a like Note.

8   *Alteration* onely fals out in perfect degrees.

R   *9 Alteration*

9   *Alteration* comes for want of one Note, when you haue reckoned after the *Ternary* numbring.

10   As oft as two alterable Notes are placed betwixt two imperfectible Notes without a *Pricke* of Diuision : the second is always altered, as the Example following doth shew.

[69]

Altera.   Tenor.   *Altera.*

Base.

11   If a *Rest* together with the figure, to which it is of equall value, be enclosed betwixt 2. perfect notes; thē either the rest goes before the figure, or followes it; if the Rest go before, the figure is altered : if otherwise, there is no place for *Alteration*, because the notes only are altered, & not the Rests. Beside *Alteration* fals alwayes vpon the second, and not vpon the first, thus :

Tenor.

Base.

12   *Alteration* is taken away by the fulnesse of the notes, and by the *Pricke* of Diuision. In *Ligatures* also *Alteration* is kept, as in the following Example is cleere.

Tenor.

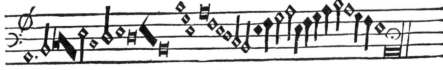

Base.

13   As oft as three alterable Notes are shut within two imperfectible   [70]
                                                       Notes,

Notes, both the imperfectible shal remaine perfect, and none of the alterable Notes is altered: becaufe the *Ternarie* number is euery where perfect.

THE THIRTEENTH CHAPTER.

Of Proportion.

Herefore *Proportion* is the nature of two compared together in
one vniuocall thing. Vniuocall I fay, becaufe in æquiuocals there
is no comparifon: for a ftill and a loud voice are not compared.
Whence is it, that proportion is properly called, when it is
found in thofe things, which are equall and vnequall, like and vnlike. Or according to *Euclide*; it is a certaine difpofition of two quantities how bigge
foeuer, (being of the fame next *Genus*) one to the other. Hence is it that
things continuate and difcreate, although they be contained vnder the
fame *Genus* of quantitie, yet are not compared, becaufe they are remote,
not neere.

Of the Diuifion of Proportion.

P *Roportions* are fome of equality, fome of inequalitie. That of equalitie
is the Relation of two equall quantities. For that is equall, which is neither greater, nor leffe than his equall. That of inequalitie, is the difpofition
of two vnequall quantities. For that is called inequall, which being in Relation with another is either greater or leffer than it.

What Proportion is fit for Mufitians.

B Ecaufe the diffimilitude, and not the fimilitude of voyce doth breede
Harmonie: therefore the Art of Muficke doth onely confider of the
Proportion of inequalitie. This is two-fold; to wit, the *Proportion* of the greater or of the leffe inequalitie The *Proportion* of the greater inequalitie, is the
relation of the greater number to the leffe, as 4. to 2. 6. to 3. The *Proportion*
of the leffer inequalitie is contrarily the comparifon of a leffe number to
greater, as of 2. to 4. of 3. to 6.

Of the 5. kindes of Proportions.

O F the *Proportions* of the greater inequalitie, there be 5. Kindes, to wit;
Multiplex, Super particular, Super partiens, and thofe be fimple: the compounded are the *Multiplex Super particular,* & the *Multiplex Super partiens.*

[71]   To thefe are oppofed 5. other kindes of the leffer Inequalitie (faith *Franchinus*) and hauing the fame names with the Prepofition *Sub,* onely fet before them: as *Submultiplex, &c.*

But feeing that *Multiplex Proportio* hath chiefe force in Muficall Confonances, and next to that the *Super particular,* and the *Super partiens* with the
two following none, we doe therefore abandon the *Super partient* with the

R 2   reft

reſt following, as vnworthy of the Harmonicall Conſort, and doe receiue the two formoſt onely.

Of the Multiplex kinde.

THe *Multiplex Proportio*, is both more excellent, and more ancient than the reſt, as when a greater number being in Relation with a leſſe, doth preciſely comprehend the whole leſſer number more than once, as ſay, twiſe, or thriſe. The kindes of this will be infinite, if you compare each number with an vnitie, as in the following quadrate you may ſee.

2	3	4	5	6	7	8	9	10
1	1	1	1	1	1	1	1	1

Dupla. Trip. Quadru. Quintu. Sextu. Septu. Octup. Nonu. Decu.

To this foreſaid kinde is oppoſed the firſt kinde of the leſſer Inequalitie, called *Submultiplex*. The one of theſe deſtroyeth the other; and this kind, making the ſame Relation of an vnitie to other numbers, doth produce out of it ſelfe the ſame *Species* which a *Multiplex* doth, and *Species* of the ſame names, by adding the Prepoſition *Sub*, and is produced in this manner.

1	1	1	1	1	1	1	1	1
2	3	4	5	6	7	8	9	10

Sub dup. Sub trip. Sub quadr. Sub quintu. ſextu. Sub ſeptu. Sub octu. Sub nonu. Sub decu.

Of the Superparticular Kinde.

SVperparticular, the ſecond kinde of *Proportions* is, when the greater number being compared with the leſſe, doth comprehend it in it ſelfe once, & beſides ſome ſuch part of it. Some ſuch part(I ſay)which being often taken doth make preciſely the whole greater number. Of this kinde the ſorts are innumerable, if you reckon each of the numbers, taking away an vnity, with the next leſſer, in manner following.

[72]

3	4	5	6	7	8	9	10	
2	3	4	5	6	7	8	9	

Sesqui altera. Sesqui tertia. Sesqui quarta. Sesqui quinta. Sesqui ſexta. Sesqui ſeptima. Sesqui octa. Sesqui nona.

The oppoſite to this, is *Sub ſuperparticular*, the ſecond kind of the leſſe Inequalitie : which doth produce the ſame *Species*, which the former doth, with the ſame names, the Prepoſition(*Sub*) being adioyned: if you will compare each of the leſſer numbers(an Vnitie I alwayes except)with the greater neighbouring, as here followeth the manner.

Subſeſ-

2	3	4	5	6	7	8	9
3	4	5	6	7	8	9	10

Sub ef-quialte-ra.	subfef-quiter-ta.	subfef-quiquar-ta.	fubfef-quiquin-ta.	fubfef-quifex-ta.	fubfef-quifep-tima.	fubfef-quioc-ta.	fubfef-quino-na.

By what meanes Proportion is made of æqualitie, and confequently one Proportion out of another.

WHen you will make a *Proportion* out of Equalitie, and one proportion out of another, you fhall thus truely worke it by this Rule of *Boëtius*, Difpofing three equall numbers, fay vnities, or any other, let three other be placed vnder them, fo that the firft may be euen with the firft; the fecond with the firft, and the fecond; the third, with the firft; the two feconds, and the third, and you fhall find it a *Duple*, thus :

1	1	1	2	2	2	3	3	3
1	2	4	2	4	8	3	6	12

   Dupla.   *Dupla.*   *Dupla.*

[73]   Now if you wil make *Triples*, placing the *Duplaes*, which you haue made in the higher ranke, let three numbers be placed vnderneath, according to the Tenor of the forefaid Rule, and you haue your defire ; thus:

1	2	4	2	4	8	3	6	12
1	3	9	2	6	18	3	9	27

   Tripla.   *Tripla.*   *Tripla.*

Now if we place thefe *Triples*, which we haue thus found in the vpper ranke, we fhall produce *Quadruples*, by the concordant, and regular oppofition of the numbers vnwritten, of *Quadruplaes, Quintuplaes*; and alfo out of *Quintuplaes, Sextuplaes*, and fo forward infinitely.

1	3	9	1	4	16	1	5	25
1	4	16	1	5	25	1	6	36

   Quadrupla.   *Quintupla.*   *Sextupla.*

And if out of *Duplaes*, you will create *Sefquialteraes*, inuerting the numbers of the *Duplaes*, fo that the greater may be firft, and the leffer fucceed in a naturall order: let there be vnder placed three other numbers, as often as the faid Rule requireth, and you haue that, as followeth.

S

                                              Sefqui-

4	2	1	8	4	2	12	6	3
4	6	9	8	12	18	12	18	21

    Sefquialteræ.   *Sefquialteræ.*   *Sefquialteræ.*

Now as of *Duples* you make *Sefquialteraes*, fo of *Triples* you may make *fefquitertiaes*, and of *Quadruplaes fefquiquartaes*, by conuerting the numbers, as was faid of *fefquialteraes*, and fo you may goe infinitely, in manner following.

9	3	1	16	4	1	25	5	1
9	12	16	16	20	25	25	30	36

    Sefquitertiæ.   *fefquiquartæ.*   *fefquiquintæ.*

[74]

Out of what Proportions Muficall Concords are made.

THe *Proportions*, which make Muficall Confonances, are fixe, (as *Boêtius* and *Macrobius* witnefle) three in the *Multiplex* Kind, to wit, the *Dupla, Tripla, Quadrupla*: 3 in the *fuper particular*, to wit, *fefquialtera, fefquitertia*, & *fefquioctaua.* Of which fpecially the allowed Interuals of Muficke are compounded (as faith *Plutarch.*) Where relinquifhing others, wee thought fit to make plaine by fhort precepts and examples thefe only, which confift and are defcribed in Notes. So keeping the naturall order, we will begin with the *Dupla*, becaufe it is both worthyer and betterknowne, than the reft.

Of the Duple Proportion.

DVpla *Proportio*, the firft kind of the *Multiplex*, is when the greater number being in relation with the lefle, doth comprehend it in it felfe twife: as 4. to 2 : 8. to 4 But Mufically, when two Notes are vttered againft one, which is like them both in nature and kinde. The figne of this fome fay is the number of 2 : others (becaufe *Proportion* is a Relation not of one thing, but of 2) affirme that one number ⎰2.4.6.⎱ is to be fet vnder another, thus; And make no doubt but in all ⎱1.2.3.⎰ the reft this order is to be kept.

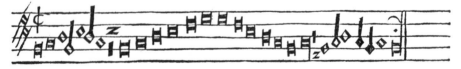

    Tenor Duplæ.

    Baffus duplæ.

I would

I would not haue you ignorant,that the duple *Proportion*,and all the o-
ther of the *Multiplex* kind, are marked by certaine Canons,saying thus,
Decrescit in duplo,in triplo, and so forth. Which thing becaufe it is done
either to increafe mens diligence, or to try their cunning, wee miflike not.
There be that confider the whole *Proportion* in figures, which are turned
to the left hand-ward with fignes,and crookes,saying,that this C.is the duple of this ◯. and this ʄ of ɪ and in Refts that this ꓶ is the duple of this ʃ

I thinke onely vpon this reafon, that *Franchinus praet. lib.2.cap.4* . faith that
the right fide is greater and perfecter than the left: and the left weaker than
the right. Againft which opinion neither my felfe am. For in *Valerius Probus*
a moft learned Gramarian in his interpretation of the Roman letters faith,
that the letter C. which hath the forme of a Semicircle fignifies *Caius* the
man,and being turned, fignifies *Caia* the woman. And *Fabius Quintilianus*
in approouing of *Probus* his opinion faith ; for *Caius* is fhewed by the letter
C.which being turned fignifies a woman:and being that men are more perfect than women,the perfection of the one,is declared by turning the Semicircle to the right hand,& the weakneffe of the other by turning it to the left.
By this occafion the Mufitians thought fit to take away the halfe left fide
from the right, thus; ꟸ ♯ ◗ C ꓶʃ

Rules of Proportions.

FIrft,Euery *Proportion* is either taken away by the comming of his contrary proportion,or is broken by the interpofition of a figne. As by the
comming of a *fubduple*,a *dupla* is taken away,and fo of others.

   2   Euery *Proportion* refpecteth both Refts and Notes.

   3   Euery *Proportion* of the great Inequalitie doth diminifh the Notes
and Refts with his naturall power: but the *Proportion* of the leffe Inequalitie doth increafe them.

   4   *Alteration* and *Imperfection* are onely in thofe *Proportions*,which are
in perfect degrees,neither are they in all figures, but in thofe onely, which
thofe degrees doe refpect with their perfection,or to which thefe accidents
befides the *Proportion* doe belong.

   5   The *fefquialtera Proportion* doth exclude the *Ternarie* perfection of
figures,vnleffe they haue it from a figne.Wherefore when the figne denies
it ; they receiue neither *Alteration*, nor *Imperfection*.

Of the Triple.

THe *Triple Proportion*, the fecond kinde of the *Multiplex* is, when the
greater number, being in Relation with the leffe, doth comprehend it
in it felfe 3.times,as 6.to 2 : 9. to 3. But Mufically,when three Notes are vttered againft one fuch, which is equall to it in kind. The figne of this is the
number of three fet ouer an Vnitie, thus ;

Tenor Triplæ.

Baſſus Triplæ.

[76]

Of the *Quadrupla.*

THe *Quadrupla* is the third kind of the *Multiplex*, and is, when a greater number doth comprehend a leſſe in it ſelfe foure times, as 8. to 2 : 12
to 3. But Muſically, when 4. Notes are ſounded to one: the ſignes of it are
theſe $\begin{Bmatrix} 4.8. \\ 1.2. \end{Bmatrix}$ as thus :

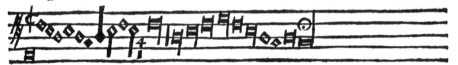

Tenor Quadrupla.

Baſſus Quadrupla.

Of the *Seſquialtera.*

THe *Seſquialtera* is the firſt ſort of the *Super particular*, and is, when a
great number doth comprehend a leſſe once, and ſome other part of it:
as 6. to 4 : 9. to 6. But Muſically, when three Notes are ſounded againſt two
of the ſame kinde : the $\begin{Bmatrix} 3.6.9. \\ 2.4.6. \end{Bmatrix}$ as in the Example following.
ſignes of it are theſe ;

Tenor Seſquialteræ.

Baſſus ſeſquialteræ.

There be, which adde the colour to the figures which are made *ſeſquial-*
terate by the Caraĉters of the numbers : and contrarily *ſeſquialterating* the
ſeſquialteraes.

[77]

ſeſquialteraes. And theſe men (as *Franchinus* witneſſeth) haue this fault, that they make of two *ſeſquialteraes,* not a duple *ſeſquialtera,* (as they thinke) but a duple *ſeſquiquarta.* Some put *Imperfection* & *Alteration* in the *ſeſquialte-rates* of the imperfect time, meſuring a *Breefe* Reſt with one Tact: although in the Notes they ſet 3 *ſemibreefes* in one Tact. But vpon what ground they doe it, excepting of an Aſſe-headed ignorance, I know none. For *Imper-fection* admits not the *Imperfection* and *Alteration* of ſignes, neither doth *Proportion* exclude Reſts.

Of the Seſquitertia.

THe *Seſquitertia* Proportion, which they cal *Epitrite,* becauſe it is made by an *Epitrite, Macr.* ſaith, it is when the greater number of Notes, doth containe the leſſer in it ſelfe, & beſides his third part: as 4. to 3: 8 to 6: 12. to 9. But Muſically, when 4. Notes are ſounded againſt 3. which are like them-ſelues. The ſignes of it are theſe, ⎰ 4 8.12. ⎱ There be that aſcribe an in-uerted *ſemicircle* to this *Proportion,* ⎰ 3.6 9. ⎱ but *Tinctor* ſeemes to be a-gainſt that.

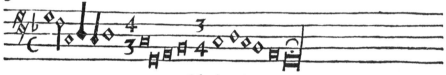

Tenor ſeſquitertiæ.

Bſſus ſeſquitertiæ.

Of the ſeſquioctaua.

THe *ſeſquioctaua* Proportion is, when a greater number being compared with a leſſe, doth comprehend it once, and with it his 8 part, as 9. to 8: 18 to 16. But Muſically, when 9. Notes are ſung to 8, which are like them-ſelues. The ſigne of it is the number of 9. ſet ouer 8, thus; ⎰ 9 ○ ⎱
                                                     Or
                                                 ⎰ 8 8 ⎱

[78]

Tenor ſeſquioctaua.

Baſſus ſeſquioctaua.

                       T   **There**

There are befides, who (becaufe the value is diminifhed by adioyning the colours)doe confider the *Sefquialtera* by the fulnes of the Notes;which alfo they call *Hemiola*.For *Hemiola* is that,which *Sefquialtera* is, faith *Aulus Gellius lib*.19.*cap*.14. Yet this blacking of the Notes, is accidentall to it neuer, but vnder the imperfect quantitie, as *Franchinus* writeth.

Tenor Hemiola.

Baffus Hemiola.

Though there be many other kindes of *Proportions*, which the Mufiti-ans doe obferue in Harmonicall *Concent*, yet haue I omitted all thefe for briefenefle fake, leaft children(for whom this Booke is made) fhould haue their wits rather clogged than helped hereby. Therefore the learned may pardon me, becaufe this is written for them that are hungry, not for thofe that haue a delicate mawe. Yet (by the grace of God)all that now for breui-tie fake,or vpon other occafions I now omit, fhall be painefully fet downe in a greater volume with more diligence and care. Meane while, I intreat yong men to exercife themfelues with thefe fmall precepts,that when they are to goe to higher matters they may be fit.

The end of the fecond Booke.

TO *PHILIP SVRVS* OF *MJL*·

TENBVRGH A SHARP-WITTED MAN, MASTER OF
Art, and a moſt cunning *Muſitian*, Chappel-Maſter to the Count
Palatine the Duke of *Bauaria: Andreas Ornithoparchus* of
Meyning, ſends greeting.

Oſt deere Philip, *in that a man is the moſt worthy of all
Creatures, a creature made like to God, by nature milde,
of ſtature vpright, prouident, wiſe; of memory, witty; by
reaſon, ſuſceptible of Lawes and learning; by his Crea-
tours great gift, farre preferred before all vnreaſonable
Creatures in al things, but ſpecially in two, to wit, Speech
and Reaſon; it followes that Ignorance in him is ſo much
the fowler fault, by how much hee is more worthy than
other Creatures. Now this as it is a fowle ſhame for all men, ſo for Scoollers it is
the fowleſt diſgrace: the courſe of whoſe life is ordayned for this, that by liuing
well they may ſhew others an example of good faſhions, learning and honeſty, en-
creaſing feruent Faith in the people, and (which is their chiefeſt Office, by praiſing
God in Hymnes and ſongs, ſtirring vp deuotion in the hearts of the faithfull.*

*By obſeruation whereof (moſt kinde friend) I was ſtirred vp to helpe learners
in that kinde alſo, and after the handling of* Concent, *which in the former bookes
we haue deliuered, to deliuer the Eccleſiaſticall Acc nt. A matter ſurely hard, becauſe it requires both a* Grammarian *and a* Muſitian, *and alſo becauſe it is to be
had rather by vſe than by writing: and further becauſe either none or very few
men haue handled this point: by this difficulty the worke was a while hindred
from ſeeing the light; now being ſet out and perfected, I commit it to your tui-
tion, and ſubiect it to your cenſure, beſeeching you both to mend the errours you
find in it, and to defend it from the inuaſion of enuious men: becauſe thou art
able, learned, godly, and beſides other gifts of nature, haſt an elegant ſtile, a ſweet
vain, and in ſinging a gracefull cunningneſſe, wherin thou doeſt exceed thy fellow-
Muſitians, in entertaining ſtrangers (as I to your coſt found) a liberall humour.
Whence it is come to paſſe, that all the Maſters of the* Budorine *vniuerſity, which
they call* Heydelberg, *do ſingularly loue, honour, and reſpect you. Farewell, (worthy Sir) and defend thy* Andreas *from the enuious backebiter.*

T 2   THE

THE THIRD BOOKE OF ORNɟ-

TOPARCHVS HIS *MVSICKE*, TOVCHING THE
ECCLESIASTICALL ACCENT.

The Argument of Mafter *Choterus* vpon the Third Booke.

THE FIRST CHAPTER.   [81

In Praife of Accent.

Ccent hath great affinitie with *Concent*, for they be brothers: becaufe *Sonus*, or *Sound*, (the King of Ecclefiafticall Harmony) is Father to them both, and begat the one vpon Grammar; the other vpon *Muſicke*, whom after the Father had feene to be of excellent gifts both of body and wit, and the one not to yeeld to the other in any kind of knowledge, and further that himfelfe (now growing in yeeres) could not liue long, he began to thinke, which he fhould leaue his kingdome vnto; beholding fometime the one, fometime the other, and the fafhions of both. The *Accent* was elder by yeares, graue, eloquent, but feuere: therefore to the people leffe pleafing. The *Concent* was merry, frollicke, liuely, acceptable to all, defiring more to be loued, than to be feared: by which he eafily wonne vnto him all mens minds. Which the Father noting, was daily more and more troubled, in making his choyfe. For the *Accent* was more frugall, the other more pleafing to the people. Appointing therefore a certaine day, and calling together the Peeres of his Realme, to wit, Singers, Poets, Orators, morall Philofophers, befides Ecclefiaftical Gouernors, which in that Function held place next to the King, before thefe King *Sonus* is faid to haue made this Oration: My noble Peeres, which haue vndergone many dangers of warre, by land and fea, and yet by my conduct haue caried the Prize throughout the whole world; behold, the whole world is vnder our Rule, wee haue no enemy, all things may goe profperoufly with you; only vpon me death increafeth, and life fadeth, my body is weakned with labor, my foule confumed with Care, I can expect nothing fooner than death. Wherfore I purpofe to appoint one of my Sonnes Lord ouer you, him (I fay) whom you fhall by your common voyces choofe, that he may defend this Kingdome, which hath been purchafed with your blood, from the wrong and inuafion of our enemies.

When he had thus faid, the Nobles began to confult, and by companies to handle concerning the point of the common fafety; yet to difagree, and fome to choofe the one, fome the other. For the Orators and Poets would
haue

haue the *Accents*, the Mufitians, and the Moralifts chofe the *Concent*. But the Papale Prelates, who had the Royalties in their hands, looking more deepely into the matter, enacted that neither of them fhould be refufed, but that the kingdome fhould be diuided betwixt them, whofe opinion the King allowed, and fo diuided the Kingdome, that *Concentus* might be chiefe Ruler ouer all things that are to be fung (as *Hymnes, Sequences, Antiphones, Refponfories, Introitus, Tropes*, and the like : and *Accent* ouer all things, which are read; as Gofpels, Lectures, Epiftles, Orations, Prophecies. For the Functions of the Papale kingdome are not duely performed without *Concent*. So thefe matters being fetled each part departed with their King, concluding that both *Concent* and *Accent* fhould be fpecially honoured by thofe Ecclefiafticall perfons. Which thing *Leo* the Tenth, and *Maximilian* the moft famous Romane Emperour, both chiefe lights of good Arts, (and fpecially of *Muficke*) did by generall confent of the Fathers and Princes approoue, endow with priuiledges, and condemned all gaine-fayers, as guilty of high Treafon; the one for their bodily; the other for their fpirituall life. Hence was it, that I marking how many of thofe Priefts, (which by the leaue of the learned I will fay) doe reade thofe things they haue to read fo wildly, fo monftroufly, fo faultily, that they doe not onely hinder the deuotion of the faithfull, but alfo euen prouoke them to laughter, and fcorning with their ill reading) refolued after the doctrine of *Concent* to explaine the Rules of *Accent*, in as much as it belongs to a *Mufitian*, that together with *Concent*, *Accent* might alfo as true heire in this Ecclefiafticall kingdome be eftablifhed. Defiring that the praife of the higheft King, to whom all honour and reuerence is due, might duely be performed.

The Second Chapter.

Of the Definition, and Diuifion of Accent.

Herefore *Accent* (as *Ifidorus lib.* 1. *eth. cap.* 17. writeth) is a certaine law, or rule, for the rayfing, or low carrying of fillables of each word Or, it is the Rule of fpeaking. For that fpeaking is abfurd, which is not by *Accent* graced. And it is called *accent*, becaufe it is *ad Cantũ*, that is, clofe by the fong, according to *Ifidore* : for as an aduerbe doth determine a Verbe, fo doth *accent* determine *Concent*. But becaufe thefe defcriptions doe rather agree with the Grammaticall *accent*, than with the Muficall, I hold it neceffary to fearch out by what means the Ecclefiafticall *accent* may rightly be defcribed. Therefore *accent* (as it belongeth to Church-men) is a melody, pronouncing regularly the fyllables of any words, according as the naturall *accent* of them requires.

Of the Diuifion of accent.

NOw it is three-fold, as *Prifcian* and *Ifidore* witneffe, the *Graue*, the *Acute*, and the *Circumflex*. The *Graue* is that, by which a fillable is carried low:

V but

but to fpeake mufically, it is the regular falling with finall words, according to the cuftome of the Church. Of which there be two forts. One which doth fall the finall word, or any fyllable of it by a fift: and this is properly called *Graue*. Another which doth fall the finall word, or any fyllable of it onely by a third, which by the Mufitians is called the middle *Accent*. Neither haue the Grammarians caufe to be angry, if they find any thing here contrary to their lawes. For we goe not about to handle the Grammaticall *Accent*, which *Prifcian*, and others haue throughly taught, but the Ecclefiafticall, as here followeth :

Medius.   Grauis.
Parce mihi domi ne,   ni hil enim funt di es me i.

[83]

An *acute Accent* grammatically, is that, by which the fyllable is raifed. But mufically, it is the regular eleuation of the finall words or fyllables according to the cuftome of the Church. Wherof there are likewife two kinds: one which reduceth the finall fyllable or word to the place of his difcent, keeping the name of *Acute*. The other, which doth raife the fecond fillable not to the former place of his difcent, but into the next below. Which is alfo called *Moderate*, becaufe it doth moderately carry a fillable on high, as appeareth in the example following :

Moderatus.   Acutus.
Il lu mi na re Hie ru fa lem   qui a   glo ri a   do mi ni   fuper te or ta eft.

The *Circumflex* is that, by which a fillable firft raifed is carried low. For it is, as *Ifidore* witneffeth, contrary to the *acute*, for it begins with the *acute*, and ends with the *graue*, vnknowne to Church-men. Yet the Monkes, and efpecially thofe of the Ciftertian order, haue the *Circumflex accent*, as at the old Cell a Monaftery of the fame order my felfe haue tried, and I my felfe haue feene many of their bookes in the fame place.

Now farewell they that forbid Church-men to vfe Muficke; what folace   [84] (fetting finging afide) can they haue either more healthfull, or more honeft? For whilft we recreate our felues with finging, all euill thoughts, and fpeech, all backe-biting, all gluttony and drunkenneffe, are auoyded. Wherefore Song-Muficke both plaine and Menfurall, becommeth the moft religious, that they may both fing praifes to God, and make themfelues merry at fit times of recreation. But leauing this difcourfe, let vs returne thether whence we digreffed, and fend thofe which would bufily enquire the nature of the *Circumflex accent*, to *Mich. Galliculus*, who hath fet out the matter fo briefly, that it need no other explayning.

The

The Third Chapter.

Of the generall Rules of Accent.

Ecause to proceed from easie things to harder, is the naturall method, we thought fit first to explaine the generall Rules of accent, and secondly the speciall.

1 Euery word of one syllable, or indeclinable, or barbarous, requires an *acute accent* : as *Astarot, Senacherib, me, te, sum.*

2 Greeke and Hebrew words in Latine terminations retaine the Latine *accent*, as *Parthenopolis, Nazarenus, Hierosolima.*

3 Greeke and Hebrew words hauing not the Latine Declension, are a-cuted, as *Chryson, Argyrion, Ephraim, Hierusalem.*

4 A *graue accent* is made in the end of a complete sentence, an *acute* likewise, the *Moderate* and *Meane* onely in the end of an imperfect sentence.

5 A *graue accent* must not be repeated, if no other come betwixt, vnlesse the speech be so short, that another cannot come betwixt, as thus :

Factum est vespere & mane dies secundus dixit quoque Deus.

The Fovrth Chapter.

Of the speciall Rules of Accent.

Irst, A word that is of one sillable, indeclinable, barbarous, or Hebrew, which wee saide must haue an *acute accent*, either is in the end of a compleat sentence, and is thus acuated; or in the end of a sentence not compleat, and is thus. From this Rule are excepted Encletical Coniunctions, which are marked with a *graue Accent*, thus:

[85]

Dominus locutus est clama te ad me & ego exaudiam vos Deus dominusque.

2 The first sillable of a word which hath two sillables, doth alwaies receiue the *accent*, whether it be short or long, thus :

Et fugit velut vmbra. Et in amaritudinibus morabitur oculus meus.

3 A word of many sillables put in the end of a speech, either hath the last saue one Long or Short : if Long, the *accent* fals vpon it, if short, then the last saue two receiues the *accent*.

Lignum si præcisum fuerit rursum virescit. Et rami eius pullulant.

V 2

4 A

4   A ſpeech with an interrogation,whether it haue in the end a word of one ſillable, or of two ſillables, or more, the *Accent* ſtill fals vpon his laſt ſillable, and that muſt be acuated. Now the ſignes of ſuch a ſpeech are,*who, which,what,*and thoſe which are thence deriued, *why,wherefore,when,how, in what ſort,whether,*and ſuch like.

Vnde es tu   Quid eſt homo?   Quantas habe o in i qui tates & pecca ta?

To theſe are ioyned Verbes of asking as *I aske, I ſeeke, I require, I ſearch, I heare, I ſee,*and the like.

THE FIFT CHAPTER.

Of the Points.

Ecauſe the Eccleſiaſticall *accent* is commonly knowne by *Points,* it is neceſſary to deliuer the nature of certaine *Points* fitting this purpoſe.

1   The *Point,* which they call a *Daſh,*if it be placed betwixt more words of one part of a ſentence, it ſhewes they are to be reade diſtinctly.

2   Two Pricks,or one Prick ſet directly on the middle of the right ſide,   [86] is a marke of the middle *accent,*which diſcends by a third.

3   A Pricke in the end of any ſentence raiſed a little aboue the middle, doth repreſent either the *acute,* or moderate *accent,* according as the ſentence giues it.

4   A Prick a little below the middle of the word,is a marke of the *Graue accent.*

5   A *Point* of Interrogation, which is made thus (?) being found in ſome place,doth ſhew that the laſt ſillable of the word,(to which it is ioyned) is to be pronounced with an *acute accent.* The euidence whereof followes in the example following.

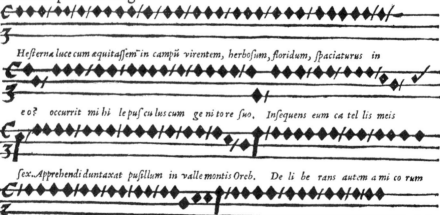

Heſterna luce cum æquitaſſem̄ in campū virentem, herboſum, floridum, ſpaciaturus in

e o?   occurrit mi hi le puſ cu lus cum ge ni to re ſuo.   Inſequens eum ca tel lis meis

ſex. Apprehendi duntaxat puſillum in valle montis Oreb.   De li be rans autem a mi co rum

Le po ri as iſtas carnes eſſem con dò na tu rus? inte rogans comitem meum quid eſſet

ſuaſurus?

sua surus? Sano mi hi con si li o di xit.   Hortor eum fi du ci a e as   do no da ri

con su li de Brunswick.Tu autē domine, mi se re re nobis.

[87]

THE SIXT CHAPTER.

Of Accent in the Epistles.

 He totall *Accent* of Epistles is diuers, (according to the diuersity of Diocesse and Religions) yet the partiall is the same withall, because it proceeds from the quantitie of Sillables, as by the vnderwritten rules is cleere.

1 Euery *accent* of Epistles and Gospels are taken out of the sillables of the finall sentences, and their number?

2 When in the end of a sentence is placed a word of one sillable, the *accent* is varied according to the varietie of the words going before.

3 If a word of one sillable goe before the like finall word, and before it a third of the same sort, the first is to be raised, thus :

Sic in fla ti sunt quidam tanquam non ven tu rus sit ad nos.

Now by what meanes (according to the Monkes) that *accent* is distinguished, Friar *Michael de Muris Galliculis* in his Treatise, which hee wrote both truely and learnedly, hath worthily shewed.

4 If a word of two sillables come before a word of one sillable finall, then the first sillable of it must be raised, whether it be long: or short, thus :

Om ni a e nim vestra sunt si quis di li git de um ex e   o est.

5 If a word of three sillables come before a word of one sillable finall, then is it to be raised, if it haue the last saue one *Long* : if short, then the *accent* is to be translated to the last saue two.

In pa ce Deus vo ca uit   vos. Dispen sa ti o mi hi credita   est.

6 If a word of two sillables be placed in the end of a speech, then the last syllable saue one of the word going before must be raised, it it be long ; If it be short, the last sauing two, thus :

[88]

Et dix it mi hi, Et in ple ni tu di ne Sanctorū de ten ti o me a.

X

7 If

7 If a word of three ſyllables be placed in the end of a ſpeech, and a word of one ſillable goe before it, then this is to be raiſed : but if a word of two ſyllables, then let the firſt ſyllable of it be raiſed, whether it be long, or ſhort. If a word of three ſyllables goe before a word of three ſyllables, it raiſeth the laſt ſaue one, if it be long : If it be ſhort, the laſt ſaue two, thus :

Tu ſcis om ni a   nonne dix it do mi nus   cantantes   De   o glori am.

At il li dix e   runt do mi no nouit om ni   a domi nus.

8 If in the end of a ſpeech be placed a word of more ſyllables than three, then the firſt ſyllable of it muſt be raiſed, if it be long : if it be ſhort, the *accent* fals vpon the word going before, thus:

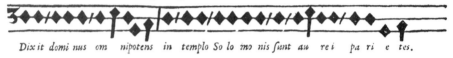

Dix it domi nus om   nipotens   in   templo So lo mo nis ſunt au   re i   pa ri   e tes.

THE SEVENTH CHAPTER.

Of the Accent of Goſpels.

He totall *accent* of Goſpels, is differing in diuers Dioceſſe and Religions. But the partiall, which is the ſame euery where, is comprehended in the Rules following.

1 If the ſpeech end with a word of one ſyllable, and another goe before it, and a third before that, the *accent* is taken from the firſt, thus:

2 If a word of two ſyllables goe before a word of one finall, the firſt ſyllable of it receiues the *accent*, whether it be long or ſhort, thus.

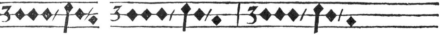

Surrexit non eſt hic.   Om ni a   ver ba hæc.   Do mi nus dedit hoc.

3 If a word of many ſyllables goe before a word of one ſyllable finall, the *accent* fals vpon his laſt ſyllable ſaue one, if it be long ; if it be ſhort, vppon the laſt ſaue two.

Dolentes que re ba mus te   nonne dix it om ni a hæc.

4 If the ſpeech end with a word of two ſillables, the laſt ſillable ſaue one of the word going before muſt be raiſed, if it be long ; if ſhort, the laſt ſaue two, thus :

Vt de ſcri be retur v ni uer ſis   Or bis Abraham au tem ge nu it Iacob.

[89]

5 If

5 If the speech end with a word of three syllables, hauing the last saue one Long, then the *accent* fals vpon the last syllable of the word going before. But if it be short, then the last sillable saue one of it shall receiue the *accent*, thus:

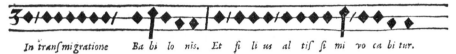

6. If the finall word of a speech be of more syllables than three, the *Accent* fals vpon the first sillable of it, if it be long : if it be short, the last sillable of the word going before is raised.

Of the Accents of Prophecies.

THere is 2. waies for *accenting Prophesies.* For some are read after the maner of Epistles, as on the Feast daies of our *Lady*, the *Epiphany*, *Christmas*, and the like, & those keep the *accent* of Epistles: some are sung according to the maner of Morning Lessons, as in Chrifts night, & in the *Ember* Fasts: and these keep the *accent* of those Lessons But I wold not haue you ignorant, that in accenting oftentimes the maner and custome of the Country and place is kept; as in the great Church of *Magdeburgh*, *Tu autē Domine*, is read with the middle sillable long, by reason of the Custome of that Church, whereas other Nations doe make it short, according to the Rule. Therefore let the Reader pardon me, if our writings doe sometime contrary the Diocesse, wherein they liue. Which though it be in some few things, yet in the most they agree. For I was drawne by my owne experience, not by any precepts to write this booke. And (if I may speake without vain-glory) for that cause haue I seene many parts of the world, and in them diuers Churches both *Metropolitane* and *Cathedrall*, not without great impeachment of my state, that thereby I might profit those that shall liue after mee. In which trauell of mine I haue seen the fiue Kingdomes of *Pannonia*, *Sarmatia*, *Boemia*, *Denmarke*, and of both the *Germanies* 63. Diocesses, Cities 340. infinit fashions of diuers people, besides sayled ouer the two seas, to wit, the *Balticke*, and the great *Ocean*, not to heape riches, but increase my knowledge. All which I would haue thus taken, that the Readers may know this booke is more out of my experience, than any precepts.

The end of the Third Booke.

TO THE WORTHY AND INDVSTRIOVS, MASTER

Arnold Schlick, a moſt exquiſit Muſitian, Organiſt to the Count Palatine, Andreas Ornithoparchus of Meyning, ſends health.

Ere Arnold, *whereas mans intellect in it beginning is naked and without forme, and hath nothing in it, but a poſibility to receiue formes, many haue doubted why the high Creatour did not giue knowledge naturally to man as well as to other ſenſible creatures. For ſome haue naturally the art of ſpinning; ſome of making hony; ſome of weauing; ſome of doing other things: but man is borne naked, vnarmed, without any Art, crying the firſt day of his birth, and neuer laughing til he be* 40. *dayes old (as* Pliny *writeth in the Prologue of the* 7. *booke of his* Nat. Hiſt.) *Is man therfore inferiour to beaſts? in no ſort, for that nakednes of man doth not argue his vnworthineſſe, but his nobleneſſe. For that which is within, hinders not that which would be without. Hence is it, (we ſee) that thoſe animals, which haue arts naturally, can doe nothing but that naturall Art. But man wanteth all Arts, that he may be fit for all: which is proued by the natural deſire hee hath to knowledge. For Arts are deſired by all, though they be not bought by all; and are praiſed* [91] *by all, though they be not ſearched after by all. The hindrance is ſloath, pleaſure, vnorderly teaching, and pouerty. And though we haue naturally the deſire of all Arts, yet aboue all we doe deſire and loue the Art of Singing. For that doth entiſe all liuing things with the ſweetnes; draw them with the profit; and ouercome them with the neceſſity of it: whoſe parts (thogh they be al both ſacred & diuine) yet that which we cal the Counter-point, is more ſweet, worthy, & noble, than al the reſt. For this is the dwelling place of al the other, not that it cōtains in it al the difficulties of* Muſicke; *but becauſe to make it, it requires a learned and perfect Muſitian. Wherfore hauing diſcuſſed of the reſt, leaſt our Office be fayling in this laſt point, I thought good to handle the Counter-point, placing it in the laſt place (as it were a treaſury) wherin al the ſecrets of* Muſick *are laid vp: not that hereby all men, to whom nature is not ſeruiceable, ſhould fall to compoſition, but that all men may iudge whether thoſe things which be compoſed by others, be good or bad. Yet who ſo can, let them compoſe by our writings: they which cannot, let them proceed, as farre as they can.*

But not to digreſſe too wide, (worthy Sir) I haue in this laſt booke, collected the Rules *of the* Counter-point, *out of diuers places, for the common good of learners; which I bring to you to be weighed, that after your cenſure, it may be ſubiected to the carps of the malicious. For from your ſentence no man will euer appeale; becauſe there is no man either learneder, or ſubtiler in this Art, than your ſelfe, who beſides the practiſe, haſt wiſdome, eloquence, gentleneſſe, quickneſſe of wit, & in al kinds of* Muſick *a diuine induſtry, and further the knowledge of many other ſciences. Thou wanteſt the bodily lamp, but in thy mind ſhineth that golden light: thou ſeeſt nothing without thee, within thee thou ſeeſt al things. Thou wanteſt the cleereneſſe of the eyes, thou haſt the admirable quicknes of wit: thy ſight is weak, thy vnderſtanding ſtrong; Wherfore not onely by thy princes, who are to thee moſt gracious, but euen of all men (like* Orpheus *and* Amphion) *art thou loued. Farewell, the honour and delight of* Muſicke, *and protect thy* Andræas *from* Zoiliſſes *and* Therſitiſſes.*

THE FOVRTH BOOKE
OF *ORNITHOPARCHVS* HIS
Muficke, declaring the Principles of
the *Counter-point.*

[92]

The Argument of Mafter *Cotherus.*

THE FIRST CHAPTER.

Of the Definition, Diuifion, and difference of the names of the Counterpoint.

NIcomachus the Mufitian faith, That the Art of *Muficke* was at firft fo fimple, that it confifted of a *Tetrachord.*And was made with the voice *Affa,*that is,one Voyce alone(for *Affa* the Ancients called alone,whereof it is called *Vox affa,*when it is vttered with the mouth, not adding to it other Muficall *Contents,*wherein the praifes of the Ancients was fung, as *Phil. Beroaldus* writeth in the Tenth booke of his Commentary vpon *Apuleius.* Yet by the meanes of diuers authors,the *Tetrachord* from foure Cords grew to fifteen. To which the after-ages haue added fiue and fixe Voyces, and more. So that a Song in our times hath not one voyce alone, but fiue, fixe,eight,and fometimes more.For it is euident,that *Ioannes Okeken* did compofe a Mottet of 36. Voyces.Now that part of Mufick which effecteth this,is called of the Mufitians,the *Counterpoint.*For a *Counterpoint* generally,is nothing elfe than the knowledge of finding out of a Song of many parts. Or it is the mother of *Modulation,*or (as *Franchinus lib.*3. *cap.* 1. writes) it is the Art of bending founds that may be fung,by proportionable Dimenfion, and meafure of time.For, as the clay is in the hands of the Potter; fo is the making of a Song in the hands of the Mufitian. VVherefore moft men call this Art not the *Counter-point,* but *Compofition.* Afsigning this difference of names, and faying, that *Compofition* is the collection of diuers parts of Harmony by diuers *Concords.*For to compofe is to gather together the diuers parts of Harmony by diuers *Concords.*But the *Counter-point* is the fodaine, and vnexpected ordering of a plaine Song by diuers Melodies by chance·VVhence *Sortifare* fignifies to order a plain Song by certain *Concords* on the fodaine. Now it is called *Counterpoint*(as *Bacchus* faith)as it were a concordant *Concent* of Voyces fet one againft another, examined by Art.

Y   *of*

Of the Diuiſion of the Counter-point.

THe *Counter-point* is two-fold : Simple and Coloured. The Simple *Coun-ter-point* is the concordant ordering of a Song of diuers parts by Notes of the ſame kind. As when a plaine Note is ſet againſt a plaine Note, a *Breeſe* againſt a *Breeſe*, thus:

Diſcantus.   *Tenor.*   *Altus.*   *Baſſus.*

[93]

The Coloured *Counter-point* is the conſtitution of a Song of diuers parts by diuers figures, and differing *Concords*, thus :

Cantus.   *Tenor.*   *Altus.*   *Baſſus.*

The Second Chapter.

Of Concords and Diſcords.

BEing that *Concordance* (as ſaith *Boëtius*) is the due mingling of two or more voices, and neither can be made without a *Sound*, nor a *Sound* without *beating*, nor *beating* without *Motion*, it is neceſſary motion be diuided. Of *motions* therefore ſome be equall, ſome vne-quall. Now it is plaine, that out of the equality of *Motions* doe proceed equall ſounds, and out of the inequality of it, vnequal ſounds: and out of the mean inequalitie doe proceed conſonant Sounds, out of the greater inequalitie, *Diſcords*. Hence is it, that the *Pythagoreans* concluded, that no *Concord* could be beyond the *Diſdiapaſon* (as before appeared *lib*. 1. *cap*. 5.) becauſe of the too great diſtance of the extreames. By how much therefore *Sounds* are neerer one another, they are ſo much the ſweeter? and the further they are diſtant one from another, the leſſe they agree. Which I doe chiefly proue to come by the inequall falling of ſuch ſounds into the eares, becauſe a Con-ſonance is a mixture of two Sounds, falling into the eares vniformely. For high Sounds are heard ſooner, than baſe Sounds. As a ſharpe Sword pier-ceth quicker, whereas a blunt one doth not ſo, but enters ſlowly : euen ſo when we heare an high forced Voyce, it ſtrikes into one : but a baſe voyce doth dully, as it were thruſt at one, ſaith *Cælius lib*. 10. *cap*. 53.

Of Voyces.

BEcauſe the likeneſſe of Voyces, doth not breed *Concord*, but the vnlike-neſſe. Therefore Voyces are called ſome *Vniſons*; ſome not *Vniſons*. *Vni-ſons* are thoſe, whoſe Sound is one. Not *Vniſons* are thoſe, whereof one is

[94]

deeper,

deeper, another higher. Of not *Vnisons*, some are *æquisons*; some *Consones*; some *Emmeles*; some *Dissonant. Aequisons* are those, which being stroke toge-ther, make one sound of 2. as *Diapason* and *Disdiapason. Consones* are those, which yeeld a compound or mingled Sound, *Diapente* and *Diapason diapente. Emmeles* are they, which being not *Consones*, yet are next to *Consones*: as those which sound thirds, sixts, or other imperfect *Concords. Discords* are they whose Sounds mingled together, doe strike the sence vnpleasingly

---

What Concord is.

B Y that which hath been said appeares, that Consonance (which other-wise we call *Concordance*) is the agreeing of two vnlike Voyces placed together. Or is (as *Tinctor* writeth) the mixture of diuers Sounds, sweetly pleasing the eares. Or according to *Stapulensis lib.3.* It is the mixture of an high, and lowe sound, comming to the eares sweetly, and vniformely. Of which (among the Practickes) there are two vsed, although some by repea-ting the former, haue more.

$$
Viz. \begin{cases} \text{Vnison,} \\ \text{Third,} \\ \text{Fift,} \\ \text{Sixt,} \end{cases} \begin{matrix} 8 \\ 10 \\ 12 \\ 13 \end{matrix} \begin{cases} 15 \\ 17 \\ 19 \\ 20 \end{cases} \text{\textit{Vnisonum \& eundem causant sonum,}} \\ \text{\textit{quia fiunt in octauis.}}
$$

Of Discords.

A *Discord* (as saith *Boëtius*) is the hard and rough thwarting of two sounds, not mingled with themselues. Or, (as *Tinctor* saith) it is the mixture of diuers sounds, naturally offending the eares, whereof there be Nine:

$$
Viz. \begin{cases} \text{Second,} \\ \text{Fourth,} \\ \text{Seuenth,} \end{cases} \begin{matrix} 9 \\ 11 \\ 14 \end{matrix} \begin{cases} 16 \\ 18 \\ 21 \end{cases} \text{\textit{Vnum \& eundem causant sonum,}} \\ \text{\textit{quia fiunt in octauis.}}
$$

THE THIRD CHAPTER.

Of the Diuision of Concords.

[95]   O F *Concordances* some be simple or primarie, as an *Vnison*, a third a fift, and a sixt. Others are repeated or secundary; which are also *æquisons* to them that goe before, proceeding of a duple di-mension. For an eight doth agree in sound with an vnison; a tenth with a third; a twelfth with a fift; and a thirteenth with a sixt. Others are tri-pled, to wit, a fifteenth, which is equall to the sound of an Vnison, and an Eight. A seuenteenth, which is equall to a third, and a tenth; a nineteenth which is equal to a fift, & a twelfth; a twentieth, which is equall to a sixt and a thirteenth, and so forth. Of *Concords* also some be perfect; some imperfect. The perfect are those, which being grounded vpon certaine Proportions, are to be proued by the helpe of numbers. The imperfect, as not being pro-

Y 2   bable,

bable, yet placed among the perfects, make an Vnison sound; whose names are these:

$$\text{The Perfects are} \begin{Bmatrix} \text{Vnison,} \\ \text{Fift,} \\ \text{Eight,} \end{Bmatrix} \text{and} \begin{Bmatrix} 12 \\ 15 \\ 19 \end{Bmatrix} \text{Imperfects are} \begin{Bmatrix} 13 \\ 17 \\ 20 \end{Bmatrix}$$

Each whereof simply carryed, doth receiue only two Voyces, although by corruption it receiue more.

Rules of Concords.

First, Two perfect *Concords* of the same kinde, are not suffered to follow themselues, but Cords of diuers kindes may well. Yet an Eight, so that they proceed by different and contrary Motions, saith *Franchinus lib.* 3. *cap.*3. thus :

Discantus.   *Tenor.*

2 Two imperfect *Concords* or more, are allowed to follow themselues together, ascending or descending.

3 Let alwaies the next perfect follow the imperfect *Concords*, as an Vnison after an imperfect third; a fift after a perfect; a fift after an imperfect sixt; an eight after a perfect, as *Gafforus lib.*3.*cap.* 3. declareth.

4 Many perfect *concords* of the same kinde immouable are allowed to follow one another, but the moueable not.

5 A *Minime,* or his *pause* is not sufficient to come betwixt perfect *Concords* of the same kinde, because of the little, and as it were insensible sound it hath, although by most the contrary be obserued.

6 It may fall out so, that a *Minime* or a *Crochet*, may be a *concord* in parts contrarily proceeding, for such a *discord* is hidden, nothing at all offending the eares. Yet must you take heede, least two or more be ioyned together.

7 A *Breefe* or a *Semibreefe* discording, is banished from the *Counterpoint.* Yet be there, that admit a *Breefe* discordant diminished in a *Quadruple*, and a *Semibreefe* diminished in a *Duple.*

The Fovrth Chapter.

[96]

Of the generall Rules of the Counter-point.

First, If you desire to compose any thing, first make the *Tenor*, or some other Voyce; according as the *Tone* by which it is ruled doth require.

2 The vnusuall *Moodes* are by all meanes to be auoyded: for they all are *Discords*, except the tenth.

3 In perfect Concordances neuer set a sharpe Voyce against a flat, nor contrarily;

contrarily,but set a *Sharpe* againſt a *Sharpe* ; a *Flat* againſt a *Flat*,or at leaſt againſt a naturall. For the Naturals are doubtfull, and will agree with ♮ *Dures*,and *b Mols*, thus ?

Tenor.   Baſe not good.   Baſe is good.

4 If the *Tenor* in the plaine Song goe too deepe, tranſpoſe it to a fift,or to a fourth if need be, as you may ſee in the *Hymne, Quem terra.*

5 All the parts of the Song in the beginning and end were by the anci-ents made of perfect Cords : which Rule with vs is arbitrarie.

6 When one Voyce goes vpward or downeward,you need not vary the reſt : becauſe to an immouable voyce,many mouable voices may be fitted.

7 In euery Song ſeeke for the neereſt *Concords* : for they which are too farre diſtant,doe taſte of *Diſcord*, ſay the *Pythagoreans.*

8 Let the *Tenor* together with the reſt haue ſweete *Melodie*,in wandring Collations.

9 If the *Tenor* touch the *Meanes* and *Trebles*, the *Meane* may deſcend to the place of the *Tenor.*

10 If the *Tenor* fall to touch the *Baſe*,let the *Baſe* goe vp into the place of the *Tenor*,according as the *Concords* ſhall require.

11 Euery Song,muſt be often adorned with formall *Cloſes.*

12 If the *Tenor* ſhall haue the Cloſe of the *Meane*; the *Meane* on the other ſide ſhall haue the Cloſe of the *Tenor*, by ending either from a tenth in an eight,or from a third in an Vniſon, thus :

Diſcantus.   Tenor.

13 If the *Baſe* take the Cloſe of the *Tenor*, the *Tenor* ſhall take the Cloſe of the *Meane* ; Or if the *Baſe* take the Cloſe of the *Meane*, the *Tenor* ſhall take his Cloſe,as in the Rule going before is ſhewed, thus :

[97]

Tenor.   Baſe.

14 The *Meane* doth ſeldome take a fift aboue the *Tenor* : but the im-fect *Concordance* oft times.

15 The *Baſe* muſt ſeldome or neuer be placed in a ſixt vnder the *Tenor*, vnleſſe an Eight ſtreight follow , but in the perfect *Concords* it may often.

Z   16 If

16 If the *Baſe* haue a fift vnder the *Tenor*, let the *Meane* be ſet in a fift aboue the *Tenor*, by ending in a third, thus :

    Diſcantus.   *Tenor.*   *Baſſus.*

17   Let the *Meane* ſeldome leape by a fift vpwards, but by a ſixt and an eight it may oft: to which alſo an eight downeward is forbidden, though all the other Interuals be graunted.

18   A *Baſe* may not leape a ſixt, it hath all the other *Moodes* common.

19   In Fourths *Mi* doth not agree with *Fa*, becauſe it maketh a *Tritone*.

20   A Fourth though being ſimply taken it is a *Diſcord*; yet being ioyned to a *Concord*, and mingled therewith, it maketh a Concordant midling with the extreames, ſaith *Franchinus*.

21   A Fourth is admitted onely in two places in the *Counter-point* : firſt when being ſhut betwixt two Eights, it hath a fift below. Becauſe if the fift be aboue, the *Concord* is of no force : by that reaſon of *Ariſtotles* (whom *Plato* calleth *Anagnoſtes*, that is an vnwearied Reader of Bookes) whereby in his Problemes he ſhewes, that the deeper Diſcordant ſounds are more perceiued than the higher. Secondly, when the *Tenor* and *Meane*, doe goe by one or more ſixts, then that Voyce which is midling, ſhall alwayes keepe a Fourth vnder the *Cantus*, and a third aboue the *Tenor*.

          The higher Voyce.

         The middle Voyce.

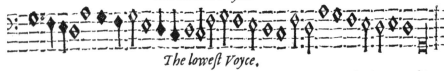

[98]

         The loweſt Voyce.

21   The moſt famous manner of the *Counter-point*, as (ſaith *Franchinus*) is, if the *Baſe* goe together with the *Meane*, or any other Voyce, being alſo diſtant by a tenth, whilſt the *Tenor* doth goe in *Concord* to both, thus :

         Tenor huius.

     The Treble out of the Baſe in the Tenth.

                                         23 If

23 If you ioyne not the fame *Concord*, you fhall make two parts *Concords* in Tenths.

24 It is neceffary for yong beginners to make a Scale of ten lines, then to diftinguifh it by bounds, fo that they may write each time within each bound, by keyes truly marked, leaftthe confufed mingling together of the Notes hinder them; yet is it better to compofe without a Scale, but becaufe it is hard, let yong men begin with a Scale, thus:

[99]

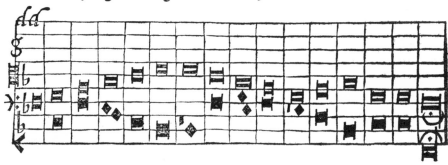

Neither muft young learners thinke it a matter of no weight, how the fignes are fet together, for by the vnorderly referring of them, fo many errours haue fprung in Muficke, that it is hard to be knowne, in what path a man may goe fafe. Wherefore if a man will compare one figne with another, let him carefully marke the nature of the Diminution and Proportions, leaft referring this to that, the meafure of the one be too great, or too little.

THE FIFT CHAPTER.

Of the Parts and Clofes of a Song.

He Ancient fimplenefle of Muficke, knew not the diuers parts of a Song, which the fubtilenefle of our age requires. For the whole being encreafed, al the parts are increafed. Now the parts which Mufitians at this time vfe, are many, to wit; the *Treble*, *Tenor*, high *Tenor*, *Melodie*, *Concordant*, *Vagrant*, *Contratenor*, *Bafe*; yea, and more than thefe. But becaufe they be not all commonly vfed, we will fpeak fomewhat of thofe which are moft commonly vfed; of the reft nothing.

Of the Difcantus.

THe *Difcantus* (as *Tinctor* faith) is a Song made of diuers voyces. For it is called *Difcantus*, *Quafi diuerfus Cantus*, that is, as it were another Song. By which name the ancients did call euery Menfurall Song. But we, becaufe *Difcantus* is a part of a fong feuered from the reft, will defcribe it thus. *Difcantus* is the vppermoft part of each Song. Or it is an Harmony to be fong with a Childs Voyce.

Z 2   *of*

Of the Tenor.

100

A Tenor is the middle voyce of each Song, or (as *Gafforus* writes *lib.3. cap.5.*)it is the foundation to the Relation of euery Song : so called a *Tenendo*, of holding, because it doth hold the Consonance of all the parts in it selfe, in some respect.

Of the Baritone.

THe *Bassus*, (or rather *Basis*) is the lowest part of each Song. Or it is an Harmony to be sung with a deepe voyce, which is called *Baritonus*, a *Vari*, which is low, by changing *V* into *B*, because it holdeth the lower part of the Song.

Of the higher Tenor.

THe high *Tenor*, is the vppermost part, saue one of a Song: or it is the grace of the *Base* : for most commonly it graceth the *Base*, making a double *Concord* with it. The other parts euery Student may describe by himselfe.

Of the formall Closes.

BEing that euery Song is graced with formall *Closes*, we will tell what a *Close* is. Wherfore a *Close* is (as *Tinctor* writes) a little part of a Song, in whose end is found either rest or perfection. Or it is the coniunction of voices (going diuersly) in perfect *Concords*.

Rules for Closes.

FIrst, Euery *Close* consists of three Notes, the last, the last saue one, and the last saue two.

2   The *Close* of the *Discantus* made with three Notes, shall alwayes haue the last vpward.

3   The *Close* of the *Tenor*, doth also consist of three Notes, the last alwayes descending.

4   The *Close* of the *base* requires the last Note sometime aboue, and sometime beneath the *Tenor*. Yet commonly it thrusts it an eight below, and sometimes raiseth it a fift aboue.

5   The *Close* of a high *Tenor*, doth sometime rise, sometime fall with the last Note; sometime makes it an Vnison with others. Which being it proceeds by diuers motions, the sorting of it is at the pleasure of the Composers.

6   The *Close* of the *Discantus*, doth require the last Note saue one aboue the *Tenor* in a sixt : or in a fift, if the *Base* hold a sixt below.

101

7   The last Note saue one of a *Tenor*, is flatly placed a fift aboue the *Base*· and a sixt also, if the *Base* take the *Close* of the *Tenor*, and the *Tenor* the *Close* of the *Discantus*.

8   If the *Close* of the *Tenor* end in *Mi*, as it is in the *Deutero*, or otherwise the last Note but one of the *base* being placed not in the fift. But in the third beneath

beneath the *Tenor*, may fall vpon the fift Finall without any hazard of
Defcant, as is declared in the vnder-written *Concent*.

    Tenor.   *Baritonus.*

9 If the *Clofe* of the *Tenor* end in *Re*, as commonly it doth in the firft
Tone, the *Bafe* fhall very finely end from a fift to a third vpward, not varying
the *Difcantus*, although it may alfo fall into an eight.

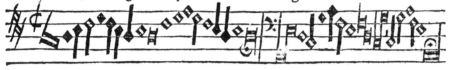

    Tenor.   *Baffus.*

10 Euery Song is fo much the fweeter, by how much the fuller it is of
formall *Clofes*. For fuch force there is in *Clofes*, that it maketh *Difcords* be-
come *Concords* for perfection fake. Therefore let Students labour to fill their
Songs with formall *Clofes*. Now that they may the more eafily doe this, we
thought fit here to fet downe an Exercife or Store-houfe of *Clofes*, that fuch
as Students fing here, they may know they are in their owne Songs to make.

Here followeth the Exercife and forme of Clofes.

[102]

        Difcantus.

        Tenor.

   Baffus.   *A a*

THE SIXT CHAPTER.

Of the ſpeciall precepts of the Counter-point.

Auing deliuered thoſe things which we thinke neceſſarie for the Art of ſetting, now will we in moſt ſhort Rules open eſſentially the matter it ſelfe, as it is.

1 The *Cantus* being ordered with a *Tenor* in an Vniſon, the *Baſe* requires a third below, and the *Altus* the ſame aboue. Or the *Baſe* a fift below, and the *Altus* a fourth aboue. But if the *Baſe* hold an eight below, the *Altus* ſhall agree moſt fitly in a third aboue, or in a fourth below. But if the *Baſe* hold a tenth below, the *Altus* requires a third aboue, or the ſame, or a ſixt below, as you may ſee in the figure following.

Exm. Prim.	Secundi.	Tertij.	4ᵗⁱ membri.
	Altus ◊		
Altus ◊		Altus ◊	Altus ◊
Diſcā: Tenor ◊	Diſcā: Tenor ◊	Cantus: Tenor ◊	Dis: Tenor ◊
Bassus ◊			Altus ◊
		Altus ◊	Altus ◊
	Baſſus. ◊		
		Baſſus ◊	
			Baſſus ◊

2 As oft as the *Diſcantus* is placed a 3. aboue the *Tenor*, let the *Baſe* be placed a third below, and the *Altus* a ſixt aboue, or in an Vniſon. But if the *Baſe* haue an eight below, for a fift it cannot haue, the *Altus* ſhall hold a fourth below. But if the *Baſe* hold a tenth below, the *Altus* requires a third, or a ſixt below. Which a Student may proue by ſuch a Scale as goes before.

3 If the *Diſcantus* hold place in a fift aboue the *Tenor*, which it ſeldome doth, the *Baſe* ſhall be in a ſixt below, and the *Altus* in a third aboue, or in a fourth below. But if the *Baſe* be in an eight below, the *Altus* requires a third aboue, or a fourth, or a ſixt below.

4 If the *Diſcantus* be in a ſixt aboue the *Tenor*, the *Baſe* ſhalbe in a fift below, and the *Altus* in a third below, or a fourth aboue. Or if the *Baſe* be in an eight below, the *Altus* ſhall onely agree in a third aboue; but when the

[104]

Baſe

Bafe is in a tenth below, the *Altus* fhalbe in a third aboue, or in the fame below. It might alfo be in an eight below, and found a thirteenth with the
Difcantus.

5 If the *Difcantus* be placed in an eight aboue the *Tenor*, the *Bafe* will
agree well in a third below, & the *Altus* in a third or fixt aboue, or in a fift
below. But when a *Bafe* be in the fame below, the *Altus* fhalbe in a fourth or
fixt aboue, or in a third below. If the *Bafe* be in an eight below, the *Altus* fhall
fweetly agree in a fift or third aboue. But if the *Bafe* fall to a tenth below, the
Altus fhall hold a third or fixt aboue, or the fame below.

6 As oft as the *Difcantus* doth reft in a tenth aboue the *Tenor*: the *Bafe*
fhall be in a third below, and the *Altus* in a third, fixt, or eight aboue. But if
the *Bafe* be found in a third aboue, the *Altus* fhalbe in a third below, or in a
fift or eight aboue. But if the *Bafe* be in a fift aboue the *Tenor*, (for below it
cannot) the *Altus* fhalbe in a third aboue, or an eight below. But if the *Bafe*
fall to an eight below, the *Altus* may be in a fourth below, or in a third or
fift aboue.

7 When the *Difcantus* is in a twelfe aboue the *Tenor*, the *Bafe* muft be in
an eight below, & the *Altus* in a third, fift, or eight aboue. But when the *Bafe*
is in a third aboue, the *Altus* fhall be in a fift, eight, or tenth concordantly.

8 If the *Difcantus* be in a fourth aboue the *Tenor*, the *Bafe* requires a
a fift below, & the *Altus* a third or fixt aboue. Contrarily (if you make your
Bafe firft) you fhall make it with the *Difcantus*. But if a man will make more
than 4. parts, let him take the *Concords* aboue or below, as other parts fhall
require, obferuing thofe things which are to be obferued, which we referre
to the Setters iudgement.

The Seventh Chapter.
Wherefore Refts are put in the Counter-point.

He placing of *Refts* in a *Counterpoint*, is for many caufes
tollerated.

1 To auoide difficulty. For whilft two parts of a fong or more
are fo fitted together that it is hard to fit the other parts, we fet
Refts for fo long, till that difficultie ceafe.

2 To auoide *Fict* Voices, and the forbidden Interuals.

3 To diftinguifh two perfect *Concords* which cannot mutually follow
one another, vnleffe a Note or paufe come betwixt.

4 For the making of Signes. Now a figne is the fucceffiue diftribution
of one and the fame Clofe, in the beginning or any other place, by diuers
parts of a Song Or it is the repetition of the fame Clofe in diuers parts of
the fong thus :

[105]

Difcantus   *Tenor.*   *Baffus.*

A a 2   5 *Refts*

5 *Rests* are admitted for taking breath, least by the swiftnesse of the Song, either the Singer might be out of breath, or breed confusion by taking his breath at vnfit times.

6 That the *Intrinsecall* signes and markes of Musicall degrees, consisting in their perfection, may be perceiued. For a perfect *Mood* is inwardly noted by a rest of 3.times. A perfect time by 2. *Semibreefe* Rests, placed with a *Semibreefe*, as before is said in the fift Chapter of the second booke.

7 Because of the many parts of a song For when a song goes with more parts than foure, it is necessary that some Rest, whilst others sing : least the sweetnesse be dulled either by the too much prolonging of the Voices, or by the vnelegant commixtion of *Concords*, and so the Consort seeme rather to make a noyse, then a Concordant sound.

THE EIGHT CHAPTER.

Of the diuers fashions of singing, and of the Ten Precepts for Singing.

Very man liues after his owne humour; neither are all men gouerned by the same lawes, and diuers Nations haue diuers fashions, and differ in habite, diet, studies, speech, and song. Hence is it, that the English doe carroll; the French sing; the Spaniards weepe; the Italians, which dwell about the Coasts of *Ianua* caper with their Voyces; the other barke : but the Germanes (which I am ashamed to vtter) doe howle like VVolues. Now because it is better to breake friendship, than to determine any thing against truth, I am forced by truth to say that which the loue of my Countrey forbids me to publish. *Germany* nourisheth many Cantors, but few Musitians. For very few, excepting those which are or haue been in the Chappels of Princes, doe truely know the Art of Singing. For those Magistrates to whom this charge is giuen, doe appoint for the gouernment of the Seruice youth Cantors, whom they choose by the shrilnesse of their Voyce, not for their cunning in the Art; thinking that God is pleased with bellowing and braying, of whom we read in the Scripture, that he reioyceth more in sweetnes than in noyse, more in the affection, than in the Voice. For whē *Salomon* in the *Canticles* writeth, that the voice of the church doth sound in the eares of Christ, hee doth presently adioyne the cause, because it is sweet. Therefore well did *Baptista Mantuan* (that moderne *Virgil*) inueigh euery puffed vp, ignorant, bellowing Cantor, saying;

> *Cur tantis delubra Boum mugi:ibus imples,*
> *Tu ne Deum tali credis placare tumultu.*

Whom the Prophet ordained should be praised in Cymbals, not simply, but well sounding.

Of the Ten Precepts necessary for euery Singer.

BEing that diuers men doe diuersly abuse themselues in Gods praise; some by mouing their body vndecently; some by gaping vnseemely; some by changing the vowels, I thought good to teach all Cantors certaine Precepts, by which they may erre lesse.

[106]

1 When

1 When you defire to fing any thing, aboue all things marke the Tone, and his Repercuffion. For he that fings a Song without knowing the Tone, doth like him that makes a fyllogifme without Moode and Figure.

2 Let him diligently marke the Scale, vnder which the Song runneth, leaft he make a Flat of a harpe or a Sharpe of a Flat.

3 Let euery Singer conforme his voyce to the words, that as much as he can he make the Concent fad when the words are fad;& merry,when they are merry Wherein I cannot but wonder at the Saxons (the moft gallant people of all Germany, by whofe furtherance I was both brought vp, and drawne to write of Muficke)in that they vfe in their funerals,an high,mer- ry and ioconde Concent, for no other caufe (I thinke) than that either they hold death to be the greateft good that can befall a man (as Valerius in his fift Booke writes of Cleobis and Biton two brothers) or in that they beleeue that the foules (as it is in Macrobius his fecond Booke De fomnio Scip.) after this body doe returne to the original fweetnes of Muficke,that is to heauen. Which if it be the caufe,we may iudge them to be valiant in contemning death,and worthy defirers of the glory to come.

4 Aboue all things keepe the equalitie of meafure. For to fing without law and meafure,is an offence to God himfelfe, who hath made all things wel!,in number,weight,and meafure.Wherefore I would haue the Eafterly Franci(my countrey-men)to follow the beft manner,and not as before they haue done;fometime long;fometime to make fhort the Notes in Plain-fong, but take example of the noble Church of Herbipolis,their head,wherin they fing excellently.Which would alfo much profit,and honour the Church of Prage,becaufe in it alfo they make the Notes fometimes longer,fometime fhorter, than they fhould Neither muft this be omitted, which that loue which we owe to the dead,doth require. Whofe Vigils (for fo are they com- monly called)are performed with fuch confufion,haft,and mockery (I know not what fury poffeffeth the mindes of thofe, to whom this charge is put o- uer);that neither one Voyce can be diftinguifhed from another, nor one fil- lable from another, nor one verfe fometimes throughout a whole Pfalme from another.An impious fafhion to be punifhed with the feuereft correcti- on. Think you that God is pleafed with fuch howling fuch noife,fuch mum- bling, in which is no deuotion, no expreffing of words, no articulating of fyllables ?

5 The Songs of Authenticall Tones muft be timed deepe, of the fubiugall Tones high,of the neutrall,meanly.For thefe goe deep,thofe high, the other both high and low.

6 The changing of Vowels is a figne of an vnlearned Singer. Now, (though diuers people doe diuerfly offend in this kinde) yet doth not the multitude of offenders take away the fault. Here I would haue the Francks to take heede they pronounce not u for o, as they are wont, faying nufter for nofter.The countrey Church-men are alfo to be cenfured for pronoun- cing, Aremus in ftead of Oremus.In like fort, doe all the Renenfes from Spyre

B b　　　　　　　　　　　　　　　to

to *Confluentia* change the Vowel *i* into the dipthong *ei*, saying *Mareia* for *Maria*. The *Westphalians* for the vowel *a* pronounce *a* & *e* together, to wit, *Aebs te* for *Abs te*. The lower Saxons, & al the *Sueuians*, for the Vowel *e*, read *e* & *i*, saying, *Deius* for *Deus*. They of lower *Germany* doe all expresse *u* & *e*, in stead of the Vowel *u*. Which errours, though the *Germane* speech doe often require, yet doth the Latine tongue, which hath the affinitie with ours, exceedingly abhorre them.

7 Let a Singer take heed, least he begin too loud braying like an Asse, or when he hath begun with an vneuen height, disgrace the Song. For God is not pleased with loude cryes, but with louely sounds: it is not (saith our *Erasmus*) the noyse of the lips, but the ardent desire of the Art, which like the lowdest voice doth pierce Gods eares. *Moses* spake not, yet heard these words, *Why doest thou cry vnto me?* But why the Saxons, and those that dwell vpon the Balticke coast, should so delight in such clamouring, there is no reason, but either because they haue a deafe God, or because they thinke he is gone to the South-side of heauen, and therefore cannot so easily heare both the Easterlings, and the Southerlings.

8 Let euery Singer discerne the difference of one holiday from another, least on a sleight Holiday, he either make too solemne seruice, or too sleight on a great.

9 The vncomely gaping of the mouth, and vngracefull motion of the body, is a signe of a mad Singer.

10 Aboue all things, let the Singer study to please God, and not men; (saith *Guido*) there are foolish Singers, who contemne the deuotion they should seeke after? and affect the wantonnesse which they should shun: because they intend their singing to men, not to God: seeking for a little worldly fame, that so they may loose the eternall glory: pleasing men that thereby they may displease God: imparting to other that deuotion, which themselues want: seeking the fauour of the creature, contemning the loue of the Creatour: to whom is due all honour, and reuerence, and seruice. To whom I doe deuote my selfe, and all that is mine, to him will I sing as long as I haue being: for he hath raised me (poore Wretch) from the earth, and from the meanest basenesse. Therefore blessed be his Name world without end, *Amen.*

The end of the Worke.

The Epilogue and Conclusion of the Booke.

 Am to intreat the curteous Reader fauourably to view this Worke of Musical Theorems, which I haue before this some yeres past searched out, & now at last put into the forme of a booke and printed, not out of any arrogant humour, as some enuious persons wil report, but out of a desire to profit the Youth of Germany, whilst others are drousie. If the basenes of the stile, or simplenes of the words offend any man, I intreat him to attribute that to the matter which we handle, and the persons for whom it is written, namely, Children. I doubt not but there will be some, that will be soone ready to snarle at it, and to backbite it, contemning it before they read it, and disgracing it before they vnderstand it. Who had rather seeme than be Musitians, not obeying Authors, or Precepts, or Reasons : but whatsoeuer comes into their hairebraind Cockscombe, accounting that onely lawful, artificiall, and Musicall. To whom I intreat you (gentle Readers) to lend no eare. For it is a thing praise-worthy to displease the eu ll. Yea, (to vse the sentence of Antisthenes the Philosopher) to be backbited is a signe of greatnesse ; to backebite, a token of meanesse. And because the praise of one wise man is better than the commendation of Ten fooles; I pray consider not the number, but the quality of those detractors : and thinke what an easie matter it is to silence those Pyes, and to crush such Fleas euen betwixt two nayles. Neither hearken ye to those that hate the Art : for they dissuade others from that which their dulnesse will not suffer them to attaine to, for in vaine it is to harpe before an Asse. But account that this I speake to you as a Master, because I haue passed the Ferrular. For the cunning men in each Art must be beleeued, as the Emperours Maiestie saith. Wherefore let those courteous Readers (that be delighted with Ornithoparchus his paines taken) be contented with these few things, for as soone as I can but take breath, they shall see matters of greater worth.

Bb 2

A TABLE OF ALL THAT IS CONTAINED
IN THE FIRST BOOKE.

The Table of all that is contained in the second Booke.

The Table of all that is contained in the Third Booke.

The Table of all that is contained in the Fourth Booke.

FINIS.